THE
COMPLETE
IDIOT'S
GUIDE
WITHDRAWN

Being a Model

Second Edition

*by Roshumba Williams with
Anne Marie O'Connor*

ALPHA
A member of Penguin Group (USA) Inc.

ALPHA BOOKS

Published by the Penguin Group

Penguin Group (USA) Inc., 375 Hudson Street, New York, New York 10014, U.S.A.

Penguin Group (Canada), 10 Alcorn Avenue, Toronto, Ontario, Canada M4V 3B2 (a division of Pearson Penguin Canada Inc.)

Penguin Books Ltd, 80 Strand, London WC2R 0RL, England

Penguin Ireland, 25 St Stephen's Green, Dublin 2, Ireland (a division of Penguin Books Ltd)

Penguin Group (Australia), 250 Camberwell Road, Camberwell, Victoria 3124, Australia (a division of Pearson Australia Group Pty Ltd)

Penguin Books India Pvt Ltd, 11 Community Centre, Panchsheel Park, New Delhi—10 017, India

Penguin Group (NZ), cnr Airborne and Rosedale Roads, Albany, Auckland 1310, New Zealand (a division of Pearson New Zealand Ltd)

Penguin Books (South Africa) (Pty) Ltd, 24 Sturdee Avenue, Rosebank, Johannesburg 2196, South Africa

Penguin Books Ltd, Registered Offices: 80 Strand, London WC2R 0RL, England

Note: This publication contains the opinions and ideas of its authors. It is intended to provide helpful and informative material on the subject matter covered. It is sold with the understanding that the authors and publisher are not engaged in rendering professional services in the book. If the reader requires personal assistance or advice, a competent professional should be consulted.

The authors and publisher specifically disclaim any responsibility for any liability, loss, or risk, personal or otherwise, which is incurred as a consequence, directly or indirectly, of the use and application of any of the contents of this book.

Most Alpha books are available at special quantity discounts for bulk purchases for sales promotions, premiums, fund-raising, or educational use. Special books, or book excerpts, can also be created to fit specific needs.

For details, write: Special Markets, Alpha Books, 375 Hudson Street, New York, NY 10014.

Publisher: *Marie Butler-Knight*
Editorial Director: *Mike Sanders*
Managing Editor: *Billy Fields*
Senior Acquisitions Editor: *Paul Dinas*
Production Editor: *Megan Douglass*
Copy Editor: *Krista Hansing Editorial Services, Inc.*
Cartoonist: *Richard King*

Cover Designer: *Rebecca Harmon*
Cover Photo: *Eric Scot*
Book Designers: *Trina Wurst/Kurt Owens*
Indexer: *Julie Bess*
Layout: *Ayanna Lacey*
Proofreader: *Mary Hunt*

Contents at a Glance

Contents

Foreword

There's no doubt that a professional career in modeling is like winning the lottery! Most successful models start their career at an early age and experience an exciting and glamorous lifestyle of travel, culture, success, and money. Modeling can also open many doors to other long-term careers. As a professional model, you learn so much about fashion, style, photography, management, and business. There are also opportunities to represent the major fashion and cosmetic companies as a spokesmodel.

To a young woman who aspires to become a model, it can all seem unattainable and very confusing! That's why it's important to learn about the modeling business before spending lots of money on unnecessary portfolios, modeling classes, photos, etc. Very often Elite finds new models on our open calls or via pictures submitted through the mail or e-mail. At Elite, we prefer to develop and manage a young model from the very beginning of her career. We guide her as she learns to work with photographers, stylists, makeup artists, and clients; develops a working portfolio; develops a personal style; and learns to walk the runway and pose. Most important, we come up with a management plan for each model.

Roshumba's book, *The Complete Idiot's Guide to Being a Model*, now in its second edition, is a must-read for anyone interested in a modeling career. She provides a wealth of information from her years of personal experience as a top model. I have had the pleasure of working with Roshumba on the Elite Model Look USA Tour. Roshumba was Elite's spokesmodel and mentor to thousands of young people across the country. Her advice was always sincere, direct, and priceless! She is a true professional!

Roshumba is a well-known and respected woman in the entertainment business. She has worked with all the top clients in the modeling industry and is most famous for being the first black model to grace the cover of *Sports Illustrated*. Modeling led Roshumba into many other accomplished careers, such as author, spokesperson, TV host, and actor.

I've had the pleasure of knowing Roshumba personally for many years; not only is she smart, determined, dedicated, and beautiful, but she's a great friend, too!

Sincerely,

Cathy Gould

Cathy Gould is director of Elite North America modeling agency. A former model, Gould was instrumental in helping develop the Elite Model Look and Ford Models' Super Model of the World contests. She also re-imaged the Ms. Universe, Ms. Teen, and Ms. USA competitions and was an executive producer of *Search for the Supermodel* and *Making of a Supermodel* on E!

Introduction

It seems that nearly everyone, at one time or another, dreams of becoming a model. Maybe you're a magazine junkie who loves looking at your favorite models in the pages of *Vogue, Glamour,* or *Seventeen.* Or maybe you've watched fashion shows on TV or at a local store, and you think strutting up and down the runway looks like your kind of fun. Or maybe you love perusing catalogs and wonder how those models get hired. Although it can be a tough business to break into and aspiring models face many pitfalls, I'm living proof it can be done.

I was once sitting in my bedroom at home in Peoria, Illinois, looking at magazines and dreaming of a career on the runway and in front of a camera. And with a lot of luck, hard work, and determination—and despite a lot of rejection and numerous setbacks—I managed to go from my small hometown to appear on magazine covers and in fashion shows.

In *The Complete Idiot's Guide to Being a Model, Second Edition,* I share my hard-won knowledge and experiences with you. I explain how the modeling business works and take you step by step through the process of getting an agent and getting started in the business, while warning you about all the hazards I've seen in my years in the business.

Every model has a reason for wanting to be in front of the camera or on the runway. Some love clothes and are attracted to the fashion industry; some just want to make a lot of money and then get on with their life. Others want to be as famous as their favorite supermodels. No matter what your reason, to get started in the modeling industry, you need to convince a lot of people that you have what it takes to shine in their magazine, ad, website, or catalog. Becoming a model isn't all about the way you look. It's also about a great personality and a good attitude. To give you an edge up, I explain my secrets for making a (good) impression that lasts.

Not only can the modeling industry be difficult to break into, but it can be very harsh and crazy once you're a part of it. On the other hand, it can be every bit as glamorous and exciting as you've heard. In this book, I give you my advice on giving the modeling world your best shot, and I also share with you my tips for establishing the kind of career that is long-lived and lucrative and enhances your life. Finally, I give you guidance on avoiding the many pitfalls and scams that every model faces.

How to Use This Book

The modeling industry is easy to understand once you break it down into its six major components. Each part of this book explains a different aspect of the industry. By the time you've read them all, you'll have a firm grasp on everything you need to know to give a modeling career a try.

Part 1, "Modeling: The Ultimate Dream," examines the many reasons people want to get into modeling. It gives you a realistic assessment of what it takes to make it and whether you have what it takes. It also talks about how world fashion trends can affect your career and how you can stay on top of industry developments.

Part 2, "Breaking Into the Business," is where you find out all you need to know to conquer the first major hurdle to becoming a model: finding an agent. Here, I explain the materials you'll need (don't worry, they're minimal and inexpensive) and everything you need to do to stand out when you start looking for an agent. Next, I talk about the pros and cons of open calls, model searches, model conventions, and modeling schools. Finally, there's a special chapter just for parents of aspiring models.

Part 3, "Now That Your Foot's in the Door, What's Next?" discusses the challenges you face once you've found an agent. I explain how an agency works and the model musts you need to be familiar with (test shoots, portfolios, composites, vouchers), as well as give you a behind-the-scenes look at a test shoot. I also talk about go and sees—those all-important job interviews for models—and tell you my secrets for shining at them.

Part 4, "Oh My God, I've Booked a Job, Now What?!" tells you everything you need to know to get through your first few photo shoots with grace and style. I share tips on preparing for that all-important first job. I also explain who everyone at the shoot is, give you hints for working with them, and discuss the differences between working in the studio and working on location.

Part 5, "There's Something for Everyone," discusses the many aspects of modeling, including magazines, fashion shows, advertisements, and catalogs. I talk about the pros and cons of each, and I also discuss opportunities for models who don't meet the stringent criteria for fashion modeling, including plus-size models, elegant (older) models, and real-people models. I also talk about how men and children can get started in the business.

Part 6, "Personal and Career Management," tells you everything you need to know about making the most of your career when it's up and running. I talk about establishing clientele, finding a niche, and managing your finances. In addition, I share my thoughts on staying sane in a crazy business. Finally, I give you my tried-and-true advice on keeping your outer self picture-perfect.

And to make sure you don't get confused by modeling lingo, a glossary contains all the terms you'll need to sound like an insider in conversations with agents, editors, fashion designers, and casting directors. I've also included a list of must-read books and websites for aspiring models, a directory of modeling agencies around the country and abroad, and a list of key tourist offices in major modeling centers.

Extras

In every chapter, I give you the insider secrets on the modeling industry. These boxes contain four different types of information:

Model Scoop

In these boxes, I tell you fun stories about various models and their exploits, both exemplary and cautionary.

Roshumba's Rules

These are my best tips on making the most of your modeling career. You can't go wrong following the rules!

Reality Check

These are warnings about the worst aspects of the modeling industry. Read these carefully, and avoid these pitfalls at any cost!

Catwalk Talk

Modeling terms are defined for you here so you'll always be fashion-forward when the talk turns technical.

Acknowledgments

From Roshumba:

I would like to thank God for giving me the inspiration and dedication needed for this book. I would also like to thank the following: Gail Parenteau, Sheree Bykofsky, Anne Marie O'Connor, Paul Dinas, Kevin Brown, Cathy Gould, Karen Lee, Elite Model Agency, Eric Scot, Rodney Ray, and George Lowrey.

From Anne Marie:

I would like to thank my very funny friend Janet Rosen, the warm and wonderful agent Sheree Bykofsky, the beautiful Roshumba Williams; some of the people who helped us with this book: Gail Parenteau, Debra Hall, Erin Lundgren, Ellen Harth, Calvin Wilson, Karen Lee, Laura McClafferty, Ryan Kopko, Kwame Brathwaite, Alvaro, Natalie Laughlin, Christiana Cordel, Christopher Cordel, Patti Abbott-Claffy, M. L. McCarthy, Corynne Corbett, Christiana Anbri, Stephen

Schmidt, Nikki Suero-O'Brien, and Andrea Fairweather; as well as my model friends and family.

Trademarks

All terms mentioned in this book that are known to be or are suspected of being trademarks or service marks have been appropriately capitalized. Alpha Books and Penguin Group (USA) Inc. cannot attest to the accuracy of this information. Use of a term in this book should not be regarded as affecting the validity of any trademark or service mark.

Part 1

Modeling: The Ultimate Dream

So you think you want to be a model! You've probably seen *America's Next Top Model* and want to experience the glamour, excitement, and big money of a modeling career yourself. Maybe your friends and family tell you you should be a model, or perhaps strangers stop you and ask if you're one.

The modeling industry can be full of pitfalls, scams, and other trouble for the naive and uninformed. So I start out by talking about everything you need to know about modeling before you launch a successful career. I look at the modeling business itself, how it all works, and what you need to be aware of. I also talk about the physical and mental prerequisites for becoming a professional model.

Since the best models are the ones who know and understand the fashion industry, I also talk about the preparations necessary for a successful career. Finally, you find out about the different types of models and learn which type you are and how that affects your career. To find out if you have what it takes, and for more information on getting started, keep reading!

Why Become a Model?

In This Chapter

- The reality of modeling
- The different levels of modeling
- What type of modeling is right for you?

The million-dollar paychecks. The closets full of designer clothes. Jet-setting from Paris to New York to Jamaica. Flocks of men pursuing you. Your face on the cover of magazines. Fans from all over the world asking for your autograph. Dressing up and getting your hair and makeup done—and getting paid for it. Who wouldn't want to be a model?

But the truth is, this is the side of modeling you see only in the movies, on TV, and in magazines. Sure, for a very fortunate few supermodels—perhaps 5 to 10 women in the world at any one time—this is a true picture of a modeling career. But behind all the glitz and glamour lies a completely different reality and a lot of blood, sweat, and tears. Although female models garner more attention than male models, men face many of the same obstacles. (For more information on male models, see Chapter 20.)

The Dream vs. the Reality

The reality is, the vast majority of models will never reach the supermodel stratosphere of limos, champagne, and million-dollar paydays. To give you just one example, of the thousands of girls every year who enter modeling contests to find the next generation of models, only a few of them end up with modeling contracts. Maybe just one of them—if she's lucky—may go on to *supermodel* status.

> **Catwalk Talk**
>
> A **supermodel** is a model who is so successful she becomes a household name, well known to an audience outside the fashion industry. Supermodels include Cindy Crawford, Heidi Klum, Tyra Banks, Gisele Bündchen, and Roshumba Williams.

Although the rewards can be incredible for those fortunate few, a professional modeling career at any level involves a lot of hard work and sacrifice. Many models have to leave their friends, boyfriends, and family behind to move to a big city where they can pursue a career. They also usually need to leave or defer going to school so they can model, or make special arrangements to complete their basic education.

Because most models travel so much, they may need to live out of a suitcase, wearing the same few outfits for weeks at a time, spending more time sitting on planes than at home. Before you decide whether you want to pursue modeling, it's important that you get a realistic picture of what a career entails.

Missing Out on Fun

Many professional models who rise to the top of the industry start their careers when they're as young as 13. (Age 15 or 16, however, is the average.) Usually, they continue to attend high school and may model on Christmas break, during spring vacation, and during the summer. Other times, they may choose to miss a few days of school for a very important assignment.

> **Catwalk Talk**
>
> A **go and see** is a job interview for a modeling job. It's called a go and see because a model *goes* to the client's office so they can *see* what she looks like in person.

As exciting as it may sound to spend your vacations modeling in a big city, the reality is that while your friends are having fun going to the beach or to parties, you may be exhausted from walking around a large city all day going from one job interview, known as a *go and see*, to another. (I tell you a lot more about these in Chapter 14.) Believe me, being lost on the streets of Chicago after your twentieth go and see in 95-degree heat is not fun, exciting, or glamorous.

Modeling sounds more glamorous than it really is. In reality, it involves a lot of exhausting schlepping around big cities going from one appointment to another—and often getting lost.

Rejected and Dejected

We've all had some disappointment or rejection in our lives—we didn't make the school play, didn't get that cushy lifeguard job, didn't ace the test we studied for all semester. Models have to deal with that rejection every day, all day. I've gone on as many as 15 go and sees in 1 day without getting a single job.

There's probably no other business in the world in which one human being can receive as much rejection as in the modeling industry. So if you decide you want to become a model, get ready! Plan to have doors slammed in your face and hear very blunt criticisms of your body and features: *her hips are too wide; his shoulders are too small; we don't want any black girls* (yes, I really did hear that once!); *no Asian girls; her jaw's too square;* and so on.

It's even more nerve-wracking because you're spending a fortune on rent, subways, a cell phone, and food—and despite all your efforts, no money is coming in.

Roshumba's Rules

If you're just starting out on a modeling career and things are slow getting started, consider getting a supplemental job. Not only will you earn money to live on, but staying busy will keep you from becoming dejected.

Even after a week or month of meetings and go and sees, you may still not have gotten even one modeling job; some models have a harder time than others getting a career off the ground (and others find that theirs never takes off). One client after another may decide you're not exactly right for them. You may be completely broke living in a teeny two-bedroom apartment with six other models and surviving on peanut butter and jelly sandwiches. Besides not having any money, you can become extremely depressed expending all that time and energy trying to find a modeling job, only to be rejected again and again.

Meanwhile, your friends at home may still live in their own rooms in their parents' house, with full access to a well-stocked refrigerator, a TV, a stereo, video games, a phone, and a car with gas already in it. Except for the occasional problem at school or work, they live pretty cushy and stress-free lives. But if you want to be a model, you may have to forego these comforts of home. (I discuss how to deal with rejection in Chapter 22.)

The Downside of the Glamorous Life

Many of the things that make modeling sound so exciting—the travel, the cute guys who flock around successful models, the parties—can actually be negatives. Your fifth plane flight in a week isn't as much as that first time. Those cute guys can turn out to be con artists and predators, and too many parties can take their toll on your looks and career. So before you say yes to modeling, you need to take a closer look at the darker side of some of its (so-called) fringe benefits.

On the Road

Most successful models travel constantly, all around the world. This *sounds* great, but the downside is that you may also not get to see your family and friends as much as you'd like. Even though I've seen some incredible sights—the Louvre Museum in Paris, the pyramids in Egypt, the beaches of Jamaica—I've also missed a lot of fun at home, including my best friend's birthday, my brother's graduation, and many Christmases with my family.

Roshumba's Rules

A good way to stay close to your loved ones is to set aside quality time to spend with them. When I first moved away from home, my mom and I would set up specific times when we were both free to have heart-to-heart telephone chats. This helped me stay close to my family.

Traveling so much also means spending a lot of time alone; although I enjoy this, some models find that they often feel very lonely and isolated. On top of that, it's exhausting and stressful to always be running to catch a plane, train, or automobile to get to the next job.

The reality of modeling is traveling all the time and rushing through airports, dragging heavy suitcases.

A Scam a Minute

Models at all stages of their careers, from beginners to supermodels, are targeted by con artists hoping to profit from their hopes, dreams, and naiveté. Aspiring models are generally very young, and their desire to model may occasionally cloud their judgment. Often their parents don't know much about the business, either, which is why there are so many horror stories about disreputable people who offer drugs to young models, who coerce them into modeling nude, who demand sex in exchange for a modeling job, or who want the model to pay them to get a job.

Reality Check

If a photographer tries to convince you to spend a lot of money (more than $300) on a photo session and/or pictures, either he is not knowledgeable about the modeling industry or he is scamming you. In either case, refuse to give him any money. The truth is, once you have an agency, it will arrange for any necessary professional photos. Any professional photos taken without an agency's guidance may be useless.

Catwalk Talk

Your **portfolio** is an album of specially selected pictures you bring with you on job interviews; your **composite** is an 8½×11-inch or 5×7-inch card with several photos on it that your agent sends to potential clients.

Beware, too, photographers who try to get young, just-starting-out models to pay hundreds (or thousands) of dollars for photos, *portfolios*, and *composites*. They will insist these materials are necessary to find a modeling agency that will represent a beginning model, or that they're needed to get started in the modeling business. Don't fall for this common scam; professional photos are definitely not necessary to get started as a model. In fact, they can actually hurt your chances of making it. (For more on scams, see Chapters 8 and 9.)

The Four Basic Levels of Modeling

Although the big-time models on the cover of *Vogue* get most of the attention, there are actually four different levels of modeling:

- Hobby modeling
- Local- and secondary-market modeling
- Big-time modeling
- Celebrity modeling

Each has its own requirements, which means opportunities exist for many different types of models.

Maybe you're not ready to leave your friends, family, and education for a modeling career in a big city such as New York or Paris. Maybe you just want to have some fun, express yourself creatively, and get involved with the fashion industry. In this case, you may want to consider hobby modeling at local malls, in local TV commercials and ads, and for hometown newspapers. Hobby models generally earn little or no money. (For more information on hobby models, see Chapter 8.)

Maybe you'd like to make some money and get a chance to be the center of attention, but you don't want the stress and loneliness of traveling all the time and never seeing your friends and family. In this case, you may want to pursue modeling in local markets (small cities) or in secondary markets (larger regional centers such as Miami, Chicago, and Los Angeles. Local and secondary-market models appear in catalogs, advertisements, local runway shows, and regional publications. Although models in small, local markets may have difficulty finding work on a full-time basis, many models in secondary markets manage to carve out lucrative careers without the continual travel, competition, and stress of big-time modeling.

Or maybe you're prepared to make the necessary sacrifices to give big-time modeling a shot. Maybe you've been dreaming of seeing your face on a magazine cover or on a billboard in Times Square, and you're ready to leave your friends and family to work harder than you ever have before to give big-time fashion modeling a try. Although the rewards are great, so is the competition. Even though you realize you might not make it, your dream is so strong you're willing to risk everything to give it a shot.

The final category is celebrity modeling. Celebrities are appearing more and in magazines, in print advertisements, and in TV commercials. As the name suggests, the famous names in this category have established themselves as stars in another field.

Why Do You Want to Model?

Most models get into the business for more than one reason. They may love fashion, they may be attracted to the glamour of dressing up and posing for the camera, they may want to get out of their small hometowns, or they may want to express themselves creatively. Some may harbor a secret desire to become rich and famous—or at least to make some extra money and be the center of attention for a short time. Your reasons for wanting to get into modeling, and how much you're willing to give up to pursue your dream, can help you determine what kind of modeling career to pursue.

Your physical characteristics—height, weight, body type, facial structure (see Chapter 3 for more details)—play a part in determining the path of your modeling career. But before you take your first step down the *runway*, you need to figure out why you want to model.

Catwalk Talk

The **runway** (also known as the *catwalk*) is a long, narrow stage that juts out into the audience. At a fashion show, the models walk down the runway, which allows the audience to see the clothes up close.

There are as many reasons to model as there are models. Are any of the following reasons yours?

- I love clothes and makeup and want to be more involved with the fashion and beauty industries.

- I love to perform and be the center of attention.

- I'd like to be famous.

- I want to make a lot of money.

- I want to express myself creatively.

- I want to build my self-esteem.

- I want to be independent.

- I want to travel the world and experience new things.

- All of the above!

Learning from My Experience

In this book, I give you the benefit of my many years of experience in the modeling business. I've been where you probably are now—sitting in your bedroom, reading *Elle* magazine, dreaming of becoming a model.

Since then, I've experienced modeling on every level. I began modeling for local stores in Peoria. I spent a year in a secondary market (Chicago) struggling to break into the business with little to show for all my efforts. Then I went to Paris with just $150 and a return ticket, and with an incredible bit of luck, I ended up getting hired my first week by fashion designer Yves Saint Laurent. I've hit some bumps in the road, but I've always managed to move ahead. So I think I can confidently say I know the modeling business inside out.

You'll vastly increase your chances of success and avoid common pitfalls and scams if you're knowledgeable about the modeling industry, so in the chapters ahead, I give you the inside scoop on what modeling is really like, and I give you advice that will give you your best shot at success!

The Least You Need to Know

- The reality of modeling is a lot less glamorous and a lot more harsh than the image.

- Models can be exposed to rejection, loneliness, scams, and drug and alcohol abuse.

- There are several levels of modeling; the one you choose depends on your reasons for getting into the fashion industry.

Chapter 2

The World of Modeling

In This Chapter

- ◆ The many different aspects of modeling
- ◆ Modeling's relationship to advertising and marketing
- ◆ How models and celebrities embody certain images and fashion trends

Now that you know a little about the pros and cons of modeling as a career, you probably want to know more about the work itself. Modeling encompasses everything from appearing on the cover of a top fashion magazine, to posing for pictures in a catalog, to walking around a store in the local mall dressed in the latest styles. In this chapter, I discuss the major types of modeling: print (magazine and newspaper), catalog, runway, fittings, advertisement, TV, and endorsements.

It's also important that aspiring models understand how the modeling business affects the fashion industry, the advertising business, and the corporate world in general. So in the second half of this chapter, I talk about why the modeling business really is a *business*.

Cover Girl: The ABCs of Editorial Modeling

Editorial work, modeling for magazines, is one of the most important and most prestigious sources of work for models. Large national publications

Catwalk Talk

Modeling for a magazine is referred to as **editorial work** because the models appear in the editorial stories (the pages created and written by the publication's staff) as opposed to the advertisements.

such as *Vogue, Glamour, Marie Claire,* and *Seventeen,* as well as local magazines such as *Chicago* and *Boston* magazines, hire models to appear on their covers and in their stories.

Editorial work includes modeling in fashion stories, which showcase the latest style trends (the newest look in coats, the must-have shoes for spring). A second major type of editorial story is beauty related, which means anything having to do with skin care, hair care, makeup, or cosmetic procedures, such as facials and massages. Models are also used to illustrate lifestyle pieces, stories about relationships, jobs, money, food, health, and fitness.

Editorial is generally considered the most high-status type of modeling because magazines set the standard for the fashion industry as a whole. They decide what styles are in, what designers are important, and which models and celebrities embody the look of the moment. Although models used to appear on nearly all magazine covers, celebrities have mostly taken their places. The famous actor, actress, or singer gets to promote the latest movie, TV show, or CD, while the magazine gets a recognizable face that will hopefully sell a lot of copies.

The downside of editorial work is that it doesn't pay well, but models who appear in a lot of magazines actually end up making the most money. Doing editorial work establishes a woman as a top model, and then everyone else (fashion designers, advertisers, catalogs, websites) is soon clamoring to hire her. (I talk more about the pros and cons of editorial work in Chapter 18.)

The Lucrative World of Catalog/Website Modeling

Catalog/website work—posing for photos that will appear in retailers' catalogs and on their websites—generally doesn't get as much attention as magazine and runway work, but in reality, catalogs and websites employ more models than any other sector of the industry. In addition, this type of modeling pays very well. Many models make a good living doing catalog/website work alone.

Who uses catalog models? That's easy: specialty retailers such as J. Crew, Spiegel, and J. Jill, and department stores such as Neiman Marcus, Nordstrom, and Saks Fifth Avenue. Department stores often produce a dozen or so different types of catalogs. One might feature designer clothing, another might show bridge lines (designers' secondary, less-expensive lines, such as DKNY, Lauren by Ralph Lauren, and Anne Klein

New York), and a third might include moderate merchandise. They may also publish catalogs with seasonal themes, such as Christmas and Mother's Day. For each different catalog, a separate team of models is hired.

With website modeling, you're likely to work for national chains like Gap.com, JCrew.com, Anthropologie.com, and UrbanOutfitters.com, as well as for department stores like NeimanMarcus.com, Barneys.com, and Macys.com.

Catalog/website work is not fancy or creative—I like to call it bread-and-butter work. The purpose of a catalog or website is to sell merchandise, so every shot is designed to show the clothing at its best, prompting people to buy it. The models are chosen because of their ability to make the clothes appealing and desirable. (In contrast, editorial modeling is about creating an artistic image or selling an attitude.)

Modeling for catalogs/websites is one of the most lucrative types of modeling as it can pay a very high *day rate*. Also, because there are so many catalogs, there's a lot of work available in cities around the country.

Roshumba's Rules

Studying the models in catalogs is a great way to learn how to model clothes in ways that show off their best attributes. Notice how the models stand, where they place their arms, and which direction they face.

Catwalk Talk

A model's **day rate** is the amount of money she earns for a full day of work. A model's experience, her popularity, and the caliber of the client all determine her day rate.

On the Runway

You've no doubt seen footage of fashion shows on TV or in magazines, where models strut up and down a long, narrow stage (called the runway or catwalk) dressed in the newest fashions. Runway shows allow fashion designers to present their latest creations to the press, clothing store executives from around the world, and wealthy customers. Top designers today prefer using the most popular editorial models for their shows, although many designers, especially in Paris and Milan, are also always on the lookout for fresh new faces.

Some models specialize in doing runway, and travel continually doing fashion shows in second-tier fashion cities around the world (including London, Tokyo, Sydney, and Singapore). They may also model in designers' showrooms and at trunk shows (private showings of a designers' line in local stores).

Although generally only the top fashion designers' shows are showcased on television, online, and in the press, many other types of fashion shows hire models, including local events at malls and stores around the country. These shows are known as consumer fashion shows, and they give local shoppers an idea of the newest design trends and styles. (Hopefully, the audience will buy the fashions they saw on the runway.)

The very top models can earn up to $20,000 for a half hour on the runway, but for most models, that figure is about $1,500 an hour. Models who specialize in runway in second-tier fashion cities can earn anywhere from $100 to $250 an hour, while models at consumer fashion shows often earn nothing. (For more information on runway modeling, see Chapter 18.)

Modeling on the Small Screen

Models also appear in many of the national and local commercials you see on television. TV commercials generate a lot of potential work for all types of models, from the Classic Beauty to the "real-person" model (a model who doesn't meet the prerequisites for fashion modeling but who embodies a specific character type, such as the mom, the student, or the businesswoman; see Chapter 5 for more on the types of models).

The bad news about TV commercials is that models are competing not only with other models, but also with actors and "real-people" types to land those spots. (For more information about real-people models, see Chapter 20.) Often it doesn't necessarily matter how beautiful someone is; the most beautiful girl in the world could be turned down if her personality and look don't match what the client is trying to sell.

Commercials generally pay well, especially at the national level, and offer a model an opportunity to try her hand at a new medium, working in front of a *live-action camera*. But because working in front of a live-action camera is much more complicated than modeling in front of a *still camera*, filming TV commercials can be very demanding, repetitive work. (For more information on television commercials, see Chapter 19.)

Roshumba's Rules

To increase your chances of landing a TV commercial, consider taking acting and/or commercial technique classes. These teach you the skills necessary to perform your best in front of a live-action camera.

Catwalk Talk

A **live-action camera** is a camera that captures more dimensions: walking, talking, and movement. **Still cameras** capture only the dimension of a still photo; movement is captured frame by frame.

Salespeople: Advertisement and Endorsement Modeling

Appearing in a magazine, newspaper, or billboard advertisement can be a very lucrative job for a model. Of course, these lucrative jobs are harder to land.

Models who score advertisement bookings often have physical attributes that relate to the product. If it's a hair ad, she'll have healthy, beautiful hair. If it's for exercise clothes, she'll have an extremely fit, athletic body.

Other times, the model needs to embody the image of the product. (I discuss image more later in this chapter.) A model appearing in an iPod ad will need a trendy, cool, young look. A model posing as a doctor in a medical ad, however, will need to look older, more professional, and responsible. So although it can be difficult to find the right match for your exact look, the good news is that there is modeling work for many different types of looks (and hopefully yours, too!).

Reality Check

Don't think you can't model in advertisements because you don't live in New York or another very large city. Even smaller and midsize cities have local ad agencies that create advertisements for area clients, such as clothing stores, hair and beauty salons, health clubs, restaurants, banks, appliance stores, and car dealerships. Often local models are hired to appear in these ads because local clients typically don't have budgets to fly in big-name models or celebrities.

Even more lucrative and prestigious than advertising are endorsements. Landing an endorsement deal is as fabulous (and as rare) as winning the lottery. With an endorsement deal, a company signs you to represent its products and the company for a certain period of time, usually at least a year. As part of the deal, you may appear in all of that company's advertisements and represent it at various events for consumers at malls and stores. You may even be asked to meet the company's employees and investors at major corporate meetings.

All models covet endorsement deals because they (usually) pay so much. (Some models live off endorsement deals alone.) For example, L'Oréal might hire a model to endorse its hair-care, makeup, and skin-care products for 3 years at a rate of $1 million a year. But the model may be required to work only a relatively few number of days—20, perhaps—to earn that money. Granted, only a very few models—less than 1 percent—ever land endorsement deals, but if you become one of them, you've hit the modeling jackpot!

In the last few years, celebrities—in particular, actors and actresses—have been hired for many of the endorsement deals that used to be given to models. (Think Angelina Jolie for St. John fashions, Gwyneth Paltrow for Estée Lauder, and Heather Locklear and Milla Jovovich for L'Oréal.) Advertisers hire them because they are even more recognizable than any model, and they may feel they're more relatable for consumers.

Model Scoop

More and more often, companies are hiring celebrities instead of models for advertising campaigns and endorsement deals. Revlon, for instance, has hired Halle Berry, Eva Mendes, Julianne Moore, and Rachel Weisz to appear in its ads, while Kristin Davis appears in Maybelline ads. Teri Hatcher is featured in Clairol ads, while Sarah Jessica Parker works for Garnier hair color. Destiny's Child and Queen Latifah were hired to help give some razzle-dazzle to Wal-Mart's image in another ad campaign. Jessica Alba has appeared not only in ads for beauty products (for L'Oréal), but also in JC Penney and Nintendo ads and in the Got Milk? campaign. Even celebs with less glamorous images have landed advertising gigs, like David Spade, who appeared in humorous commercials for Capital One credit cards.

The Business of Modeling

When people think about modeling, they mostly think about the glitz and glamour of photo shoots and fashion shows. But behind all the fabulousness is a business, a very big business, that is an intrinsic part of the fashion industry and myriad other corporations that sell consumer products, such as soft drinks, potato chips, cars, stereos, videos, sports equipment, and so on.

Models and celebs are responsible for the bottom lines of many companies because it's their pictures that sell the mascara, the soft drink, the shoes, and the candy bars. This is why major corporations pay top models and celebs so much to help market a wide range of products. If a desirable image is connected to a product, that product can be transformed from an obscure and unprofitable item to a multimillion-dollar success.

Creating an Image

Say someone has an idea for a new perfume. She knows her perfume has a lovely scent, but it needs a desirable presentation to launch it in the marketplace. What does her company do? It hires an advertising agency to create an *image* for the product and design an advertising campaign that will create desirability and, thus, demand for the product. This is where models/celebs come in, to lend their image, personal style, physical looks, and personality to the product.

Catwalk Talk _____

An **image** is a physical embodiment of an idea or concept. A company hires a model who best represents its image. For instance, edgy cosmetic company M.A.C. chose Pamela Anderson to represent the company because of her sexy, over-the-top image.

The Face of a Product

One way to build an image for a product is to hire a particular model whose looks and personality lend a specific aura to a product. A good example of this is the care fashion designers take in selecting a model or celeb to be featured in their advertisements. A lot of money is spent designing beautiful garments, developing advertising campaigns, and manufacturing and distributing the merchandise. That's why designers pay so much attention to models who will embody what they feel is aesthetically perfect, to make their products look as appealing as possible.

Models give life to fashion trends, like the halter top, capri pants, and feathered handbag shown here.

Model Scoop _____

Cosmetic companies use models to embody their name and company image. For example, Estée Lauder has established itself as an upscale, classic line of beauty products, primarily through an advertising campaign featuring one or two models who are signed to exclusive contracts. Carolyn Murphy and Liya Kebede currently embody the Estée Lauder image. In consumers' minds, their classic features, beautiful skin, and lovely smiles are associated with Estée Lauder products. On some subliminal level, buyers think they can become just as beautiful if they use those products.

Fifteen Minutes of Fame: How Fashion Trends Originate

Besides helping to create an image for a product and sell that product to consumers, models are key players in helping to initiate fashion trends. Every time a new style comes in and is embraced by even a segment of the population, millions of dollars change hands. Models and celebrities play an essential role in making that happen.

Whenever you've been shopping, reading a magazine, or watching a TV show about fashion, you've probably wondered who decides what's in and what's out. It often happens that you see a story in a magazine with a model or celeb wearing the new short skirts, the new flat shoe, or the new brown nail polish. Then the next time you go to the mall, there are the new short skirts, the new flat shoes, and the new brown nail polish in all the stores.

That doesn't happen by accident. It's a large, well-coordinated effort on the part of the fashion industry to inform you about the newest fashion trends—and, more important, to encourage you to buy them.

Catwalk Talk _____

A **fashionista** is a woman or man, often someone who works in fashion or retail, who follows every trend. She or he is always wearing the latest styles, carrying the most fashionable purse, and sporting the hottest sunglasses.

The fashion industry, which includes clothing designers and manufacturers, magazine editors, advertisers, photographers, hairstylists, and makeup artists, is constantly redefining what's considered beautiful and what's "in." These people, fondly called *fashionistas*, can take a new idea (or recycle an old one), refine it, package it, and make us want to buy it.

Ralph Lauren can declare that Bermudas are the new look for spring and feature them in a big ad campaign. Before long, just about everyone in the country is wearing them. *Allure* magazine can print pictures of a new red lipstick, and suddenly we all need it to feel hip and modern. *W* can put actress Kirsten Dunst on the cover of the magazine, dressed in a 1970s-style coat, which may inspire us to copy her hairstyle and buy the makeup and clothes she's modeling.

Why do fashion trends change so much? Partly to keep the fashion designers and magazine editors busy working. Partly to keep people's attention. But mostly to keep people buying and buying and buying—the latest clothing, makeup, shoes, hats, belts, coats, and nail polish.

Roshumba's Rules

If you're on a budget, fashion experts suggest splurging on classics that don't go out of style (jackets, turtlenecks, tailored shirts and pants) and buying cheaper versions of trendy items (platform shoes, halter tops).

Wherever a trend originates, be it from a designer, a Hollywood, or the street, it takes a model to bring it alive and to inspire people across the country to want to copy it (translation: buy it). This is why models are so essential to business success.

The Least You Need to Know

◆ Modeling work encompasses photo shoots for magazines, catalogs, and advertisements, as well as TV commercials and runway shows.

◆ Modeling is an intrinsic part of advertising and marketing.

◆ Fashion changes continually in an effort to keep consumers buying.

Chapter 3

Do You Have What It Takes?

In This Chapter

- ◆ The physical requirements fashion models must possess
- ◆ The mental and emotional requirements of modeling
- ◆ Taking responsibility for your modeling career
- ◆ Do you have the right stuff? A quiz

Have you been told that you look like a model, or that you should give modeling a try? Many pretty girls have been told at one time or another that they should become models. But to be a successful fashion model—the type of model who appears in magazines, catalogs, and fashion shows—a person needs to be more than just pretty. Because fashion models need to be able to fit into special sample-size garments and to look a certain way when photographed, it's also necessary that they meet other requirements: they need to be tall, slim, and well proportioned; be within a certain age range; and have photogenic features, including beautiful skin, hair, teeth, and nails.

As you read this chapter, keep in mind that these physical requirements apply to fashion models only. So even if you don't meet all these requirements (for instance, many people who are interested in modeling aren't tall enough), don't despair! Other modeling opportunities are available to you,

Catwalk Talk

Parts models specialize in modeling specific body parts—legs, hands, or feet. These body parts must be free of scars and bruises and kept well maintained. **Real-people models** appear mainly in ads and TV commercials (not fashion magazine covers and fashion shows). They generally represent a type, such as a mom, a cute kid, a kindly granddad, a balding "regular Joe," or a businesswoman.

including *parts modeling* (in which only one part of your body, such as your hands, legs, or feet, is photographed) and "real-people" modeling (which relies as much on personality type as physical qualifications). I discuss the special requirements for *real-people models*, male models, plus-size models, petite models, and elegant (older) models in Chapter 20.

But there's a lot more to being a model than meets the eye—literally. A lucrative modeling career, like anything else, requires hard work, dedication, a good attitude, and good physical and mental health. Many otherwise beautiful models have seen their careers fizzle out because they were immature, irresponsible, or disorganized, or didn't manage their careers in a businesslike manner. Others couldn't handle the stress and rejection of the modeling industry, while others got involved with abusive relationships; developed mental problems, depression, or eating disorders; or abused drugs or alcohol. In the second part of this chapter, I talk about the mental and emotional requirements for a modeling career.

Finally, at the end of this chapter is a fun quiz that will help you figure out if modeling is for you.

Basic Physical Requirements

There's no getting around the fact that fashion models are hired for the way they look; therefore, height, weight, body structure, skin, hair, and other physical attributes are extremely important. Fortunately, there's a demand for many different types of fashion models—whether it's a magazine looking for a classically beautiful cover girl, a designer looking for an exotic-type model to walk in her runway show, or an advertiser looking for an athletic model to represent its new line of sneakers.

Height

People often ask me, "I'm 5'2". Why can't I be a model?" The answer is, when designers make garments to be shown on the runway, in a photo shoot, or in an advertisement, they make a sample size to fit one body type; a full range of sizes has not yet been manufactured. Models need to fit into that one sample available, which is generally a woman's size 4 or 6. Samples are cut longer to fit a taller model. Long, lean bodies move and look better on the runway. That is why models' body proportions, especially height, are so important.

The minimum required height for a fashion model in the fashion capitals is usually about 5'9" to 6'. Although there are exceptions to this rule (Kate Moss, for instance, is only about 5'7"), they are extremely rare. In certain secondary markets, such as Chicago and Los Angeles, where models are needed for the many teen and junior catalogs shot there, a fashion model may be as short as 5'8" to 5'11".

For celeb models, parts models, and real-people models specializing in TV commercials, height is not an issue. Real-people models can range from short, computer-genius guys in tech commercials, to 5'5" mom types, to towering giants.

Weight

Naming an ideal weight for a model is tough because people have different body structures, muscle tones, and heights. In general, fashion models need to be tall and slim to fit into the single sample-size garment that's available for a shoot or fashion show. Generally, models weigh 10 to 15 pounds less than the generic height/weight tables.

Instead of judging aspiring models on weight, many agencies look at their bust, waist, and hip measurements. "Hips should probably be no bigger than 35 inches," reports Cathy Gould, director of Elite Models North America. "Usually hips are the biggest problem we have with girls. Bust size is not as important," she says. "Some models are busty; some models are really flat-chested—it's not a major issue."

Roshumba's Rules

Don't think you need breast implants to make it as a model. It's actually preferable that fashion models be smaller rather than larger in the chest because then clothes tend to hang better.

The ideal waist measurement is your hip measurement minus 10 inches. So if your hips are 34 inches, your waist should be around 24 inches.

Again, for real-people models, weight is not an issue. The same goes for parts models, as long as the part they're modeling (hands, legs, feet) still looks attractive.

 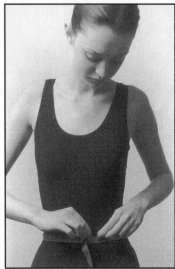 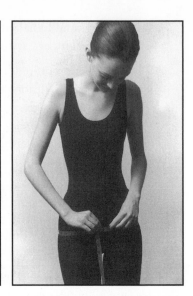

Body measurements, not weight, are used to evaluate models' figures. Here, a model takes her bust, waist, and hip measurements with a tape measure.

(Photographer: Kwame Brathwaite; model: Laura McLafferty)

Preferred Body Types

Many people don't realize that being tall doesn't automatically make you fashion-model material. Body proportion is also important. You want to project an impression of length, and that usually means long, long legs (as opposed to a long torso and short legs). You should have a toned, lean body so you can fit into sample-size clothing. (Of course, there are exceptions to the rule, such as lingerie and swimsuit models, who are fuller in the bust and hip areas.)

Real-people models come in all shapes and sizes. Parts models need to have attractive, well-proportioned parts, but the rest of their body proportions are not important.

Acceptable Clothing Size

Generally, fashion models should be no smaller than a women's size 2 and no larger than a women's size 6.

Real-people and parts models don't need to meet any specific requirements when it comes to clothing size.

Age Range

Beginning fashion models can range in age from 12 up to 21, although again, there are exceptions. In general, *modeling agents* start to scout models around the age of 14 (occasionally, they work with even younger girls), though models usually work part-time until they finish high school.

As Cathy Gould explains, "It takes a while to get a girl marketed, to get her developed, to get her book [portfolio] out there. It could take a year before something really starts to happen. So we start scouting [them] around 14.

Catwalk Talk

A **modeling agent** (often just referred to as your "agent") finds girls who have the potential to be successful models, signs a contract to represent them, markets them to clients (including magazines, advertisers, and fashion designers), and guides their careers.

"That doesn't mean they're a full-time model at 14. It means a girl may come to New York for a week to put a portfolio together. Then maybe she'll come back over the spring holiday to start to go see the magazines, then maybe she'll come for a week in the summer. She may do that for a year or two, until she's 16 or 17. It's a good gauge to see how clients are responding to the model, how the model is responding to the industry, and whether or not she has a career once she graduates high school.

"Once a girl hits a certain age, I'd say after 21, it's a little difficult [to get a career started in a major market like New York or Paris] because it takes a while to get a girl developed. In New York, we like to have the models up and running between 18 and 21, as opposed to just starting out at 21. In other cities, like Miami, Chicago, or Los Angeles, it's probably skewed a little older." So if you're over 21 and want to become a fashion model, your best bet is to try to break into a secondary market, such as Miami, Chicago, or Los Angeles.

Real-people models can be of all ages, from quirky kids featured in cereal ads to feisty old ladies in fast-food commercials. Parts models can also be of any age, as long as their "part" looks young and beautiful or fits the image of the product being advertised: for example, rugged, outdoorsy hands in a lawn fertilizer ad.

Model Skin

Healthy, clear, beautiful skin is a must for models because bad skin doesn't photograph well. People with skin that's sun damaged or marked from acne and blemishes, or

Reality Check _____

Although young children can often get away with eating anything, a bad diet (lots of fried foods, chips, candy, cookies, and soda) is unhealthful, tends to make you gain weight, and starts to show up in your skin when you become a teenager. So instead of eating junk food or fast food, eat more fresh fruits and vegetables, whole grains, fish, and chicken

people who look tired and have dark circles under their eyes from lack of sleep may have problems launching a modeling career because of their skin.

But even if you think the condition of your skin could be an impediment, don't worry—all hope is not lost. Fortunately, your skin is something you can actually improve. First of all, even at a young age, it's important to learn how to take care of your particular type of skin properly. (Check out Chapter 21 for my skin-care advice.) You can also ask your doctor or pharmacist for advice on the best ways to cleanse, moisturize (if necessary), and care for acne-prone skin. If you have more serious problems with acne (as many teenage girls do), see a dermatologist (get your parents' permission first).

It's also important to stay out of the sun and to wear sunscreen every day. Sun damage can start to show up on the skin as young as 16. Your face is your fortune, and you need to take care of yourself.

A Cover-Girl Smile

Healthy, pretty, well-maintained teeth are also crucial to modeling success. I've seen many otherwise beautiful girls turned away by modeling scouts because their teeth were discolored, crooked, or just not in good condition.

The ideal teeth are straight and white. Even if yours are not, there are many things you can do to make them look better. Consult your dentist about what you can do to get your teeth in tiptop shape. But don't sign up for expensive cosmetic dental procedures such as bonding or laminates except on the advice of an agent, and only with your parents' permission, if you're under 18.

Having braces doesn't mean you can't be a model; it means only that you'll have to delay your career just a bit. Agents would much rather see girls with braces than girls with bad teeth!

Healthy teeth and a pretty smile are key elements for success for both male and female models.

(Photographer: Kwame Brathwaite; models: Ryan Kopko and Laura McLafferty)

Hair, Beautiful Hair

Aspiring models often ask me, "What is good hair?" Good hair is healthy hair that's clean, well cut, and not overcolored, overpermed, overprocessed, or overstyled. "Hair is an individual thing," says Cathy Gould. "We're not looking for any specific hair type; anything goes today. That's the exciting thing—you see all different styles of hair [and] all different colors."

Fortunately, girls aren't usually disqualified from modeling because of the condition of their hair, but it's a good idea to keep yours looking its best. Work with a hairstylist you trust to be sure your cut suits your face and that it's a modern, youthful style. Also ask your stylist for tips on keeping your hair its healthiest.

Reality Check

When agents look at your hair, they're checking to see what can be done to it, not admiring what you did to it, so in general, the simpler the style, the better. When you're going to meet an agent, whether it's at a model search, a modeling convention, or the agency itself, shampoo and condition your hair, style it simply, and skip all the gels, sprays, and hair goos.

Real-people models can have almost any kind of hair, from balding guys, to curly haired girls, to white-haired older women. For parts models, hair is generally not an issue.

Nailing It

For all types of models, nails should be short, clean, manicured, and polished with a clear or natural-colored polish. No bitten nails! Another turnoff is nails that are long, scraggly, or unmanicured. And skip the outrageous black or green nail polish. (For more information on taking care of your nails, see Chapter 21.)

Mental and Emotional Requirements for Modeling

Modeling is a business, and like any business, it wouldn't be very profitable if the employees (the models) didn't show up for *bookings*, were late for jobs, stole half the merchandise, treated the other employees rudely, or threw tantrums every time something didn't go their way. Believe me, models have done all those things, and many of them are not modeling anymore. That's why it's important to know the kind of behavior that's acceptable for a model.

Catwalk Talk

When a model is hired for a job, whether it be to pose for a magazine or advertisement or to appear in a runway show, she is said to be "booked" for the job; a **booking** is any job a model is hired to do.

There's no denying the fact that models face rejection constantly. On my first day looking for an agency in Paris, I was rejected six times, by six different agencies. These constant rebuffs are hard to deal with even if you're happy, self-confident, and well adjusted; for a model who's very young, who's insecure, and who has low self-esteem, this endless rejection can be devastating. That's why it's so key that an aspiring model have the mental stamina necessary to survive in the business.

Finally, models face many temptations: partying, drugs, adorable boyfriends who turn out to be abusive monsters. Being able to say no to things that will cause you and others harm is equally important.

In the next sections, I cover the most important emotional and mental requirements for a model, and talk about why they are vital to a successful career—and a happy life.

A Strong Sense of Responsibility

Being responsible is key for a model. Modeling is a job, and your behavior affects a lot of people. If you're late to a booking or decide you just don't feel like working that day because you're tired or not in the mood, your irresponsibility will cause a lot of time and money to be lost and may have a negative impact on many people.

The model who is booked for a job is the center of attention. The photographer is paid a lot of money to shoot her; hairstylists, makeup artists, and fashion stylists are hired to prepare her. A studio or location is rented for the shoot. If a model doesn't show up, or shows up late, this could cost the client (be it a magazine, a fashion designer, a cosmetic company, or a catalog) a lot of time, money, and energy. So it's important to be on time, be pleasant to work with, and be willing to give your best effort.

Roshumba's Rules

If you're often late getting to places, start practicing getting there on time. Figure out in advance how you're going to get where you're going and how long it will take you to get there, and then allow yourself extra time, just in case.

Finish What You Start

Responsibility also involves knowing exactly what an assignment entails and then following it through to completion. A model who decides to fly home halfway through a 5-day shoot on location in the jungle because she doesn't like the food or is exhausted is just as bad as one who doesn't show up at all.

If you want to make it to the top, you need to be the type of person who finishes what she starts, even when the going gets tough. A good time to start learning how to complete what you start is when you're still at home contemplating a modeling career.

Motivate Yourself

Responsibility means being self-motivating—taking the initiative to do things on your own without being asked or having to be reminded 25 times. The staff at a modeling agency will tire quickly of a model who has to be told over and over that she has an assignment or an appointment, and they may soon decide that it's not worth the trouble to book that model for jobs. That's why being self-motivating is so important.

While still at home and in school, test your self-motivating skills by knowing what your assigned chores and homework assignments are and doing them without being asked. When you need extra spending money, don't depend on your parents for handouts; find your own part-time job. Taking small steps to be more self-reliant will make a big difference when your career gets going.

Roshumba's Rules

Buy a date book or PDA such as a BlackBerry, and start using it. No model worth her Louis Vuitton bag goes anywhere without hers. It contains her whole life: where she's going, when she has to be there, and what time the car is coming to pick her up.

Get Organized!

Responsibility also requires being organized. The model who forgets to put her portfolio in her backpack for an audition, leaves her date book or PDA at the photo studio where she was shooting, or is always losing things may find her career cut short. That's why it's so important to be organized, to plan ahead, and to know what you'll be doing and what you'll need for the next day. The night before, check your date book or PDA, lay out your clothes, and pack everything you'll need.

Acting Your Age

Maturity is also necessary for a successful modeling career. Models who whine, complain, and pout when things don't go their way quickly find themselves highly unpopular and eventually realize their behavior costs them jobs—and, ultimately, their careers.

Instead of getting upset about difficult situations, find a peaceful, mutually agreeable way to deal with them. It may be hard, but believe me, learning the mature way to act pays off numerous dividends once your career takes off!

Avoiding Pitfalls

It sounds old-fashioned, but knowing right from wrong is key to being a model. The reason? The temptations and pitfalls are even greater in the modeling world than in your hometown. I won't lie—drugs, alcohol, and sex are common in the fashion industry, and if you give in to them, you could find yourself addicted, unemployed, or even dead in just a matter of months.

Even minor indulgences such as going to parties, shopping, eating too much, and falling in love can be hazardous to your health, your well-being, and your career if you don't know when to say when. I like to have a good time as much as the next person. I like going to clubs and dancing with my friends to the wee hours of the morning, I love to shop, I love to eat, and I love men. But I do these things selectively and in moderation because overdoing any of them will have a negative impact on my life and my career.

Model Scoop _____

One model was incredibly popular from the moment she was discovered. She was on many magazine covers, and all the designers wanted her for their shows. But she had some very bad habits that ended up costing her career. She had a reputation of being a compulsive liar—you couldn't trust anything she said. Then she stole another model's credit card and used it to buy expensive clothes and airplane tickets. The model she stole from found out who had taken her credit card by calling one of the stores where her card had been used; then she called the police. The model/thief's agency had to pay thousands of dollars just to keep her out of jail. Even though she was absolutely gorgeous, she's hardly ever worked since then.

Develop Other Talents

When I entered the modeling business, I was fortunate in that I already had a strong sense of self-confidence. I got good grades in school, so I knew if modeling didn't work out, I could go back to school and pursue another profession. I could speak and move well, so if I didn't succeed in modeling, I could get into dancing or acting. In other words, my sense of self was not totally based on what I looked like; I knew I wouldn't be devastated if I didn't make it in an industry where looks are key. Although my ego was often put to the test, I knew I would be okay because I had other talents.

Some ways to develop self-esteem include focusing on school work and getting involved in extracurricular activities that allow you to find and nurture your own unique talents, such as excelling at academics, getting involved in sports or drama, volunteering, or developing a skill such as cooking.

Independence Day: Can You Survive?

Living independently means Mommy and Daddy aren't there to buy and cook your meals, do your laundry, clean your room, get you out of those little jams, and put up with your bad moods. The staff at the modeling agency may help you a great deal when it comes to career-related issues such as scheduling, personal maintenance, traveling, getting paid, and job selection. But at the end of the day when you've finished working, then what?

You'll need a place to live and food to eat. You'll need to buy your own food, do your own laundry, and clean your own apartment. You'll have to pay your bills and maintain your health. You may even need to find a job outside modeling until your career takes off. In other words, you will be entering the adult world of responsibility.

Reality Check _____

If you're determined to start your career and move away from home before you're 18, you'll need a parent or guardian to accompany you, at least in the beginning. You will need someone to be legally responsible for you, who can co-sign all the various legal forms involved with modeling. That's why most agencies recommend that you wait until you're 18 to begin modeling full-time.

Quiz: Do You Have What It Takes to Be a Model?

Answering the questions in this quiz (truthfully!) will help you figure out if you have what it takes to be a model:

1. You need a step stool to reach:

    A. The bathroom sink

    B. The top shelf of your locker

    C. The place where your mom hides the cookies on top of the refrigerator

    D. The moon

2. You're old enough to:

    A. Cross the street

    B. Baby-sit

    C. Drive

    D. Get your ears pierced

3. The four words that best describe your diet are:

    A. Candy, chips, and soda

    B. Hamburgers and french fries

    C. Cereal, sandwiches, and juice

    D. Fruits, vegetables, and fish

4. You were supposed to start working on an important book report a month ago. It's now the night before it's due. You:

    A. Call your friend to see if she has the book

    B. Are almost finished reading the book

    C. Are halfway finished writing the report

    D. Put the finishing touches on the finished product

5. You're sitting in your favorite class next to your best friend. How long can you go without talking to her?

    A. 10 seconds

    B. 10 minutes

    C. You don't say anything to her, but 10 minutes before the bell, you pass her a note about your after-school plans

    D. The whole class

6. The clothes you wore yesterday are:

    A. On the floor where they fell off your body

    B. On the floor under the bed where you kicked them

    C. In the family hamper

    D. Washed, dried, folded, and put away—you do your own laundry

7. The cutest guy in the school wants you to go for a swim at a romantic but dangerous cove where a bunch of kids have been hurt. You:

    A. Buy a new swimsuit and shave your legs

    B. Practice your crawl in the school pool in case something happens

    C. Agree to go, but invite along some friends who took lifesaving courses

    D. Politely decline—a guy who doesn't care about your safety and well-being isn't worth dating

8. How did you pay for your most recent clothing purchase?

    A. You whined until your mother gave you the money

    B. You hit your dad up for money when your mother was out of the room

    C. You paid for half with your baby-sitting money and your mom paid for the other half because you also needed money for a new CD

    D. You saved up your money from your part-time job

9. You have an 11 P.M. curfew. As the clock strikes 11, you're:

    A. Just starting another game of pool

    B. Looking for your car keys

    C. Careening home in your car, breaking every speed limit

    D. Walking in the door

10. You joined the school drama club because you really love to act. But instead of playing the lead, you're stuck painting backdrops and hauling furniture backstage. You:

    A. Quit as soon as you learn about how you were cheated out of a part

    B. Miss a lot of rehearsals to show them how unhappy you are

    C. Do everything you're asked, but really slowly and sullenly

    D. Act as cooperative as possible because a good attitude may help you land a part next time

How did you do? For every A answer, give yourself 1 point. For every B answer, give yourself 2 points. For every C answer, give yourself 3 points. For every D answer, give yourself 4 points.

If you scored 28 points or more, congratulations! You're definitely on the right track to a successful modeling career.

If you scored 16 to 27 points, you may have what it takes to be a model, but you may need to work on some things. Look at the questions where you scored only 1 or 2 points, and work on improving those things.

If you scored 15 points or under, you're probably a lot of fun and the life of the party, but you have a way to go before you're ready for the responsibilities of a professional modeling career.

The Least You Need to Know

◆ Fashion models need to be a certain height, weight, and age, and have good body proportions. The requirements for real-people and parts models are less stringent.

◆ Models need to have healthy, beautiful skin, teeth, hair, and nails.

◆ Models need to be responsible and mature to have a successful career.

◆ A successful modeling career won't cure all your problems.

Chapter 4

Doing Your Homework

In This Chapter

- ◆ Catching up on the latest trends
- ◆ Checking out fashion magazines and books
- ◆ Must-see TV shows for aspiring models
- ◆ Online fashion and modeling resources

This may sound funny, but to properly manage and get the most out of your modeling career, it's important to first do some homework. Believe it or not, it is to your advantage to study for a successful modeling career. These studies may not be formal (and they actually can be a lot of fun), but they are really important. The more you know about your new profession, the better prepared you will be so you can avoid common pitfalls and make the most out of what already tends to be a short-lived career.

This is as true of modeling as any other profession. Can you imagine an aspiring actress who doesn't know Meryl Streep, Jodie Foster, or Susan Sarandon? Or a newcomer to the pro basketball leagues who has never heard of Michael Jordan?

A Great Place to Start: Fashion Magazines

Fashion magazines are inexpensive, easily accessible, and fun to read. Monthly magazines such as *Vogue, Harper's Bazaar, Elle, Glamour, Seventeen, Allure,* and *Cosmopolitan* are must-reads for any aspiring model. Although they all may seem alike, these magazines actually have different editorial missions, readerships, and advertisers. They provide necessary information on fashion, makeup, and hair trends. They can teach you how to dress and present yourself so your best assets stand out. When you know the latest trends, you can be sure your look is current.

Vogue

Vogue is the fashion bible. It's extremely sophisticated and elegant in both look and tone. It features fashions by all the most important high-end designers, and it's read by everyone in the fashion industry and by some of the wealthiest, most style-conscious women in the world. Appearing in the pages of *Vogue* is one of the most prestigious assignments a model can land; once she graces the cover of *Vogue*, a model's career is pretty much made (although these days, she's competing with celebs for the privilege).

Harper's Bazaar and W

Harper's Bazaar and *W* are two other high-fashion magazines that are bold, edgy, and arty in their photography, fashion, and style. They're read by urbane, sophisticated women. They feature the highest-end and most avant-garde designers and take a lot of risks in the photographers, models, and types of stories they run. The models these two magazines book tend to be very dramatic, expressive, and exotic.

Roshumba's Rules

It's not necessary to buy every fashion magazine. You can browse through issues at your school library or the public library. You can also check them out at hair salons and coffeehouses. If you do want to buy them, keep in mind that buying a subscription is cheaper than buying single issues.

Elle

Elle is a fashion magazine that incorporates cultural and design influences from all over the world, including Africa, India, and Asia. In addition to high-end fashion, it features the work of more cutting-edge and avant-garde designers. *Elle*'s readers are young and adventurous. The models, who are often athletic or exotic types, are often pictured in motion—running, jumping, or skipping.

Glamour

Glamour takes beauty and fashion trends from the runway and translates them for working women. The fashions it features are more practical and less expensive than the fashions in high-end magazines. *Glamour* is also great for learning how to take care of your skin, hair, and body, and how to apply makeup. The models are fresh, healthy, girl-next-door types.

Seventeen and Teen Vogue

Seventeen and *Teen Vogue* are the first fashion magazines most girls ever read. They're geared toward young teenage girls and interpret beauty and fashion to make them accessible and appropriate for their readers. Both feature lots of helpful how-to hints on styling your hair, taking care of your skin, dealing with acne, applying makeup, dressing stylishly, working out, and eating right. These two magazines use mainly models who are just starting out; in fact, *Seventeen*, which has been around since the 1940s, has launched many models' careers.

Allure

Allure is *the* beauty magazine. It focuses on beauty trends, products, breakthroughs, and news. It keeps readers abreast of beauty trends and offers how-to advice on applying makeup, choosing makeup colors, taking care of your skin and hair, and related topics. *Allure* uses a wide variety of models because it wants to show all women how to be beautiful.

Cosmopolitan

Cosmopolitan is more of a lifestyle magazine, which means it focuses more on relationships, sex, jobs, self-image, and personal experiences. But its huge circulation makes an appearance in its pages or on its cover an important notch in any model's portfolio.

Other Magazines

Other publications you may want to pick up include two men's magazines: *GQ*, an upscale men's magazine that features the top

Reality Check

Now that you're reading so many fashion magazines, you may feel the urge to follow every trend you read about. Don't do it! Models should be beautiful blank slates on which clients can create their visions. Although it's good to project a modern image, there's a big difference between buying a cool new eye shadow and dyeing your hair the newest shade of purple!

menswear designers and male models with classic good looks, and *Details*, a magazine for younger men that features cutting-edge designer clothes and uses young, funky, artistic-looking models. You should also check out the music magazines *Rolling Stone* and *Vibe*, which profile top performers in the music industry and spotlight cool downtown fashions. Finally, for everything you ever wanted to know about celebrity fashion and beauty, there's *In Style*, *People*, *Star*, and *US Weekly*.

Spotting Fashion Trends

While you're reading these magazines, be on the lookout for fashion trends. Are platforms in again? What's the hot new color for the season? Being aware of fashion trends can also influence your personal style and help you embody and project a modern, contemporary image. Can you make subtle changes in your look that incorporate the newest trend? Maybe the look of the season is soft sweaters and tapered knee-length skirts complemented by a low-key beauty. Small changes, like a new lipstick, haircut, or highlights in your hair, could freshen up your look and give you the necessary edge to enhance your career.

The more an aspiring model knows about fashion and beauty trends, the better. Study magazines to learn about the ins and outs and do's and don'ts of style.

Beauty Products to Know and Love

Magazines also keep you up to date on the newest beauty products, including skin-, hair-, and body-care items. It's important to know which products are which and who makes them. Models, hairstylists, and makeup artists constantly refer to these products, and you'll want to know what they're talking about. Also, a makeup artist or hairstylist will probably use these products on you at some point in your career. You may also want to experiment with some of them so you'll know in advance how your skin/body/hair will react.

It's a good idea to try out some of the new looks you see in magazines to see how well they suit you.

Models of the Moment

Fashion magazines can also help you learn about the top models of the moment. The hottest models will be featured in *fashion spreads*, or stories about the latest beauty trends. Also, seeing which models work for which magazines can give you the inside scoop on whether a particular magazine is into your look—at least, at that moment.

Other things to pay attention to are the poses and expressions of the important models. Learn from their poses, the way they tilt their heads, the lines and energy of their bodies, the intensity in their eyes, and their smiles. Also study the image they project: are they ice-cold and aloof, sultry and sexy, bold and aggressive, or animated and smiling? Try out the different poses you see, and learn what works for you. You can also pick up some tips on how to dress and present yourself for your own success.

Catwalk Talk

A **fashion spread** is a story spotlighting a particular fashion trend. It appears toward the back of the magazine, where there are no advertisements. Because there are no ads, the pictures can "spread" across two pages.

Other Names to Know in the Fashion Industry

Fashion magazines also help you familiarize yourself with the important people in the industry (and you may even meet them if your career takes off). Fashion insiders refer to their names a lot at shoots and runway shows ("Anna" is Anna Wintour, editor in chief of *Vogue*, for example), and it's good to know who they're talking about. The best way to find out is by reading magazines' *mastheads.*

Also check out the cover credits. This list includes the names of the model appearing on the magazine's cover, as well as the photographer who took the shot and the hairstylist and makeup artist who helped create the cover girl's image. The clothing, accessories, and makeup the model is wearing are also identified. Sometimes the name of the fashion stylist (the person who selects what the model wears) is also listed. It's a good idea to familiarize yourself with these people because they usually work with the magazine's editors to create the look and the appeal of the magazine.

> **Catwalk Talk**
>
> A **masthead** lists everyone responsible for putting together the book or magazine, including the editor in chief, fashion editors, and model editor. In magazines, it usually appears between the table of contents page and the first article.

Check These Out: Books on Modeling and Fashion

Many books are available on models, modeling, fashion, designers, and photographers. Lots of models, including Kate Moss, Claudia Schiffer, and Marcus Schenkenberg, have all done semiautobiographical "picture books"—photography-oriented books with minimal text. These books feature lots of photos and take you on an interesting journey of their modeling evolution.

More biographical books on or by models are great research material. They show and tell you what life has been like for some of the most successful models, from the very beginning of their careers. Examples include *Thing of Beauty: The Tragedy of Supermodel Gia* by Stephen M. Fried, *True Beauty: Positive Attitudes and Practical Tips from the World's Leading Plus-Size Model* by Emme, and *Veronica Webb Sight: Adventures in the Big City* by Veronica Webb. (Check out Appendix B for details on all the books I mention in this chapter and more.)

> **Reality Check**
>
> Many of the books I discuss in this chapter are expensive art books, some of which cost as much as $80. So unless you have a lot of disposable income, I suggest looking for them at your local public library. If you can't find them, ask the librarian about interlibrary loans, which allow you to borrow books from other libraries' collections.

Modeling: The Big Picture

Books about the modeling industry tell the stories of the models who came before us and explain useful tidbits about the business in general. Two good ones are *Skin Deep: Inside the World of Black Fashion Models* by Barbara Summers, which is the history of African American women in the modeling industry, and *Model: The Ugly Business of Beautiful Women* by Michael Gross. *Model* gives biographical background on dozens of models, including some of the most important: Dovima in the 1950s, Twiggy in the 1960s, Cheryl Tiegs in the 1970s, Christie Brinkley in the 1980s, and Christie Turlington in the 1990s. It also provides a thorough history of the modeling business, which is both interesting and important to know.

Model Scoop

Dovima was the top model of the 1950s, and some consider her the greatest model of all time. Diagnosed with rheumatic fever at age 10, she spent the next 7 years in bed. But then she arose, like Sleeping Beauty, to almost instant success and acclaim. Almost immediately she began charging the top rate of the time—$30 an hour. She was soon so busy she was forced to change clothes in taxis and in telephone booths. Dovima appears in one of the most famous fashion photographs of all time, *Dovima and the Elephants* by Richard Avedon. The gazellelike Dovima is pictured in an elegant evening gown flanked by two enormous circus elephants.

Books About Fashion Photographers

Major fashion photographers such as Herb Ritts and Richard Avedon have published books featuring their work. Check these out to familiarize yourself with their style of photography. (Photography books tend to be very expensive, so you might want to get them from the library or look at them in the bookstore.) Other important fashion photographers whose works are available in books include Irving Penn, Peter Lindberg, Arthur Elgort, Bruce Weber, and David La Chapelle.

Books About Fashion Designers and Fashion History

Books about fashion designers and fashion history are really great to read, too. They're full of historical information, which can help you understand why and how fashion, photography, and modeling have developed and changed over the years. They fill you in on the key players of the past and how their work has affected the industry.

In fact, my favorite books to read are books about fashion designers. They tell the story of the great designers and the design houses they founded, such as Coco Chanel, Christian Dior, and Yves Saint Laurent. They inspire me so much. In addition to charting the evolution of fashion, these books capture the allure, decadence, and true art of designing clothes. They tell the stories of the designers and the visions they were trying to achieve, and at the same time, teach you about costume structure, fabrics, color, and how garments complement a woman's body. They provide information on the heart of the industry, seeing how the designers' dreams are realized. A few good ones to check out include *Christian Dior* by Richard Martin and Harold Koda; *Yves Saint Laurent 5, avenue Marceau, 75116 Paris, France* by David Teboul; *20 Years Dolce & Gabbana* by Sarah Mower; *Chanel: Her Style and Her Life* by Janet Wallach; and *Audrey Style* by Pamela Clarke Keogh and Hubert de Givenchy.

Great books on fashion history include *Icons of Fashion: The 20th Century*, edited by Gerda Buxbaum; *Fashion, Italian Style* by Valerie Steele; and *Fashion Now* by Terry Jones. *Hair and Fashion* by Lee Widdows and Caroline Cox is a fascinating look at the history of hairstyles through the ages.

Beauty Books

Makeup and hair books can teach you the basics, such as how to care for your type of skin properly, pluck your eyebrows, apply foundation, change the look of your eyes with eye makeup, trim your bangs, or blow-dry your hair. They can also guide you if you want to experiment with makeup and different hairstyles. This practical, how-to information is really important to know because at some point during your modeling career, you'll be asked to do your own hair and makeup.

Good books on makeup include *Bobbi Brown Teenage Beauty: Everything You Need to Look Pretty, Natural, Sexy and Awesome* by Bobbi Brown and *Annemarie Iverson and the Art of Makeup* by Kevyn Aucoin.

The Beauty Bible: The Ultimate Guide to Smart Beauty by Paula Begoun gives you the inside scoop on which beauty products really have scientific evidence to back up their claims. For skin-care tips, check out *The Complete Idiot's Guide to Better Skin* by Lucy Beale and Angela Jensen.

For the 411 on hair, read *Andre Talks Hair* by Andre Walker and Teresa Wiltz.

Must-See Chic TV

Over the past decade, coverage of modeling, fashion, and celebrity style on TV has increased exponentially. Just a few years ago, models and celebs were seen only on a magazine cover or in its pages—but now, because of all the television shows featuring models, fashion, and, in particular, celebrity fashion, millions of people who might otherwise not read or buy *Elle* magazine get to see *and* hear models. On television, you get to know their voices, movements, and personalities on a more intimate level.

Here I am backstage at the VH1 *Fashion Awards,* one of the biggest events for the fashion industry.

America's Next Top Model

Tyra Banks hosts this show on TV's CW in which 12 model-wannabes compete to become America's next top model. And of course, cry. A lot. Although the challenges are more for entertainment than truly reflective of the reality of modeling, aspiring models can learn many things by watching, from the way the judges encourage the models to express their personality and come alive in front of the camera, to how to take criticism with an open mind. You probably won't ever see the winners on the runways of Paris or Milan or on the cover of *Vogue*, but they have created their own niche of modeling somewhere between celebrity and traditional modeling.

8th & Ocean

This documentary-type show on MTV follows 10 aspiring models who live in a Miami Beach model apartment—where else but on the beach—as they go on go and sees, to meetings with their agent, and to auditions. It includes a range of models, from the woman who's afraid she's past her prime to the new-in-town hopeful. All in all, this show is a very realistic look at the life of a model, especially the constant rejection models have to put up with—as well as the fun times young models have hanging out together.

Project Runway

On this Bravo show, 16 wannabe fashionistas bitch and moan and compete against each other to become the next Calvin Klein or Donna Karan. Not only is it interesting to see designers' creative process, but from a model's perspective, this show reveals the importance of the interaction between designer and model, how the model often inspires the designer … and how a bad model can detract from good clothes.

Roshumba's Rules

If you can't watch MTV, VH1, or E! because you don't have cable, you can still check out what celebs are wearing in magazines on each network's website: mtv.com, vh1. com, and eonline.com.

VH1, MTV, and E! Entertainment Television

Other key viewing is the celebrity and fashion coverage on VH1, MTV, and E! Watching them helps you keep informed about the newest fashion trends as well as the coolest music and the hottest movies. Whether it's Reese Witherspoon's Oscar dress or Beyoncé's hot pants in her latest video, these networks also cover major trends in the industry.

Fashion Documentaries on TV and Video

Documentaries on fashion can be great sources of information as well. A&E's *Biography* series features many models, including Iman, Lauren Hutton, and Naomi Campbell. On DVD, the *Sports Illustrated* swimsuit issue documentary and other special-interest programs such as *Supermodels in the Rain Forest* are not only entertaining, but also offer a practical look at the industry. These offer the inside scoop on what really goes into modeling—waking up at 5 A.M. for a photo shoot, lying in chilly water for a long time until the photographer gets the shot, and working with a group traveling great distances for the shoot. You can also pick up tips about how to pose in a bathing suit and how to show off your body to its best advantage.

You could also rent *Unzipped*, a documentary about designer Isaac Mizrahi as he prepares for a fashion show, and *Ready to Wear*, a fictional movie about the Paris collections and all the behind-the-scenes shenanigans. These shows give you an in-depth look at the good, the bad, and the ugly that go into creating something of beauty. And for a less realistic but utterly charming look at the fashion industry of the 1950s, check out Audrey Hepburn in *Funny Face*.

Beauty and the Internet

The Internet has tons of information on modeling and the modeling industry—but you have to be certain that the site you're visiting is legit and offers factual information. The world of cyberspace is a con artist's paradise because it's so difficult to monitor and to trace criminals. That's why it's a good idea to trust only information from sites you've already heard of, including reputable modeling agencies, such as Elite and Ford; well-known magazines such as Style.com (*Vogue* and *W*'s website), *Elle*, and *Seventeen;* or fan-run sites that focus on one of the top models.

Many magazine websites are cool because they're interactive. You can click on and participate in quizzes and chat sessions with other readers. They're filled with fun beauty tips, advice on relationships, Style.com is packed with fashion news as well and ways to eat more healthfully. It's has pictures from all the runway shows in the fashion capitals (all of which identify the model, so it's a great way to learn all the models' names).

Reality Check

Beware of entering contests or sending money to any websites. Don't give more than $100 to anyone over the Internet, and even before you do that, Google them and be sure no complaints have been registered about them, or check them out on the Better Business Bureau's website www.bbb.org. Also be sure the company's phone number and address are listed. If the site is demanding a lot of money, or if the promises they're making sound too good to be true, they're probably not legitimate.

Many modeling agencies have websites, including Ford Models (www.fordmodels.com), Next (www.nextmodelsusa.com), Elite Model Management (www.elitemodel.com), and IMG (www.imgmodels.com). These sites have pictures and other information on all the models the agency represents, as well as the agency bio and contact information in every city where they have an office—key if you're looking for an agent.

Models.com is one of the most informative websites about current models. It has lots of pictures, biographical info (including its most important editorial and advertising pictures), modeling news, lists of the top agencies for men and women, and the top models working.

Although many scams originate on the Internet, the web is also a great source of information about the many rip-offs out there. One of my favorites is www.modelingadvice.com. Written by a commercial photographer who's heard it all, it details the many modeling swindles. (It also has a bunch of great links to modeling agencies.)

Reality Check _____

Never, ever agree to meet an individual in person whom you meet over the Internet, no matter what they promise, unless you have a parent accompanying you (not a friend, a parent). Even then, you should agree to meet someone only if they work for an established agency. We've all heard horror stories about young girls abducted and/or raped by predators they met online. Unfortunately, telling an online stranger about your wish to become a model makes you even more desirable—and vulnerable—to them.

And it's always worthwhile to Google a contest or convention you're thinking about entering (especially if it's expensive) to see if it has a history of unhappy customers.

For more on these and other websites, check out Appendix B.

The Least You Need to Know

◆ Fashion magazines keep you up to date on the hottest fashions and the most popular models, and provide lots of how-to advice for looking fabulous.

◆ Books are a great source of knowledge and inspiration for aspiring models.

◆ Watching TV can be educational—when you want to learn more about fashion and modeling.

◆ The Internet can be a great resource, but be careful to avoid scams, con artists, and worse.

Chapter 5

Which Look Are You?
The Seven Basic Model Types

In This Chapter

◆ The seven basic types of fashion and celebrity models and the characteristics of each

◆ Where do you fit in?

◆ How your type affects your career

◆ How to work your type to your best advantage

Even though there are some basic qualifications for modeling, as I explained in Chapter 3, there are really a number of different types of models representing a range of looks. Every niche of the fashion business prefers a certain type. The clean-scrubbed, all-American, Abercrombie & Fitch–catalog model might have a tough time getting a job walking the runway for an avant-garde fashion designer. Meanwhile, the sexy, big-haired Barbie type who's a knockout in the Victoria's Secret catalog is way too overdone for *Seventeen*, a magazine geared toward high-school girls. Not only does each facet of the fashion industry use different types of models, but fashion is also always changing and looking for the next new thing.

So someone who couldn't get arrested a few months ago may suddenly be the next million-dollar face!

It's important to determine which type of model you are so you don't waste your time pursuing the wrong kind of work. If you're a strapping 6-footer, you may have a difficult time getting hired for the European runway shows; they're usually looking for thinner, more delicate models. On the other hand, if you're slender and fragile-looking, you're probably not going to be modeling too many bathing suits.

Basically, fashion and celebrity models fall into seven distinct categories:

- Amazons
- Classic Beauties
- Barbie Dolls
- Chameleons

- Exotic Beauties
- Oddballs
- Athletic Girls Next Door

As you read each description in this chapter, try to figure out where you fit in. The list at the end of each category will help you pinpoint your type.

The Amazon

The Amazon is a special breed of superwoman. She is often 6' tall (or just looks like she is) with a strong, imposing, big-boned body. Like Angelina Jolie as Lara Croft in *Tomb Raider* or Wonder Woman, the Amazon has a strong, defined jawbone; an intense look in her eyes; and a full head of hair.

Catwalk Talk

The Amazons were a tribe of ferocious, powerful warrior women who are celebrated in Greek mythology (although some scholars now think they may have actually existed). From birth, they were trained to fight and were known for their skill with a bow and arrow.

Heidi Klum

Tall and regal, Heidi has the strong physique, broad shoulders, and bold features typical of an Amazon. Like many Amazons, this German-born model has done it all: appeared on the covers of fashion magazines such as *Vogue, Cosmopolitan, Elle, Marie Claire, Allure,* and *Glamour,* as well as on the coveted *Sports Illustrated* swimsuit issue. She's also one of the best-known spokesmodels for Victoria's Secret. She has appeared in ads for H&M, Nike, Liz Claiborne, and Givenchy.

The Amazon is tall, strong, and imposing-looking. Think Gisele Bündchen, Jennifer Garner, and Uma Thurman.

Like many Amazons, she's managed to extend her career beyond modeling, as host of Bravo's super-successful *Project Runway* and as an actress, with roles on *Spin City*, *Sex and the City*, and *The Life of Peter Sellars*. Heidi has also branched out into designing, with her own line of Birkenstocks and clothing, beauty, and fragrance lines.

Beyoncé

Strong, womanly, and majestic, yet warm and approachable, Beyoncé is a great example of a modern Amazon. There's her gorgeous mane of hair, her big eyes and juicy lips, and also her robust body with wide shoulders, a full bust, and, of course, major bootyliciousness. But what really defines her as an Amazon is her strong sense of self.

First famous as a member of Destiny's Child, Beyoncé has gone on to launch a successful solo music career and conquer the worlds of film, fashion, and modeling— the kind of multifield success characteristic of Amazons. In addition to appearing in the movies *Austin Powers in Goldmember*, *Dreamgirls*, and *The Pink Panther*, she has started a fashion line, House of Dereon,

Roshumba's Rules

When people ask me for the secret to success, I tell them to select a favorite model and adopt her as a role model. Copy her good habits and career moves, and learn from her mistakes.

along with her mother, Tina Knowles. On top of it, Beyoncé is a successful model, appearing in a major advertising campaigns for L'Oréal and Pepsi.

You know you're an Amazon if …

◆ You're close to 6' tall or more.

◆ You have a powerful and striking physique, with wide shoulders; full breasts, hips, and thighs; and long, shapely legs.

◆ You have large, pronounced features: expressive eyes, prominent cheekbones, and full lips.

◆ Your hair is lustrous and full-bodied, and makes a statement.

◆ Personality-wise, you're outgoing, vivacious, determined, and optimistic.

The Amazon's universal appeal adds up to a lot of modeling opportunities. Amazons often do editorial work, primarily because their image is very distinctive and compelling. They project a strong sense of personality that's hard to miss, even on a crowded newsstand.

If you're an Amazon, some of the modeling jobs you may be best suited for (but are by no means limited to) include bathing suit, lingerie, and sportswear modeling; product endorsements; and beauty stories in magazines.

Many celebrities also fit into the Amazon category. Grace Jones, Uma Thurman, and Brooke Shields come to mind. Their strong features and bodies make them stand out as much on the pages of magazines as they do on movie and TV screens.

The Classic Beauty

Classic Beauties are born, not made. These are the ladylike Reese Witherspoons of the modeling world, with perfect faces—almond-shaped eyes, beautifully slim noses, high cheekbones, medium-full lips, and sleek jaw lines.

Molly Sims

The classic All-American girl, with blond hair, green eyes, and symmetrical features, Molly has appeared in fashion magazines such as *Elle*, *Vogue*, *Cosmo*, and *Marie Claire*, as well as in the *Sports Illustrated* swimsuit issue. Her universally appealing looks and personality have scored her advertising gigs for Cover Girl, Armani, Chanel, Old Navy, and Nautica, as well as for Victoria's Secret. Sims successfully made the transition from modeling to TV, starting as host of MTV's *House of Style* and then as a reporter on *Entertainment Tonight*. Most recently, she landed a part on *Las Vegas*.

Classic Beauties have perfectly symmetrical features: oval faces, almond-shaped eyes, slim noses, high cheekbones, and chiseled lips.

Halle Berry

Gorgeous enough to be cast as a Bond Girl, yet talented enough to win an Academy Award, Halle Berry is a Classic Beauty. Her luminous skin, beautiful almond-shaped eyes, coveted nose, and sensuous mouth are in perfect proportions. Starting her career as a model (she was Miss Ohio and second runner-up to Miss America), she's equally popular with men (having appeared on the covers of *GQ*, *FHM*, and *Maxim*) and women (she's been on the covers of fashion magazines *Vogue*, *In Style*, and *Cosmopolitan*). Halle has appeared in ads for Versace and also scored a coveted cosmetics contract with Revlon.

Other famous Classic Beauties include Christy Turlington, Elizabeth Hurley, and Christie Brinkley.

You know you're a Classic Beauty if …

- You're around 5'8"—Classic Beauties are usually not too tall. You're thin but not super skinny.

- You have an oval face, almond-shaped eyes, a slim and delicate nose, sculpted cheekbones, and medium-full lips.

- Your skin is nearly flawless, with no blemishes or blotches, your hair is healthy and lustrous, and your teeth are perfectly straight and pearly white.

- You're polite, ladylike, and calm.

Classic Beauties are the envy of other models because they can do almost any kind of work. Magazines editors adore them and are constantly putting them on the covers and in the pages of their publications. Their beauty can make any product look good, so they're also hired for advertising campaigns. They get many of the lucrative beauty contracts, representing huge advertisers such as Estée Lauder, Revlon, Cover Girl, L'Oréal, Lancôme, Clairol, and Chanel. Even as they age and other models their age have long since taken their last walk down the runway, Classic Beauties continue to work. Julianne Moore, who is in her 40s, still models, as does the silver-maned beauty Carmen, who started modeling in 1945 and is still modeling today at 70-something.

In smaller cities, Classic Beauties are in demand for all kinds of work: catalog, advertisements, TV commercials, and runway.

Reality Check

Being nice, polite, and cooperative are all good qualities in a model that can help advance your career. But there is such a thing as being *too* nice. Don't let people take advantage of your niceness and youth to try to coerce you into doing things you don't want to do. Remember, you always have the right to say no, at any stage of your career.

The Barbie Doll

The Barbie Doll is defined, first and foremost, by her hair, which is often blond (although many brunette and redhead Barbies do exist). It's big—really big—so much so that it can dominate her whole face. She has a round, slightly irregular face, big blue eyes, a cute little nose, and a great big smile. Her body may be thin or even slightly plump, but she's definitely bosomy. She has long legs, slim hips, and a cute tush.

Adriana Lima

This Brazilian native definitely personifies the sexy image of her native country. Although she has appeared in ads for Guess, Anna Sui Jeans, and Bebe, and in fashion shows for Cynthia Rowley, Vera Wang, and Christian Lacroix, Lima is primarily known as one of Victoria's Secrets' sexiest Angels, thanks to her large chest, to-die-for abs, gorgeous legs, and pouty, come-hither look. Proving her wide appeal, she also scored a huge contract with Maybelline.

The Barbie is the kind of model with major sex appeal. She's beguiling, often blond, and extremely curvaceous.

Pamela Anderson

Pamela Anderson is the ultimate version of the Barbie look, with huge teased blond hair, blue eyes, and long legs. And she definitely knows how to work it! In contrast to her voluptuous body is her sweet personality. Modeling for *Playboy* put Pamela on the map and helped launch her acting career. She has since appeared on *Baywatch* and her own TV series, *VIP* and *Stacked*, as well as in movies (including some infamous home videos!). In addition, she has produced her own calendars and even published two novels.

Other Barbie types include Stephanie Seymour, Brooke Burke, and Carmen Electra.

You know you're a Barbie if …

- ◆ You have long, thick hair—preferably blond.

- ◆ You have big blue eyes, a button nose, and juicy, pouty lips.

- ◆ You're 5'5" to 5'10".

- ◆ You're slender, with large breasts, slim hips, and a cute butt.

- ◆ You're friendly, outgoing, perky, and not as naive as you seem.

The Barbie look goes in and out of fashion. But when it's hot, you'll see the Barbie on magazine covers and in lots of beauty and fashion advertisements. This type also does a lot of lingerie and swimsuit modeling. Top Barbies appear in men's magazines

(*FHM, Maxim*), the Victoria's Secret catalog, and the *Sports Illustrated* swimsuit edition. Many also have their own pinup calendars.

The Chameleon

The Chameleon is constantly changing her look, dyeing her hair from brunette to blond to red to polka dot, depending on the trend. She's willing to gain 10 pounds, lose 15, get a tan, put on full-body makeup—whatever she needs to do to keep her career alive and the spotlight on her. Chameleons depend on hairstylists, makeup artists, and designer clothes to help them create their look. In fact, if you saw a Chameleon on the street, you probably wouldn't guess she was a model. What often sets her apart from other types are a creative personality and a dramatic temperament that drive her to experiment constantly with various looks.

The Chameleon is always changing her look, trying out new hair colors, new hairstyles, new makeup— whatever it takes to stay on the cutting edge of style.

Linda Evangelista

Linda Evangelista is the ultimate Chameleon model. She continues to reinvent herself, always making each new look seem effortless. Surprisingly, it took Linda several years to establish herself as a premier model. She kept experimenting with various looks before she finally found the one that made her a darling of the fashion world: at a time when all the other models had long hair, she cut hers short, instantly launching a worldwide trend.

Linda has worked with many of the hottest photographers in the business. She is willing to do whatever it takes to fulfill the photographer's vision. This strategy has paid off for her: she has been a reigning supermodel for nearly two decades and was once quoted as saying she didn't get out of bed for less than $10,000 a day (a remark she's been trying to live down ever since).

True Chameleon that she is, she has done a phenomenal amount of editorial work and has graced the cover of just about every fashion magazine in the world time and time again. She has even managed to cross over into advertising work (for Clairol, Kenar, Yves Saint Laurent, Versace, and Chanel), which is unusual for a Chameleon. Now in her 40s, Linda still has an active career.

Charlize Theron

Charlize Theron began her career as a model in her native South Africa. She then modeled in Milan and Paris before coming to the United States to pursue a film career, where she's distinguished herself by the chameleonlike transformations she goes through for her roles, including gaining weight, cutting and dyeing her hair, wearing false teeth, and being outfitted with pads to create the look of puffy eyes. She even won an Oscar for her role as a serial killer in *Monster*, in which she was barely recognizable. She also downplayed her looks in *North Country*, for which she was also nominated for an Academy Award.

Like many *Chameleons*, Charlize will do anything to disguise her natural beauty when a role calls for it. A favorite on the red carpet, she has appeared on numerous magazine covers and in ad campaigns for Dior.

> **Roshumba's Rules**
>
> Consult your agent before you make drastic changes in your appearance, such as dyeing or cutting your hair, getting a dark tan, or undergoing plastic surgery. These changes could possibly have a negative impact on your career.

> **Catwalk Talk**
>
> A **chameleon** is a lizard that's able to change its color to blend into the landscape to avoid predators or in reaction to changes in temperature or light. Chameleon models, on the other hand, change their appearance to stand out from their environments.

Other famous Chameleons include Naomi Campbell, Carolyn Murphy, and, of course, the most famous Chameleon of all, Madonna (who did some modeling early in her career).

You know you're a Chameleon if ...

◆ You meet the basic model qualifications: tall and thin body, and good hair, skin, and teeth. (See Chapter 3 for more details.)

◆ Your hair, skin, and eyes are neutral-colored (brown or dark-blond hair, medium skin, brown eyes).

◆ You have an expressive face and dramatic or unpredictable body language.

◆ You're not afraid of artistic experimentation.

◆ You prefer to be in a creative environment more than anyplace else in the world.

Reality Check

Enjoy your 15 minutes of fame when it comes, but don't start to believe the hype. Many a beautiful star has fallen from the sky when her ego got so out of hand that people found her impossible to work with. Very few models are so extraordinary they can't easily be replaced. Remember, hundreds of girls are dying to take your place.

Chameleons do a lot of editorial work, mainly in the fashion capitals, which allows them the freedom they need for creative expression. They often team up with the most famous photographers. (Some Chameleons become muses to certain photographers because they work so often and so closely together.) You may also be hired for runway work, creative ad campaigns, and art photography. Because of their high level of creativity, Chameleons can have a tough time in smaller markets, where most of the work is doing catalog. The best bet for a Chameleon in a smaller market is to find a look that appeals to the local clients and stick with it. Avoid the outrageous—bright orange hair, radical haircuts, and strange outfits.

The Exotic Beauty

Exotic Beauty models are unique, one-of-a-kind beauties who often come from far-away places, have exotic names, and were discovered completely by chance. They possess chiseled bone structures, piercing eyes, high cheekbones, pouty lips, and beautiful, radiant skin. Their bodies are lean and shapely, with gorgeous long legs. They often have to travel great distances and overcome tremendous odds to enter the modeling business. Once their personal histories become known, the Exotics are admired for the courage and quick wits that allowed them to overcome amazing odds to land on the fashion runways.

Exotic models hail from the far corners of the globe. They often face great obstacles, even danger, to break into modeling.

Iman

Iman, perhaps the greatest Exotic Beauty of all time, is my mentor and one of the main reasons I became a model. When I was an aspiring model, reading magazines and watching the fashion shows in Peoria, Illinois, she was the person I focused on most. I studied the way she moved, the energy she projected, and the mystery she exuded. I knew I had to meet her and eventually work with her.

Iman has beautiful Exotic model features: long legs, a slender and shapely body, a neck that goes on for miles, deep-set almond-shaped eyes, a perfect chiseled bone structure, and gorgeous high cheekbones. Her movements are as nimble and graceful as a lioness stalking her prey, while her bearing is that of a regal princess.

Model Scoop

To embellish her image as an Exotic model, Iman was first introduced at a press conference by photographer Peter Beard as a savage African woman whom he had found living with a nomadic tribe in the wilds of Somalia. The truth was actually quite different: Iman was a privileged student at the University of Nairobi in Kenya, and she was the daughter of a prominent diplomat. In fact, Beard had discovered her on a trip to the Sudan and then brought her to the Wilhelmina agency. The truth eventually came out, but it didn't stop Iman's rise to the top. She soon became one of the hottest models of the late 1970s.

Iman has walked the runways for many of the top designers, including Calvin Klein, Versace, and Yves Saint Laurent. She was also featured in Revlon's Most Unforgettable Women advertising campaign. In addition, she has appeared in movies and on television, and has produced her own cosmetic line.

Eva Longoria

Petite and gorgeous, with classic Latin looks, the Mexican American Eva is anything but desperate. Longoria started her career as a model, before winning roles on *Beverly Hills 90210* and *The Young and the Restless*. She has appeared on the covers of *Marie Claire* and U.K. *Glamour*, as well as *Maxim* and *GQ*. She's also been featured in ads for Pepsi, L'Oréal, Hanes, and New York and Company.

Other Exotic models include Yamila Diaz, Salma Hayek, and Lucy Liu.

You know you're an Exotic Beauty if …

- You possess the basic physical requirements of a professional model: tall and thin body, with good skin, hair, and teeth. (See Chapter 3 for more details.)

- You have exotic facial features: distinctive eyes, a pronounced nose, healthy hair, and an extra-long neck.

- You have an exotic name or come from an obscure foreign country (or just seem like you do).

- You have an uncanny ability to survive and overcome the most impossible obstacles.

Roshumba's Rules

It's a good idea, whether you're an Exotic model from a remote country or an American in Paris, to learn to speak the language of the country where you're living. This gives you a big advantage with clients.

Exotic models are often very much in demand when they first hit the fashion scene. They're promoted as the "It" Girl of the moment, and they get all the prized modeling jobs—magazine work, runway jobs, and even advertising. Because they can easily become a passing trend, Exotics must be very clever, hard working, and lucky to maintain a lasting career. They may come in with a big bang, but they can disappear just as quickly when the initial fascination is over. Some, however, manage to be continually alluring and captivating.

Because most of the work available in smaller cities is commercial (catalogs, TV commercials, advertisements), it can be tough for an Exotic Beauty to find a lot of work in a smaller market, where clients tend to want to hire models who appeal to (and look like) their customers. The exception is cities with a large local population of people of the Exotic model's background—for instance, a Latin model in Miami.

If you're the Exotic type, surround yourself with experienced agents and managers who can help you sustain and further what you've built. If you've got an incredible look and a great story, market yourself outside modeling—tell your story to magazines and go on talk shows or other television shows. Use your story as well as your looks to advance your career.

The Oddball

What can I say about the Oddball? According to all conventional wisdom, she should never even consider the modeling business! Her features are often nothing like a model's: her eyes may be too small or too big, and her nose and teeth may be crooked. She may be too tall or too short, or maybe she moves in an odd manner. Chances are, no one would ever stop her on the street and ask if she's a model. But somehow all these peculiarities, taken together, make her stand out from the crowd.

When an Oddball first gets noticed, the industry often falls head over heels in love with her. Suddenly, a slew of look-alikes appears on the scene, and for a short time, a new trend shakes up the fashion business. During this time, you can find the Oddball on the covers and in the pages of all the major fashion magazines, on the runways for the most popular designers, and in major ad campaigns. But inevitably, a more conventional look returns, and unless she's smart and lucky, the Oddball's career may be over quickly.

Roshumba's Rules

For certain types of modeling jobs, such as catalog, TV commercials, and advertising, the focus is on the product, so your best bet is to work with the photographer and the client to figure out how to best showcase what they're selling.

With their unique, quirky beauty, Oddballs defy the conventional definition of "beauty." They may have unusually large or small features, or very short or very long hair, but somehow they stand out from the crowd.

Kate Moss

When Kate first came along, no one understood her appeal, not even other models. She was short, her eyes were too close together, she had thin lips, and she was too skinny. Well, Kate laughed all the way to the bank. (She later grew about an inch and gained a little weight.) Sulky, helpless-looking Kate actually helped establish a whole new category of model: the *Waif*. What made the Waifs so successful was that they came along at a time when the industry was tired of looking at the same old high-maintenance, overdone supermodels.

Catwalk Talk

A **Waif** is a model type who is super-skinny and not classically pretty. Waifs were the talk of the fashion world in the early 1990s. Their heyday put an end (at least temporarily) to the reign of the supermodels.

But even when the Waif look was history, Kate managed to find continued success, thanks to several Calvin Klein and other designer campaigns, countless runway shows, and magazine covers.

Although Rimmel, H&M, Chanel, and Burberry dropped her from their ad campaigns after she was photographed using cocaine, her story had a happy ending, in part because of the way Kate took responsibility for her actions—she quickly checked herself into rehab, which led to numerous magazine covers and big new advertising-campaign contracts with Chanel, Virgin, and Calvin Klein.

Sarah Jessica Parker

With her large nose, closely set eyes, and super-curly hair, Sarah Jessica is a typical oddball because, taken together, her quirky features—combined with one of the fittest bodies in the business—are highly coveted by magazine editors, fashion designers, and even advertisers. As Carrie on *Sex and the City*, she made Manolo Blahnik shoes a household name, while upping the fashion quotient on all of TV. Designers clamor to have her wear their clothes on the red carpet. She also starred in ad campaigns for the Gap and Garnier hair color and for her own perfume, while still pursuing a successful acting career.

Other Oddballs include Twiggy, Lauren Hutton, and Gemma Ward.

You know you're an Oddball if …

- ◆ Your body structure is similar to a model's (5'5'' or taller, thin, and well proportioned).

- ◆ You look unusual or distinctive in photographs or are attractive in a unique way.

- ◆ You exude a strong sense of personality, and people love being around you.

- ◆ Your personal style is very fashion forward, which makes you stand out.

- ◆ You have an overwhelming desire to be a model, even though you know you don't meet the standard requirements.

Right now, Oddball models are especially in demand for editorial work in the big fashion capitals—New York, Paris, and Milan. Take advantage of every opportunity that comes your way because your career as a model may be very limited (for instance, working for only one client) or short lived.

In a smaller market, the Oddball's best bet is to try to maximize her commercial appeal with a classic haircut and makeup that makes her best features stand out and her "oddball" features less noticeable.

Roshumba's Rules

If you're tempted to cosmetically alter your look (get a nose job, have your teeth bonded), remember that the very feature you hate might be the secret to your success.

Keep a positive attitude. Sometimes when your looks are out of the ordinary (especially when you're surrounded by Classic Beauties all day), you might start to feel bad about yourself. But remember, other models may have great careers because their looks are more conventional, but your odd qualities are the secrets to your success. Work to improve yourself as a talent and a person. Surround yourself with agents and managers who can help you make the most of your 15 minutes of fame and hopefully further your career.

The Athletic Girl Next Door

The Athletic Girl Next Door models are divided into two categories: beautiful athletes who model part-time, or full-time models who look healthy and athletic. In either case, these women are usually 6' tall or taller (or just look like they are). They look like they spend hours at the gym, perfecting their strong, muscular bodies. They have broad shoulders and powerful legs, but what makes them stand out from ordinary athletes are their pretty faces. They have medium to big eyes with a fierce, competitive look in them. They have high cheekbones, perfectly proportioned (although not necessarily small) noses, medium-full lips, fresh-scrubbed skin, and healthy hair.

The Athletic Girl Next Door is pretty and healthy and has a wholesome look that appeals to many consumers.

Elle Macpherson

Nicknamed "The Body" because of her beautiful, tall, athletic figure, Elle's wholesome looks propelled the surfer chick from Down Under into one of the most successful all-around models in the world. She has appeared on multiple covers of the *Sports Illustrated* swimsuit issue, as well as on the covers of numerous fashion magazines and even the cover of *Time* magazine. She parlayed her fame as a model into a film career (including *Sirens* and *The Edge*), workout videos, and an extremely successful line of lingerie.

Reality Check

Don't freak out if your body starts to change as you mature. It's rare that a 25-year-old model is the same body type she was when she was 16. This could be a great opportunity to expand your career. As your body changes, your model type may change, too, and you might be able to do modeling jobs you never could before.

Anna Kournikova

Although she's known as much for her sex appeal as for her on-court skills, this Russian-born tennis player is one of the most successful athlete-models. A staple of men's magazines, she has appeared on the covers of *FHM*, *Maxim*, and *GQ*, and in the *Sports Illustrated* swimsuit issue. She also has her own fragrance, trading cards, and calendar, and has appeared in an Enrique Eglesias video. In addition to all that, she has endorsement deals with Adidas and Berlei bras.

Other famous Athletic Girls Next Door include Maria Sharapova, Serena Williams, Cameron Diaz, and Gabrielle Reese.

You know you're an Athletic Girl Next Door if …

- ◆ You're 6' tall or taller (or just look like you are).

- ◆ You have a strong, muscular body, and a pretty, photogenic face.

- ◆ You're an athlete and want to continue your sports career while earning extra income.

- ◆ You're competitive and driven, yet fun to be around.

If you're an Athletic Girl Next Door, you may be best suited for (but not limited to) modeling bathing suits, athletic clothes, sportswear, and other athletic products, in both editorial and advertisements. Magazines and advertisers use Athletic Girls Next Door when they want to project a healthy, natural appeal, or just want a more sporty look. This is especially true of magazines that focus on health and fitness such as *Self*, *Shape*, and *Fitness*. Catalogs are another potential lucrative source of work, although athletic models aren't usually found on the fashion runways because their bodies can be too muscular for the clothes.

Athletes who are models are really lucky because they have two potentially lucrative careers that feed off each other. You should assemble a good team of professionals who can help you harmoniously manage both careers.

In smaller markets, the Athletic Girl Next Door type is one of the most popular types of models. Her healthy and wholesome looks appeal to just about everyone, so clients such as catalogs and local advertisers love to hire her.

Once you know which model type you are, you'll have a better idea of the best strategy for pursuing a career, whether it's modeling in a local market or in one of the fashion capitals.

The Least You Need to Know

◆ There are seven basic types of models, each with its own physical characteristics.

◆ Your type depends on your facial features, body structure, and personality, to some degree.

◆ Even the most famous, successful models can be categorized as a type.

◆ It's essential that you know which type you are because it will have a big impact on your career.

Part 2

Breaking Into the Business

So now that you've learned everything you need to know about the modeling business, your next question is probably, "How do I get started?" In Part 2, I tell you everything you need to know about launching a modeling career.

The first step in becoming a professional model is finding an agent to guide and manage your career, so I start by detailing the basic materials you need to find an agent and talk about the many options for finding one. Because many successful models start their careers with unpaid modeling jobs (which are called "hobby" modeling jobs or modeling for experience), I discuss how aspiring models can find these types of jobs and how they can start modeling professionally in Miami, Chicago, and Los Angeles (the secondary markets). The next step, of course, is big-time modeling, and I describe what it's like to model in the international fashion capitals (New York, Milan, and Paris).

Finally, one whole chapter is devoted entirely to parents, telling them everything they need to know about the business so they can ensure that their child's career is a safe, successful, and happy experience for everyone. I also go into detail about the many scams common in the modeling industry so you don't get caught up in one.

Chapter 6

Getting Started

In This Chapter

◆ Breaking into the modeling biz

◆ Keep it simple: clothing, hair, and makeup tips

◆ Tips for taking the snapshots you'll need

◆ Putting together your statistics card and letter of introduction

In Part 1, you learned a lot about the modeling industry. Although it can be a difficult field to break into, the very first steps you need to take are relatively easy, painless, and inexpensive. Yes, I did say *inexpensive!* The most common modeling scams involve pricy pictures that will supposedly launch your career. But if anyone besides a model agent at a reputable agency arranges a photo session, it's probably a scam. And if anyone wants to charge more than $300 for pictures, it's definitely a scam. When you learn the real way models find agents, you'll see why.

Other schemes involve elaborate hair and makeup sessions, but in this chapter, I give you the real scoop on how you need to look to get your foot in the door (and it doesn't involve professional hair and makeup artists). When you know how to look the part, you'll want to start getting together some essential (but simple-to-assemble) materials—snapshots of yourself, an index card with your vital statistics on it, and a letter of introduction to send to agents.

Your ultimate goal is to find a modeling agency to represent you. Your agency will help develop your look, send you on auditions and job interviews with potential clients, and guide and develop your career. Agencies have special employees, called modeling scouts, who are always on the lookout for new talent. With the simple materials I describe in this chapter, you'll have everything you need to contact agencies and impress their scouts, whether it's at open calls at their offices; at modeling searches, conventions, and schools; or by mail.

Looking the Part

When you're just starting your modeling career and going to meet with an agent or a model scout for the first time, you'll probably want to look your most fashionable. Maybe you think you look your best in high heels and a sexy little black minidress. Or perhaps you're thinking about wearing that beautiful prom dress that's an exact copy of the dress Kirsten Dunst wore to the Golden Globe awards.

But believe it or not, none of those outfits is what a model scout wants to see. They're there to look at beautiful young girls, not the latest fashions. They want to see natural-looking girls who would be lovely raw material agents, fashion editors, advertising clients, hairstylists, makeup artists, fashion editors, and clothing stylists can use to turn into an exquisite image of beauty.

That's why you want to dress so they'll notice *you*— your tall and slim body, fantastic legs, thick and healthy hair, and pretty eyes—not your overstyled hair, funky fashions, and super-long acrylic nails.

> **Reality Check**
>
> There's no need to spend a lot of money on designer outfits or the latest fashions. Model scouts aren't looking for the girl who can afford the most expensive, most fashionable outfit in the whole mall; they're looking for beautiful girls who look great even in the simplest, most casual outfits. Trust me on this: keep it simple!

> **Reality Check**
>
> In general, it's a good idea to avoid decorative body art. This includes everything from long, acrylic nails, to obvious tattoos, body piercings (other than the earlobes), and other types of decorative body art. Models make their living by using their bodies to sell products, and it's best if your body is as close to its simple, natural, healthy state as possible.

Dressing for Success

To create a positive first impression, dress as simply as possible so the real you shines through. Whether it's for an open call, a convention, a model search, or your snapshots, dress in a comfortable, simple manner that's appropriate for your age and that shows your shape. Neat jeans or a fitted, above-the-knee skirt worn with a T-shirt or sweater are perfect. Flat, comfortable shoes or sneakers are also good.

Avoid high heels—agents and model scouts want to see at a glance how tall you are. (Not to mention if you're tottering around in stilettos, you'll be focusing way too much attention on staying upright, which could make you come off as nervous, unsteady, and uncomfortable.) Clothes that are too tight or low-cut or revealing often come off as vulgar or trashy—not the image you want to project. Oversize or baggy clothes hide your shape and look like you have something to hide. Also avoid anything trendy, messy, dressy, or overdone.

Makeup Tips

Another mistake a lot of aspiring models make is wearing too much makeup. When you're going to meet a model scout, don't glop on every product in your bathroom— heavy foundation and powder, big stripes of blush, tons of eye shadow, a couple layers of mascara, and a pound of lipstick.

Model scouts don't want to see girls with a lot of makeup on their faces. In fact, sometimes scouts even ask girls to go into the bathroom and wash the makeup off their faces if it's too heavy.

Ideally, you should wear little to no makeup, maybe just a little mascara to make your eyes stand out and some natural-colored lip gloss.

Model Hair

Model hair is beautiful, healthy, shiny, well cut, clean, and conditioned. Hair of all textures, from very straight to super-curly that can be used in ads for hair products— shampoos, conditioners, styling products, hair colors—is in high demand and can make models a lot of money. So keep your hair looking its best. When you're going to be meeting with a model scout, be sure

Roshumba's Rules

When you're meeting model scouts, don't load up your hair with excessive amounts of styling products, such as gels, mousses, and sprays. It can be blow-dried, as long as it looks natural, not elaborate or exaggerated.

your hair is clean, free from split ends, and lightly styled. If you're attending a model search, convention, or open call, don't pull your hair back into a ponytail; the model scout will want to see how it looks hanging free.

Be very careful about coloring your hair because certain colors can make you look older, can clash with your skin tone, or may not match your eyebrows. Also, if color is not done properly, it could damage your hair and change its texture. If you do decide to color your hair, go to a competent professional, and choose a color within a couple shades of your natural hair color. Anything else tends to look too unnatural and un- attractive. Better yet, leave your color alone. Once an agency has signed you, they will decide whether you need to have your hair colored and, if so, will send you to a color- ist they trust.

Avoid perming your hair, too. Again, the model scout wants to see what your hair looks like naturally. Plus, the chemicals in the solutions used in perms could severely damage your hair. Perms tend to be problematic once they start to grow out, too, and redoing them increases the chances of damage exponentially. African American women often chemically straighten their hair to make it easier to maintain. Although that's not a problem, just be sure it doesn't get damaged from overprocessing. Keeping it conditioned also helps.

Drastically cutting your hair is also generally not a good idea. Although short hair has its moments in the fashion spotlight, agencies generally prefer models with midlength or long hair, which is more versatile than short hair. A drastic haircut could also throw off the balance of your face and body. And remember, it's a lot easier to cut your hair later than have to sit around and wait for it to grow back.

The Photos You'll Need

As I mentioned, one big mistake that many aspiring models often make is spending tons of money on photos, portfolios, and composites before they get an agent. This is a total waste of money and time, and people who tell you otherwise either don't know what they're talking about or are scamming you.

When you have an agent, he or she will make arrangements for all the photos, test shoots, port- folios, and composites you'll need. Most reputable agencies even pay for them up front, and the cost is subtracted from the money you earn when you

Reality Check

Be wary if an agent asks you for money up front to pay for any of these photos, portfolios, or composites because it's not the usual practice.

start working. Photos taken without an agent's guidance could be essentially useless because the photos might not capture the image the agent plans to build for you and promote to the fashion industry. When agents are looking for new models, they want to develop the model's own natural beauty into a marketable style, so spending a lot of money on professional photos that probably won't project the image they're after isn't necessary.

Once you have an agency, it will provide you with a portfolio with the agency's name and logo on it and composites. It'll also post your photos on its website. Your agent will also want to put together a composite card of you. The composite usually consists of a beautiful head shot and a body shot, and maybe a couple additional photos showing your personality or exceptional attributes, such as beautiful legs or a lovely smile. The photos used in the composite are generally selected from test photo shoots the agent has set up. Or the agency may want to incorporate pictures from magazine tear sheets (pictures of you cut from the publication in which they appeared). (For more information on test shoots for your book, see Chapter 12. To learn more about composites, portfolios, agency websites, and other model materials, see Chapter 13.)

A Warning About "Photographers" and Other Model Scammers

I can't emphasize enough that you must be careful about who you deal with as a new model—even as your career takes off. Some "photographers" often prey on young, unsuspecting models and their parents, suggesting that models need loads of professional pictures, composites, portfolios, and elaborate, expensive photo sessions that include hair and makeup artists before they've found an agent or started their careers. They tell the models that agents won't accept them if they don't have a portfolio full of pictures. If you run across this type of "photographer," *beware!* He's probably trying to scare you to make money off the photo session—not to help you launch a career. If anyone tells you that you need to spend a lot of money on pictures, hairstylists, makeup artists, photographers, or clothes to get started in this business, either he's not completely informed about the modeling process or he's scamming you. In either case, grab your wallet and run!

Also watch out for people who want to charge you to post your picture on their website, promising that all top fashion editors and designers check out the site to find new models. Again, that's not how it works. Fashion editors, designers, and advertisers work only established agencies; they don't have time to look at hundreds of pictures— most of them of people who don't have the necessary requirements for modeling—on an unknown website.

Model Scoop _____

Sometimes young, inexperienced photographers will volunteer to do photo sessions with aspiring models to get experience and develop their own books. This is called a "test shoot for experience," and it can be a great learning experience for a model. But the difference here is that there is no charge, or that it's minimal (under $300), just enough to cover the processing and printing of the film. (See Chapter 8 for more information on test shoots for experience.)

Getting in the Door Is a Snap(shot)

The most you need to get your foot in the door are a few snapshots that by no means require a professional to take. As I've said, anything more is really a waste of time and money. (But if you already have test shots you would like to use, by all means, use them.)

These snapshots can be handed out at model searches, conventions, and open calls. (See Chapter 7 for more information about these.) They also can be e-mailed or mailed to agents you can't meet in person. Keep your photos simple; don't bother spending a lot of money on fancy effects or special clothes. Again, the model scouts aren't looking for fabulous photography and the latest fashions; all they want to see is what you look like, and if they can tell that from the photo, then that photo is a masterpiece.

Roshumba's Rules _____

Take at least 24 or 36 photos so you'll be able to choose the best ones. Although a digital camera lets you see whether you have the shots you need, a disposable camera is fine, too.

Ask a friend or family member who's handy with a camera to shoot you. You'll want to take both head shots, which are close-ups of your head and shoulders, and body shots, which are pictures that show your body from head to toe.

Getting Camera-Ready

In the photos, your face should be clean, and you should be wearing little or no makeup. At most, apply a little mascara and some natural-colored lip gloss; if you're having a bad skin day, use a small amount of concealer to discreetly cover a zit or two. Remember, the agent is interested in seeing the real you, not the made-up you. Be sure your hair is pulled off your face and simply styled.

For the head shots, it doesn't really matter what you wear because your clothes won't show in the photo. For the body shots, you'll want to pose in a solid-colored one- or two-piece bathing suit or leotard, which will give agents the best look at your body. Avoid anything too revealing; thongs, G-strings, and T-backs are too flashy. Leopard prints, bold graphics, or stripes on a bathing suit or leotard make it harder to see your body's natural silhouette. Also, prints may make you look chunky or make your arms and legs look shorter, so it's best to keep it simple.

Pose in front of a plain white or pale-colored background; a blank wall is perfect. Be sure the lighting on your face makes you look healthy and pretty (check yourself with a handheld mirror first).

Reality Check

Too-revealing bathing suits can be distracting and make you come off as overly sexy. If you're a naturally sexy girl, it will show through in your personality. Besides, when you meet with agents, you'll be in a public business environment, so it's best to have some decorum and be respectful.

Karen Lee, director of scouting at Elite Model Management, offers these additional tips about taking pictures:

- Do not pose.

- Wear a two-piece swimsuit.

- Take some photos with your hair up and some with your hair down.

- Be sure to put your name, address, age, measurements (bust, waist, hips, and height), and phone number on the back of the photos. (If you're e-mailing them, be sure you include your name as the name of the photo.)

Shooting Star

You'll need several different shots:

- Four head shots

- Four shots from the waist up

- Four full-length snapshots of your body

- A casual snapshot (optional)

Head shots—close-up shots of your head and shoulders—give agents a good look at your head, facial features, and smile. Take two full-frontal face shots. In one of the photos, you should be smiling; in the other, you should be relaxed and natural looking. Also take photos of your profiles (the side view of your face), left and right.

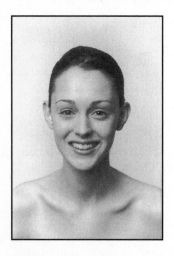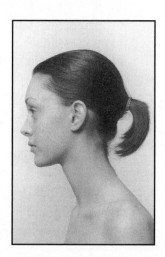

You'll want four snapshots of your head and neck: one smiling, one relaxed and natural looking, and two profile (side) shots.

(Photographer: Kwame Brathwaite; model: Laura McLafferty)

From-the-waist-up shots give agents an idea of what your body measurements and proportions are. Again, take two facing the camera, one smiling, and one with no smile. Then take two profile shots, left and right.

Full-length body snapshots give agents an idea of your overall body shape, as well as the proportions of your legs and torso. You'll want one full-length (from head to toe) shot from the front, two from the sides (left and right), and one from the back.

It's optional, but you could also include a casual snapshot. This could be a shot of you having fun or hanging out. Casual snapshots should capture your personality in a fun environment. These pictures give agents a feel for the real you, so use your imagination here.

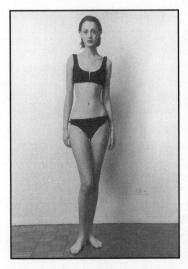 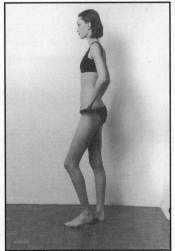 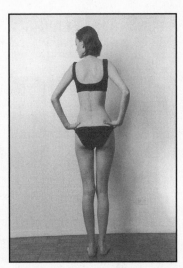

You'll want four full-length photos of your body: a frontal shot, shots from each side, and a back shot.

(Photographer: Kwame Brathwaite; model: Laura McLafferty)

A casual snapshot such as this one gives agents an idea of your personality.

(Photographer: Kwame Brathwaite; model: Laura McLafferty)

Model Scoop

I've seen girls send in all kinds of casual snapshots of themselves. One girl who was into horses sent in a picture of herself dressed in riding gear, posing on her horse. A couple of girls who were members of the school basketball team sent in photos of themselves pictured in the school gym in their basketball uniforms. Another girl was photographed posing under a tree playing the guitar. My casual snapshot showed me dressed in a leotard, stretching in the backyard—I wanted to show agents I was very health-conscious. The important thing is to capture yourself doing something you like, which allows your special talents to show through.

When you've shot the pictures you need, have them developed. (Getting them developed at the local drugstore is fine; there's no reason for expensive processing.) Choose the best shots, and have several prints made of each so you'll be able to give them out. Be sure to write your name, age, phone number, and measurements in pen on the back of each photo.

Your Statistics Card

Agents need to know your height, weight, and body *measurements* to determine what body type you are and to decide what kinds of modeling (runway, bathing suit, petite) you're best suited for. Plus, this information helps them gauge whether you'll fit in the clothes a potential client wants you to wear.

Catwalk Talk

Measurements are usually written as a series of three numbers: for example, 34-24-34. The first number is the bust size, the second is the waist measurement, and the third is the hip size. Use a measuring tape to take yours at the widest part of each area.

Your statistics card, which lists all your vital measurements, gives agents all your important information at their fingertips. To create your own statistics card to give to agents, write the following measurements on several blank 3×5-inch index cards:

- Name (or modeling name)
- Address
- Home and cell phone number (Include the best time to call.)
- E-mail address
- Age

- Height
- Weight
- Bust, waist, and hip measurements
- Dress size

- Shoe size
- Eye color
- Hair color
- Special talents (for example, you study ballet or speak a second language)

This card, along with your snapshots, is all you need to get started. Good luck!

How Do You Measure Up?

All you need to take your measurements is a measuring tape. Place the end of the tape (that begins with 1 inch) in the center of the front of your body or body part you'll be measuring. Wrap the tape around the back of your body, bringing it around until both ends meet. Pull it taut but not tight. Write down the number in inches (not centimeters).

You'll need to measure the following parts of your body:

- Bust
- Waist
- Hips

To take your bust measurement, wrap the measuring tape around the fullest part of your chest and note the number. To figure out your cup size, wrap the tape around your chest directly underneath your breasts. Subtract the second measurement (your chest under your bust) from the first (your full bust); that number is your cup size. If the difference between the two numbers is 1, you're an A cup. If the difference is 2, you're a B cup. If the difference is 3, you're a C cup, and so on. If this is too complicated, you can take the size from a bra that fits perfectly.

Measure your waist at your natural waistline, where your belly button is.

Measure your hips where your rear end is fullest.

A Letter of Introduction

The last thing you need to get started in the modeling business is a letter of introduction, which you enclose with your photos and statistics card when you're contacting agents to see if they're interested in representing you. Also include a self-addressed, stamped envelope when you're sending photos if you want the agents to return them to you. You can either snail-mail or e-mail this letter, but always address it to "New Faces Department." (I list e-mail contacts for some agencies in Appendix C, but you can also usually find this on agency websites.) If you're meeting model scouts in person at a search, convention, or open call, you can skip the letter.

Use this letter or e-mail to introduce yourself to the agent. Include such information as your age, height, weight, dress size, and eye and hair color. If you can tell them something that's unique about you (such as hobbies or special talents), be sure to mention it. Finally, ask the agency if they're interested in representing you or if they have any advice for things you can improve that will help get your modeling career off the ground. Most important, be sure it has your name, address, and phone number on it! It's also a good idea to have someone proofread your letter.

Here's one of the letters I sent to an agency when I was just starting out.

> Roshumba Williams
> 10 Main Street
> Anywhere, IL 12345
> 309-555-5555
>
> March 3, 1986
>
> To: New Faces Department
>
> Dear Sir or Madam:
>
> My name is Roshumba Williams, and I am very interested in being a model. I am 16 years old and 5'10" tall. I weigh 115 pounds, and my measurements are 34-23-33. I wear a dress size 2 or 4. My eyes and hair are brown.
>
> I live in Peoria, Illinois, where I am a high school junior. I am enrolled in my school's work-study program. I work as a receptionist at the Salvation Army.
>
> Please contact me and let me know if you think I have what it takes to be a model, and if you would be interested in representing me. If not, I would appreciate your advice on how I can improve myself, or any suggestions of other agencies that might be interested in my look.

I am enclosing some photos, my statistics card, and a self-addressed, stamped envelope. I would really appreciate it if you could return my photos and any advice or comments.

Thank you so very much.

Sincerely yours,

Roshumba Williams

If you're contacting the agency by e-mail, you can also use this letter. Just attach the photos and a file with your statistics to the e-mail (and omit from the letter the bit about returning the photos). If you're mailing the letter, also enclose your photos, your statistic card, and a self-addressed, stamped envelope. A professional but friendly letter like this one will let the agency know you're serious enough about modeling to have done your homework and know how to go about getting into the business. If you don't receive a response 2 weeks after sending the letter, contact the agency for feedback.

The Least You Need to Know

- Dressing simply, not like a model in a magazine, is the best way to impress an agent.

- When meeting with an agent, keep your hair and makeup simple.

- Don't spend a lot of money on photos; do-it-yourself ones are fine.

- List all your measurements on a statistics card to give to agents. If you aren't meeting with them in person, send or e-mail a letter of introduction along with your snapshots and statistic card.

Finding an Agent

In This Chapter

- ◆ Why a model needs an agent
- ◆ How you can shine at open calls, model searches, and model conventions
- ◆ What can a modeling school teach you?
- ◆ The easiest and least expensive way to find an agent
- ◆ Exploring other nonmodel options in the fashion industry

Finding an agent can be one of the most difficult obstacles a fledgling model must face. Fortunately, there are many ways to find an agent, including open calls at modeling agencies, regional model searches, model conventions, modeling schools, online or on a TV show, or simply sending photos of yourself to an agency. In this chapter, I tell you everything you need to know!

Why Have an Agent?

Finding an agent is the first major hurdle on the road to becoming a model, whether you're a fashion model, a celebrity, or a specialty model (a real-people model, a parts model, or a plus-size model). Agents help models get their careers off the ground. They help make the model's look as marketable as possible, send her on job interviews, and manage her career. An agent helps with testing with the right photographers and helps a model develop her portfolio, making sure it captures her best attributes. Finally, the agent is the key link between the model and her clients.

Opening Doors at Open Calls

Open calls are a little like a modeling agency's version of an open house. Agencies are always looking for new models to represent, so they invite aspiring models to come into their offices at a set time to meet them to see if they have modeling potential. Anyone who is interested in getting into modeling is free to drop by the agency during open calls to meet with the agents and bookers. Some agencies hold open calls as frequently as twice a week, others have them less often, and some don't hold them at all. To find out about open calls, call the agency you are interested in and ask when they hold open calls.

Before you go, call the agency to confirm the time, date, and location of the open call. Also ask what you should wear and what you need to bring. Usually, the agency wants you to bring a couple snapshots of your face, a few of your body in a simple swimsuit, and a shot capturing your personality, as well as your statistics card listing your age, height, weight, body measurements, hair, and eye color. (See Chapter 6 for more information on these materials.)

Making a Good Impression

You have only one chance to make a first impression, so you'll want to look your best at an open call. Don't wear your most fashionable or outrageous outfit. Instead, dress simply in clean, comfortable clothes that fit you well, and go light on the makeup and hair products.

The models in these photos are wearing the perfect type of outfits for finding an agent: casual but neat, body-conscious but not too tight or revealing.

(Photographer: Kwame Brathwaite; models: Laura McLafferty and Ryan Kopko)

What not to wear: the two aspiring models on the left have it all wrong. One is wearing way-oversize hip-hop clothes and too much jewelry; the other is over-dressed in a formal prom dress. The neatly dressed model on the right will probably get the most positive response from agents.

Keeping Your Cool

When you arrive at the open call, you'll be asked to sign in and take a seat in a special room or in the reception area until the agent comes out. I advise getting there early so you can sit down and get comfortable with the environment before you meet with the agent. Modeling agencies are frantically busy, with models rushing in and out, messengers delivering packages, phones ringing off the hook, and people running around. You also might want to check yourself in the bathroom mirror to be sure you look fresh. And then just try to relax.

Roshumba's Rules _____

While you're waiting at the open call, do whatever you do to relax and make yourself comfortable. Take a series of deep breaths or read a book of positive affirmations, such as Deepak Chopra's *The Seven Spiritual Laws of Success: A Practical Guide to the Fulfillment of Your Dreams*.

It's only natural to feel uncomfortable sitting in a room full of beautiful girls who are all trying to get the same thing you are. Try not to allow yourself to get distracted by them. Don't look at the other models' pictures or portfolios, and don't let them look at yours. Be friendly and cordial, but if they ask to see your pictures, just say, politely but firmly, "I prefer not to." Don't make the mistake of starting to compete with all the other girls; don't start thinking everyone is more beautiful. You probably have something the other girls don't have, and it may be just what the agency is looking for! Finally, try to enjoy the experience.

Show Time!

The agents or bookers will come out to meet with you or invite you into their office. They'll look at your face and figure, and view your snapshots and statistics card. They're looking to see if you meet the basic physical requirements for modeling—that you're the right height, weight, and age, and have the right body proportions. (See Chapter 3 for more specifics.)

They may ask you to walk for them, to get an idea of how you'll move in front of the camera and on the runway. They'll also evaluate your facial expressions and try to see if they can visualize you in an advertisement or on the cover of a magazine. To try to get a feel for your personality, which is almost as important as looks for a successful model, they may ask you why you're interested in modeling, who your favorite model is, what your family is like, or where you go to school.

Reality Check _____

Some girls at open calls are actually snippy to the agents, acting like they're doing the agent a favor by even coming to the open call or being mad they had to wait. Some act like, "I know I'm going to be a star. If you don't take me, somebody else will." But even if these girls do find an agent willing to sign them, with attitudes like that, chances are, their careers will be short-lived.

Often a great personality can be the clincher at an open call, so be sure to be friendly and outgoing. Also, bring up whatever is special about you, whether you are an athlete or a painter, or can speak another language. At one of the open calls I was involved with, the agent asked a girl why she wanted to model. She said she wanted to get into modeling to help launch a singing career. The agent then asked her to sing something, and this girl sang this amazing blues song that truly expressed her personality. Everyone immediately fell in love with her, and she was signed on the spot. If you're given a chance to show off a particular talent or a charming personality, go for it!

Play the Field

If you're unable to land an agent in your first few meetings, go on as many open calls at reputable agencies as you can. They're a great experience and will help you get over the shock and scariness of walking into an agency cold turkey, and your confidence will increase. Furthermore, every agency (and every agent) has different tastes in models. Some agents might represent mostly Amazons, others have more success with Classic Beauties, and others do best with the Athletic Girls Next Door. (See Chapter 5 for more information on the different types of models.) Even if 10 agencies turn you down, the eleventh might think you have that special something.

If circumstances force you to drop by an agency when they're not having an open call—maybe you're in town for only a few days—you should know in advance there's a good chance the door will be slammed in your face and you'll be told to come back during an open call. Sometimes you might need to take that chance, but be prepared for the possibility that the agency's staff may be extremely rude and dismissive.

Model Scoop

I must confess, I didn't follow my own advice. I arrived in Paris on June 27, 1987, with enough money to last only 2 weeks. I didn't have time to wait for the agencies' next open calls, so I just dropped by their offices. Some of them were polite and turned me down; others were incredibly rude and turned me down; a few said to come back at the next open call. My last stop was at a small agency called Cosa Nostra, which booked models for fashion shows. They were welcoming and supportive, and they helped me get my first job, modeling for designer Yves Saint Laurent—the very next day!

Possible Results: Yes, No, Maybe

Models the agency is interested in will usually get a *callback*, requesting that they come in for a second meeting. Congratulations! This is a very good sign that you caught someone's eye. Callbacks allow the agency to see and meet with you another time to make sure

Catwalk Talk

When an agency asks you to come back for a second interview because they're considering representing you, they are giving you a **callback.** You can get a callback by phone, e-mail, or regular mail.

you're right for them. You'll probably be introduced to the other people in the agency—bookers, department managers, even photographers—to see if they like your look, if they think you fit their company's image, and if they have ideas about how to develop your talent.

Other times, an agency may think you have modeling potential but that you maybe need to polish your presentation. (This is especially true of very young girls, say, 13- and 14-year-olds.) In this case, they may invite you to participate in a model search or model convention and ask you to keep in touch. If you're invited to participate in a search or convention, by all means attend. These competitions allow you to make contacts with professional makeup artists, hairstylists, and runway coordinators (the person who teaches models how to walk on a runway and show their personality). This process gives the agent a chance to see how you behave and blossom in an intimate modeling situation.

If the agents aren't interested in representing you, they may just politely glance at you and your pictures during the open call and then thank you for taking the time to come in. Some may be direct and tell you right then and there that they're not interested; often you'll be able to tell from their attitudes. Others will send you a letter a week or so later. In some cases, an agency may not contact you at all.

If you think you want to work with a particular agency but haven't received any feedback since meeting with them, wait a week and then call back and ask to speak with the person in charge of the open call. Let him know who you are, tell him you're interested in working with the agency, and ask him if he's interested in you. If he's not, ask why and whether he has any advice for you. It's a good idea to find out what he doesn't like because it may be a simple thing you can easily work on to improve.

Reality Check

Never harass an agency! Don't call them every day and bug them. Agencies get hundreds of calls a day, and handle the careers of hundreds of girls—they don't have time to field dozens of calls from one person. Word gets around about harassers, and these would-be models can quickly find themselves shut out of every agency in town.

Listen to what the agents tell you. If you happen to notice that people are repeating the same thing—if they're all suggesting that you cut your hair, lose weight, or wait until you're older and get your braces off—it makes sense to heed their advice. After all, they are the professionals, and following their suggestions will increase your chances of launching your career.

Looking for a Winner: Model Searches

Model searches are contests held all over the country, in cities large and small, at all times of year, to try to spot the next Tyra Banks or Carmen Kass. I've found model searches (also called model contests) to be fun and exciting. They have helped many young models get their first taste of the business.

Search contestants can range in age from 14 to 21; the average age is 15 or 16. If you're under 18, you'll need to bring your parent or guardian because you need his or her signature on the entrance form. (And it's a good idea to have an adult's moral support and common sense along with you anyway.) Often girls bring their own cheering sections—mom, dad, boyfriend, grandparents, and friends.

Catwalk Talk

A **model search** is a contest held by a modeling agency or magazine to find potential new models. They are held in cities all around the country, often at local malls.

Not only are the contests fun, but they can also be a crucial turning point in your career. Prizes vary depending on the sponsor (contests are usually sponsored by modeling agencies, magazines, and clothing and cosmetic companies), but they're often quite valuable. Some offer lucrative modeling contracts; others award magazine gigs; others offer a shot at a product advertisement.

Model searches are less expensive to attend than model conventions. Plus, they're usually smaller than conventions, so you get more of a chance to talk to the agents, ask questions, and find out the best route for your career.

Why You Should Enter a Model Search

Model searches are one of the most important ways modeling agencies scout new models. Instead of having to cough up thousands of dollars to visit New York, you can meet Big Apple modeling scouts in your hometown. These agents are also a great source of advice; they can tell you whether you have what it takes to make it in the fashion capitals or whether you're better suited to doing catalog work in a *local* or *secondary market*.

Catwalk Talk

New York is where most U.S. models work, but many models also work in other, smaller cities, such as Miami, Chicago, Los Angeles, Dallas, and Atlanta. These cities are referred to as **local** or **secondary markets**.

To Pay or Not to Pay?

The biggest searches are sponsored by the Elite and Ford modeling agencies. The best-known model search, of course, is *America's Next Top Model.* Most charge nothing (or a nominal fee, up to $20) to enter. At some searches, a number of agencies send scouts; in these cases, a more sizeable entrance fee is charged.

But if you haven't heard of any of the agencies who are sending representatives (check out the sponsors in Appendix C), or if they're charging high fees, it may not be a legitimate search.

> **Reality Check** _____
>
> Even if a search is legitimate, you need to be on your guard. Searches attract unscrupulous photographers who come and take pictures of the participants and then try to sell them the photos at exorbitant prices. Never pay a lot of money to have photos taken unless you already have an agent and she has directed you to have them taken. Even then, costs should be kept down. At this point, the agency pays for the photos and photo sessions up front, and the model reimburses them when she starts working.

How to Succeed at a Search

Be sure you're freshly showered and are wearing deodorant. Avoid strong perfume, which can leave a smell on clothes that will be worn for the contest. Keep your hair, makeup, and clothing simple and natural.

Know what events are taking place and when they start, and be where you need to be on time. It's also a good idea to bring snapshots of yourself, preferably a couple head shots and a couple body shots, to show the agency representative how you look in photographs. (See Chapter 6 for more information on photos.)

Ruling the Runway

When it's your turn on the runway, take your time and walk naturally. Even if you're nervous because you're not used to being onstage in front of an audience, don't just run on and run off. This could be the scouts' one chance to see you. And remember, they're not judging you on how well you do a model's trademark catwalk sashay; it can often come off badly if you don't know what you're doing. You're much better off walking naturally.

Pretty Is as Pretty Does

Introduce yourself to the scout and be friendly and outgoing. This shows your personality and makes it more likely that they'll remember you. And someone who is outgoing and friendly to a modeling scout is likely to be outgoing and friendly with clients—an important factor in a model's success.

Even if you don't win a search, go up and talk to the scout and ask why you didn't win and what you can do to improve your chances of breaking into the industry. Consider this a great opportunity to get some free advice, and take any criticism with an open mind—it can be the key to winning the next modeling contest!

> **Roshumba's Rules**
>
> To find out about model searches in your area, look online or for advertisements in magazines, in newspapers, or on the radio. Before you enter, do some research to be sure the contest is reputable (that is, be sure scouts from major agencies will be attending). Normally there is no cost to enter, but if there is, find out how much and what it covers before entering.

Modeling Conventions

Attending *modeling conventions* can be a good way for aspiring models to find an agent. Conventions usually draw more participants than searches (1,000 to 6,000 contestants is not uncommon at conventions, whereas usually no more than several hundred girls participate in a search). Conventions generally last from 2 to 4 days, are held in hotels in cities around the country, and have more sizeable entrance fees (sometimes from $3,000 to $5,000). Some of the better-known model conventions include IMTA and Model Search America.

> **Catwalk Talk**
>
> **Modeling conventions** are events attended by many different agents looking for new models to represent. Unlike searches, they charge sizeable entrance fees, and they usually last several days (searches take place in one afternoon).

Why You Should Consider a Convention

As an aspiring model, you might want to consider attending a convention because agents and scouts from many different agencies will be in attendance, increasing your chances of catching someone's eye. Conventions offer a great opportunity to meet agents from the big New York agencies without having to travel to New York. Also many agents from around the world—Paris, Milan, London, and even Tokyo—attend conventions looking for models.

Conventions also provide a great crash course in modeling. You'll gain experience working with hairstylists, makeup artists, and clothing stylists (at conventions where they're provided); at the very least, you'll learn how to do your own hair and makeup for a runway show. You'll find out what it's like to walk the runway and get used to people looking at you. Finally, you'll gain a lot of knowledge and information from talking to the agents present.

Conventional Wisdom

How can you tell if a convention is not a rip-off? Before you sign up or pull out your credit card, find out who the sponsors are or whether it's linked to a major modeling agency. Some of the judges should also be from a major magazine, such as *Seventeen*, or advertisers, such as Cover Girl or Keds. Also ask the convention representative what well-known models have gone on to successful careers after participating in their convention. Reputable companies will have press kits or brochures and will be willing to answer questions.

If the brochure is not clear about exactly what the fee includes, ask. Many charge extra for basics that you may assume is included (like the right of your parents to attend the events).

Roshumba's Rules

Don't be afraid to ask the sponsors of a model convention a lot of questions, especially if it's pricey. A legitimate convention will be happy to answer all your inquiries because they're proud of the work they do.

Also think twice if the price seems really high. I personally would not pay $3,000 to $10,000 to attend a convention, and I don't recommend spending that much to anyone, especially when there are no guarantees and there are other less expensive ways to jump-start a career. At the conventions I have attended, the reality is that 85 to 90 percent of the contestants do not have what it takes. If you don't meet the physical requirements to be a fashion model (see Chapter 3), going to a convention will just be a waste of money.

The Parent Trap

Most girls at conventions are accompanied by their parents or guardians. Even though you may prefer to leave them at home, they can be a great asset for you at a convention. Sometimes a young, aspiring model's desire to launch her career may overshadow her judgment, or she may find herself in a situation she isn't equipped to deal with. That's when it's key to have a parent or guardian along who can scrutinize the circumstances, ask questions, be objective, and read between the lines.

The Convention Itinerary

The first order of business at a convention is registration. Then there's usually a short interview, called a *meet and greet*. Also on the first day are rehearsals for a runway fashion show and then the show itself.

On the second day of the convention, a callback sheet is posted. The callback sheet lists all the agents' names, followed by the names of the girls in whom they are interested. The agents all have their own tables, and models line up to meet with the different agents.

At a convention, it's possible you could get a callback from five or six different agencies, in which case you would meet with each one at its designated table. Making it onto the callback list doesn't mean the agency definitely wants to represent you, just that it's interested in seeing you and meeting you again. Sometimes girls are signed on the spot; other times, they're told the agency will be in touch.

> **Catwalk Talk**
>
> A **meet and greet** is a short interview the judges and agents conduct with participants. You'll be asked basic questions, such as where you live, what grade you're in, and why you want to be a model.

Even if no one is interested in signing you, approach a couple agents and ask for their advice on how you can improve (but don't yell at them for not picking you!).

Tips for Success

Interviewing and interpersonal skills are even more essential at a convention than at a search because the agent interviews at a convention are longer and more involved. Showing some personality is key, so even if you're nervous, try to avoid giving one-word, yes/no answers.

Agents look for a good personality because it's a key element in a successful modeling career. If you shine at the interview with the judges at the convention, they'll know you can handle yourself on a go and see with a client. An enthusiastic, personable girl will also stand out from the crowd.

Nice Girls Finish First

As at open calls and searches, you should try to be as cooperative as possible. Obviously, say no to things you're not comfortable with, for instance, if you're asked to pose nude or wear something really provocative. But don't give attitude if you don't like the dress you're asked to wear, or if the photographer wants you to jump or dance and you feel stupid doing it.

If you're already saying no before you're even established, you may find it difficult to get your career off the ground.

Modeling Schools

Some people feel that _modeling schools_ are a big scam, but I don't agree. It's true that graduating from a modeling school won't guarantee you a modeling career. And it's also true that hardly any working models went to modeling school. Plus, modeling schools are expensive. But girls who attend modeling schools can learn a lot about modeling opportunities in their area, including the best agencies. They also learn to develop a sense of style, grace, poise, and self-confidence, and they learn about good grooming and beauty techniques, healthful eating, and exercise. Basic modeling skills are taught, too: how to apply makeup, walk the runway, and move in front of a camera. Still, don't let anyone tell you modeling schools are a necessity for a modeling career. Overall, I consider modeling schools more of finishing schools than true model training programs.

Like everything, modeling schools have good and bad aspects. I think the best thing they do is give girls confidence and poise, help a shy or awkward girl grow out of her shell, and give her experience in her market.

Model Curriculum

At a good modeling school, you'll learn about the modeling industry as a whole and how it works, how to develop good posture and graceful movements, how to move in front of the camera, how to walk on the runway, and how to model in groups. You'll also learn about clothes; makeup, hair, and skin care; nutrition, diet, and exercise; interviewing and social skills; and how to develop poise and self-confidence. These classes can help prepare you for anything you do in life. You'll learn how to best present yourself at a job interview or public speech, including how to dress properly and ask the right questions.

It's a good way to learn the right way to do things, and this knowledge will help boost your confidence, especially if you're shy or have low self-esteem.

Reality Check

If a modeling school insists on your having professional photos taken with a photographer of their choosing before you can enroll in their school, *run for the door!* A legitimate modeling school charges models for a full curriculum, teaching her poise, grace, how to walk on the runway, and makeup and hair tips, as well as providing test shoots, photos, and prints. These monies can be paid in advance or in installments. Only illegitimate schools that are running scams charge crazy fees for photos just to get your foot in the door. Their focus is on making money, not developing talent.

Spotting Modeling School Scams

Even though many modeling schools are ethical, legitimate businesses, others are not. These "schools" prey on the unsuspecting and the naive, so you need to be on your guard and do some research to protect yourself.

Some modeling schools are attached to modeling agencies or conventions; in fact, some of the best modeling schools are affiliated with large, reputable agencies. These affiliated schools will be able to provide you contact information for agents, agencies, conventions, and contests in your area. (But be on guard if they push you too hard to attend lots of conventions or contests; they may be making a commission when you enter, not looking out for your career.)

But other times, schools will be affiliated with agencies that are not reputable. When a modeling school is associated with an agency, the school and the agency should operate separately. You shouldn't be required to enroll in the modeling school before the agency will represent you, and vice versa. Legitimate modeling agencies make money on a commission basis, meaning they get a percentage of the fees you earn working as a model; they don't make money by insisting on being paid up front, whether it's for classes or special photos. Good schools also give you a realistic assessment of your chances to become a model, and they won't promise you work if you enroll at their school.

The Cheapest Way to Find an Agent

Say you're unable to attend a model search or convention (maybe you just missed it or the closest one is too far away). No modeling agencies are near you, and you're not able to travel to a big city for an open call. Or maybe you're not the fashion model type, but you think you could break into the industry as a parts model, plus-size model, or older model.

There's a quick and easy way to get in touch with an agent via e-mail or regular mail. All you need to do is to send several snapshots of yourself to a few of the agencies listed in Appendix C. Just ask a friend or family member who's handy with a camera to take some photos of you (follow the tips in Chapter 6). Generally, all you need is around 12 pictures. Be sure to write your name, phone number, and measurements on the back of each photo if you're mailing them.

Along with the photos, include a letter of introduction and your statistics card (see Chapter 6), as well as a self-addressed, stamped envelope. Put it all in an envelope, and send it off! (Or just e-mail it with the photos and statistics card attached.) If you don't receive a response within 2 weeks, call or e-mail to be sure your photos were received and request (politely) they return them if you mailed them, along with any comments.

Although this method of contacting an agency is easy and inexpensive, it has one big disadvantage—agents aren't getting to meet you, so they can't see what you look like in person and what a great personality you have. Still, with so little to lose, it's worth taking the chance.

Not Model Material?

If you've tried everything to break into the modeling business but have gotten no positive feedback, you may need to face the fact that fashion modeling is not for you. But this definitely does not mean you aren't pretty and attractive! Keep in mind that many famous beauties, including many Hollywood actresses, don't have the necessary requirements to be a model.

And sometimes girls with all the basic qualifications (age, height, weight) aren't able to break into the business, even after going to numerous open calls, model searches, and conventions. If you've been receiving a lot of rejections, ask for comments on your look and advice on how you can make yourself more suitable and marketable as a model.

Fortunately, modeling is just as glamorous behind the camera as in front of it. There are many other ways you can get involved in the fashion industry:

- Photographer
- Clothing designer
- Model scout
- Model booker

- Hairstylist
- Makeup artist
- Clothing stylist
- Magazine writer or editor

To find out more about careers in these fields, contact your local university, community college, art center, or art school (for more information on photography); a journalism school at a local university (for careers in magazine writing or editing); local beauty school (if you're interested in becoming a hairstylist or makeup artist); or Parsons School of Design (where *Project Runway* is shot) or the Fashion Institute of Technology in New York City (for careers in fashion design and merchandising). Another good idea is to ask the model scouts at the next model search in your area—they'll be happy to direct you to the right people.

The Least You Need to Know

- Open calls at a modeling agency are one of the best ways to find an agent.
- Model searches are great ways to be seen by model professionals from New York.
- Modeling conventions expose you to agents from a number of agencies, increasing your chances of catching someone's eye.
- Modeling schools can help you develop poise, grace, and modeling skills.
- The cheapest way to find an agent is to mail pictures of yourself to an agency.

Hobby and Professional Modeling in Secondary and Local Markets

In This Chapter

◆ Defining and breaking into hobby modeling

◆ Why hobby modeling can be a good career move

◆ Getting started—and staying—in secondary and local markets

A fashion model's career goes through three different stages: hobby modeling in her hometown (which is like an unpaid internship for fun and experience, professional modeling in local and secondary markets (various big cities around the country), and big-time modeling in the fashion capitals of Milan, Paris, and New York.

Modeling professionally in a secondary or local market is the intermediary step between hobby modeling and big-time modeling (which I tell you about in Chapter 9). Unlike hobby modeling, this stage is considered professional modeling because you're usually paid for your work. Also, professional models in secondary and local markets almost always have a modeling agent who represents them and helps them find jobs.

Some models spend their whole careers in secondary markets, for any number of reasons. Spending time in a secondary or local market can also be a great intermediary step for a model who wants to give big-time modeling a shot; it gives a model skills and experience that will be of great benefit when she moves on to the intensely competitive world of big-time modeling.

In this chapter, I discuss which types of models do best in local and secondary markets and which types may have a better shot as a big-time model. Let's see where you fit in.

Getting Started: Hobby Modeling

The first stage of modeling is *hobby modeling*, also called *modeling for experience*. A hobby model might model in fashion shows at the malls, at hair shows for a local salon, or for local newspaper advertisements. These jobs are generally done for the experience, so girls are usually not paid.

> **Catwalk Talk**
>
> Hobby modeling and modeling for experience are two terms that mean the same thing: modeling done primarily for the experience and fun of it. Hobby modeling is usually unpaid.

At this stage, a girl might also be doing test shoots for experience, which I discuss in Chapter 12. Hobby modeling can be done almost anywhere in the country. My very first hobby modeling jobs were in Peoria, Illinois—not exactly a major city!

If you're young (ages 13 to 15) and are interested in exploring the possibilities of a career on the catwalk, a hobby modeling job might be just the thing for you.

Some girls do skip this stage. Or if you have fun modeling but don't want to make a career of it, you might also fit in the hobby modeling stage. Someone who does hobby modeling generally doesn't have an agent because most of the work is unpaid. That means a hobby model needs to find her own jobs, which can be frustrating.

> **Model Scoop**
>
> I still vividly remember my first modeling job. I was hired to stand in the display window of a mall boutique and pretend I was a mannequin while dressed in some of the latest fashions. I found the job by asking managers of shops in the local mall if they used models. A manager of one upscale boutique told me they didn't normally use models, but sometimes they let girls come in and pose as dress mannequins in the display window. There was no pay, but I didn't care: I was just so happy to finally have my first real modeling job.

Although you generally don't get paid for hobby modeling, the experience and knowledge you gain from it are extremely valuable. This is your time to figure out if you have the temperament for the modeling business. Can you stand to sit still for 2 hours to get your hair and makeup done? Do you enjoy being the center of attention on a fashion runway? Do you love to have your picture taken? Modeling for experience lets you explore whether you have the necessary physical requirements, the right temperament, and the desire to pursue it further.

Models Wanted: Finding Hobby Modeling Jobs

One of the best places to start looking for modeling jobs is your local mall. Most malls have fashion shows, sponsored by individual stores, several stores, or the mall itself. The Internet, newspapers, and local news publications may print listings for models for hair shows, music videos, or exhibition conventions that come to town (car shows, etc.).

To get involved with the fashion scene at your local mall, contact the mall and ask if they have a *teen board* or *fashion board*. These boards consist of a group of local people who sign up at their local mall to be part of mall fashion events.

I believe getting modeling experience at the mall, local stores, hair salons, and school- and church-related functions is the safest way to start. Lots of con artists are waiting to prey on unsuspecting young models, and you'll probably be most vulnerable to them during this stage in your career, when you're still quite young and inexperienced with the job market in general and the modeling business in particular. Department stores, smaller chain stores, boutiques, and hair salons are all businesses that must maintain good reputations in the community to stay in business. The chances of their doing something illegal or unscrupulous to harm or take advantage of a young person are, therefore, slim.

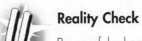

Catwalk Talk

Fashion boards, or **teen boards,** are mall-sponsored groups of models for events at the mall. They're a great way to try out modeling.

Reality Check

Be careful when answering newspaper ads because they can be scam heaven. When answering these ads, ask as many questions as possible to be sure the job is legit. Or take a parent or guardian when you answer ads in person.

Model Scoop _____

Another one of my first modeling jobs was informal, in-store modeling at a local boutique. The store would have local girls come in and model the latest collection of dresses in the store. The customers could admire how the dresses looked on the models and judge whether they wanted to buy them. After doing my own hair and makeup, I would put on a dress and then wander around the store for about half an hour. Not only did I learn a lot about how to best show fine clothes, but I grew more comfortable being around older, wealthier, more sophisticated adults, which made the transition to professional modeling much easier.

Modeling Experiences You *Don't* Want

While you are modeling for experience, you are in a particularly vulnerable state: most hobby models are very young, and their desire to model may occasionally cloud their judgment. But you should definitely just say no to anyone who offers you drugs, tries to get you to pose nude, demands sex in exchange for a modeling job, or wants you to pay him to hire you to model.

Roshumba's Rules _____

I strongly urge you to tell your parents, school guidance counselor or teacher, or another trusted adult about any negative experiences you have while modeling for experience. Let them decide whether the police should be called.

Modeling Professionally in Secondary and Local Markets

When industry insiders talk about *secondary* and *local markets* in the United States, they're basically referring to any city outside of New York City. (New York, along with the European fashion capitals of Milan and Paris, are considered the three fashion capitals of the world because so many fashion and cosmetic companies, fashion magazines, and advertising agencies are based there.)

The three major secondary markets in the United States—Chicago, Miami, and Los Angeles—don't have as many fashion designers, cosmetic companies, and advertising clients who hire models as New York. These three cities do, however, have a sizeable number of clients who hire models, including catalogs, advertisers, TV commercial producers, and, to a lesser extent, magazines and newspapers. These three cities are where the majority of models who aren't located in New York live and work.

Other big cities, such as Atlanta, Boston, Toronto, Dallas, and Nashville, are considered local markets because they have limited opportunities for models. Except for retail stores and beauty salons, few fashion-oriented businesses call these cities home. Generally, models in these cities are hired for local advertisements and TV commercials.

> **Catwalk Talk**
>
> The U.S. **secondary markets** are Chicago, Miami, and Los Angeles. **Local markets** refers to any other city in the country (with the exception of New York, which is a fashion capital)

Each secondary market is known for having specific types of clients. Following is a quick survey of each one.

Chicago

Chicago is a major catalog and advertising market. Many, many catalogs and websites are shot in the Windy City, so there's a constant stream of work for catalog-type models. The huge Spiegel catalog is headquartered in Chicago, as are many smaller catalog houses. Many of the major retailers, including JCPenney and Sears, do shoots in Chicago. Chicago also has a sizeable number of advertising agencies that hire models for everything from McDonald's commercials to hotel advertisements.

A limited amount of editorial work can be found in Chicago, mainly for the local newspapers (the *Chicago Tribune* and the *Chicago Sun-Times*) and for local magazines such as *Chicago* magazine. There's also some runway work for consumer fashion shows, as well as *in-store modeling*.

> **Catwalk Talk**
>
> With **in-store modeling** (which is also called informal modeling), the models are dressed in the clothes from the store and walk around to let the customers see the clothes up close as they shop.

Miami

Over the past 15 years, Miami has developed into a major modeling center. The enormous popularity of South Beach (an ultra-cool section of Miami Beach jam-packed with restaurants, clubs, hotels, and modeling agencies), combined with the warm weather (which makes year-round outdoor shoots possible) has contributed to the growth of the Miami's fashion market.

Model Scoop

Cindy Crawford is a textbook case of a model who started out as a hobby model then moved on to secondary market modeling. Her first modeling job was in a fashion show at a local store in her hometown of DeKalb, Illinois. Soon afterward, she volunteered to model in a Clairol-sponsored hairstyling show in Chicago, the closest secondary market. At the show, an agency agreed to represent her, but they recommended that she have her famous mole removed. She refused, and soon after she snagged her first professional job—a bra ad for local retailer Marshall Field's. After that, she was so busy modeling that she was forced to rearrange her school schedule so she could model every day in Chicago.

Although it has a reputation for being all-bathing-suit shoots, much of the modeling work in Miami is for the various catalogs shot there; the majority of clients are from national and international marketplaces. Local advertising agencies also hire models to appear in TV commercials and print ads for area businesses.

In addition to catalogs and advertisements, Miami attracts high-fashion editorial clients. Besides local publications such as *Ocean Drive*, many New York–based magazines shoot in the Miami area, as do some European publications. A limited amount of runway work is done in Miami, including consumer fashion shows and in-store modeling.

Los Angeles

Because it's home to so many TV studios, numerous TV commercials are shot in Los Angeles. L.A. is also a good destination if you're interested in getting into acting as well as modeling. Because of the large number of teen-oriented companies based in the area, L.A. also offers a lot of work for junior-type models. With the beautiful weather, you can count on a lot of swimsuit modeling as well.

L.A. has a limited amount of runway work, too, including consumer fashion shows and in-store modeling.

The Major Local Markets

Atlanta, Boston, Toronto, Dallas, and Nashville offer (at most) small numbers of fashion and beauty businesses, and more limited opportunities for models. Generally, models in these cities are hired for local advertisements and TV commercials; the occasional consumer fashion show and in-store modeling event can be found here. In these smaller markets, there is virtually no high-fashion advertising or magazine work.

Secondary Markets: The Best Choice for You?

Two kinds of models work in secondary and local markets: those who work there for their whole careers and those who spend a couple years working there gaining experience and waiting until they're old enough to move on to big-time modeling.

Many models can benefit by staying in secondary markets for their whole careers instead of trying to break into modeling in a fashion capital. Models with a commercial look, who are also called catalog or *commercial models*, can benefit from staying in a local market where their look is desirable by catalogs. *Editorial models*, on the other hand, are better suited to the job opportunities in New York.

How can you tell if you have what it takes to make it in New York and the other fashion capitals? Not only do you need to meet every one of the physical requirements (height, weight, body proportions, dress size, and so on) in Chapter 3, but you also need a high degree of perseverance, self-confidence, motivation, sense of self, and all the other mental requirements in the second part of Chapter 3.

Catwalk Talk

Commercial models work primarily in local or secondary markets and appear mainly in catalogs and advertisements. **Editorial models,** also known as high-fashion models, work in the fashion capitals, where they appear in magazine stories, designer fashion shows, and high-end advertisements.

As we've seen, much of the work in secondary markets is commercial (catalog and advertising) work. In the fashion capitals, the work is more high fashion (magazine, runway and high-end advertising). Commercial work requires a different type of model—a pretty, wholesome-looking type who will appeal to the average American consumer. Basically, the catalog-commercial girl has that "all-American girl" look—pretty, healthy looking, and appealing. She can be a Classic Beauty, an Amazon, an Athletic Girl Next Door, or sometimes a Barbie. (See Chapter 5 for more information on the different types of models.)

An editorial model, on the other hand, has more of a quirky or exotic high-fashion look. These girls are often more striking or unusual than classically pretty. Oddballs, Exotic types, Chameleons, and sometimes Amazons can be high-fashion models.

Classic Beauties who fit into the high-fashion world of modeling usually radiate a special magic or have other qualities that make them stand out. (This is another reason it's important to know your type.)

Reality Check

If you're not ready, willing, or able to deal with the full-blown crazy lifestyle of an international model—the intense competition, the high rates of failure, the grinding schedule, and the often back-stabbing atmosphere—stay in your local market.

Some models choose not to move on to big-time modeling, but instead spend their whole careers in secondary markets because they're satisfied with the quality and amount of work they're getting. They see no real reason to give up steady work to move on to New York or another fashion capital.

Some models may stay in their local markets because they are attending college or don't want to leave their families and friends behind. Besides, models in secondary markets can have longer careers than models in the fashion capitals.

Do You Need an Agent in a Local Market?

As a professional model in a secondary market, you'll need a modeling agency to represent you. Agents have the contacts necessary to find out about modeling opportunities, and they screen clients so a model is not sent into a dangerous situation. In addition, agents handle billings, collections, and other aspects of the money side of things. They also help a model fine-tune her look so she's marketable to local clients. Finally, if a model decides she wants to move on to big-time modeling, an agent in a secondary or local market may have connections to agencies in fashion capitals so she can more easily move into big-time modeling.

Roshumba's Rules

It can be difficult to find a legitimate modeling agency in a smaller city. If you can't find any by word of mouth, try calling a local advertising agency and asking them which modeling agencies they work with. Or call a big agency in New York and ask if they have any recommendations.

In Chapter 7, I talked about finding an agent, going to open calls at modeling agencies, attending model conventions, and mailing in photos to modeling agencies. These are great ways to find an agent in a secondary market, too. (See Appendix C for more help finding an agency.)

Modeling Mastery

If you know you want to give big-time modeling a try, it's still a good idea to spend a year or two modeling professionally in a secondary or local market instead of jumping right into big-time modeling without any experience.

You might not want to be in a fashion capital when you're 15 or 16 because your body may be going through some awkward changes. You might still be growing, your skin might have a tendency to occasionally break out, and even your hair might undergo changes. By 17 or 18, you'll be ready to move on—*if* you decide you want to pursue big-time modeling.

You'll gain many important additional skills and professional modeling experience working in a local or secondary market. You'll learn how to start to develop and maintain a mutually beneficial relationship with a modeling agent and agency. You'll have the opportunity to learn what it's like to be directed by professional photographers, how to best work with different personalities, and how to play up your best attributes in front of the camera.

These photos show me in two different modes. In the one on the left, I'm posing for a catalog, which is typical of the work done in local and secondary markets. In the one on the right, I'm doing a high-fashion editorial shoot, a good example of the type of work done in the fashion capitals.

(Photos by Charles Tracy)

Model Scoop

After graduating from high school, I moved to the secondary market closest to me, Chicago, to pursue modeling more seriously. My grandmother lived there, so I had a place to stay. I landed a job with a local Chicago fashion designer, Sterling Capricio, who needed a fit model on whom he could fit his designs to see how they hung. I would try on the dresses and stand, walk, or pose in the garments, whatever was required. Sterling taught me how to stand, pose, walk, and present a garment to a designer. That knowledge was invaluable when I got my first job in a fashion capital as a fit model for Yves Saint Laurent.

Are You Ready for Big-Time Modeling?

You can tell you're ready to move from hobby modeling or professional modeling in a local or secondary market to big-time modeling when you're at least 16 years old and you feel confident and adept at hobby-modeling activities, such as fashion shows at the mall and test shoots for experience. Or maybe you've done professional modeling in your local market. You should have a certain comfort and skill level in front of the camera. Also, your body should not have changed so drastically since you started hobby modeling that you no longer possess the necessary physical characteristics to be a professional model. If you feel competent and confident in all these areas, you're ready to become a professional model in a fashion capital.

The Least You Need to Know

- ◆ Hobby modeling is the first stage of modeling. It's a great way to explore modeling, learn modeling techniques, and gain self-confidence.

- ◆ Hobby modeling jobs are available almost everywhere in the country; the best place to start your search is your local mall.

- ◆ Chicago, Miami, and Los Angeles are the major secondary markets in the United States. Atlanta, Boston, Toronto, Dallas, and Nashville are local markets because the modeling opportunities are more limited.

- ◆ Secondary and local markets offer a lot of opportunities for models, including TV commercials and catalog work, and may be the best choice for models with a "commercial" look.

Chapter 9

Modeling in the Fashion Capitals

In This Chapter

- ◆ The three fashion capitals: Milan, Paris, and New York
- ◆ Opportunities in other important fashion cities
- ◆ Why waiting until you're 18 is best
- ◆ Ways to support yourself until your career takes off
- ◆ Whether or not to make the move

Big-time modeling means modeling in the three fashion capitals: Milan, Paris, and New York. This is where the majority of models you see in magazines, in advertisements, in fashion shows, and on TV live and work.

"Big-time modeling" means that modeling is your *only* career, the sole way you support yourself and make a living. By industry standards, it also means that most of your work is done with well-known clients, such as *Vogue*, Gucci, Lancôme, and Marc Jacobs. Some big-time models specialize in catalog work for famous, high-end clients, such as Saks Fifth Avenue, Neiman Marcus, and J. Crew, or do primarily advertising work for clients like Oil of Olay, Pantene, or Liz Claiborne.

But big-time modeling also means facing intense competition, dealing with a lot of rejection, and being subject to the whims of the fashion industry. It's also about being the consummate professional; always being on time, cooperative, pleasant, and professional; and not being difficult because you're hot, or tired, or you hate the outfit you're wearing. In this chapter, I give you an overview of big-time modeling and how you can give it your best shot.

Milan, Paris, and New York

There's no denying the fact that big-time modeling is extremely competitive. People come to New York and the other *fashion capitals* from every country, city, and small village around the world. It's in the fashion capitals that models can make the biggest bucks and get the best jobs. It's also where you're *least* likely to be able to break into the business.

The first step to getting into big-time modeling is finding an agent. It's impossible to break into modeling in the fashion capitals without one; most clients won't even see a model who isn't represented by an agent. (Check out Chapter 7 for more information on finding an agent.) American models generally acquire an agency in New York, which is known as their *mother agency*.

Catwalk Talk

Milan, Paris, and New York are considered the three **fashion capitals** of the world because so many fashion and cosmetic companies, fashion magazines, advertising agencies, and models are based there. Your **mother agency** is the agency that discovered you, marketed you, and developed your career. If you've changed agencies in the course of your career, your mother agency is your base agency, which is usually located in the city you call home.

Often a model's mother agency will urge her to go to Milan or Paris, especially if she's having trouble getting started in New York. The mother agency will arrange for a model to be represented by another agency in one of the other fashion capitals, and it will also take care of any necessary working papers (legal documents needed to work in places outside the country of which you are a citizen).

Each fashion capital prefers certain types of models, and each has distinct advantages that can be capitalized on and disadvantages that should be avoided. Let's take a closer look at what these are.

Milan

Milan is often the first stop for a model who wants to launch a big-time international modeling career. Clients in Milan are known for preferring new faces with a young, fresh, untouched look, as opposed to more established models who may have been around for a while.

That's why it's the perfect place to go to work professionally when you're just starting out. (Still, it's better if you have an agency in New York that has referred you to an agency overseas. New York is American models' link to the international fashion world.) Here you'll have the best chance of building your portfolio and filling it with great tear sheets from internationally recognized clients. (I tell you more about tear sheets in Chapter 13.) It's also ideal for building a name, image, and reputation on the runway and in front of the camera, and establishing your presence as an up-and-coming professional in the international market.

Another plus is that Milan offers all types of work. It's full of magazines, advertising clients, and fashion designers who are willing to give newer models a chance.

Because so many of the major fashion designers are based there, and because it's such a style-conscious city, Milan also affords you the opportunity to learn the ABCs of international style. You'll be exposed to models from all over the world, as well as to people from all walks of life.

It's also not very difficult to set yourself up in Milan. Unlike agents in other fashion capitals, agents in Milan are more willing to advance money to beginning models for basic expenses and a place to live. The city has a great public transportation system, and the people are willing to speak English and are friendly and open to strangers. They are also fascinated by other cultures and will want to get to know you. Also, Italian men love women from other countries, so you can expect a lot of attention!

Reality Check

Wherever there are a lot of models, there are also "modelizers"—playboys whose objective is to be seen with models, have sex with models, and/or have models pays all their bills. Although they exist everywhere, they're especially common in Europe. Sometimes what we Americans see initially as foreign charm is anything but. Before you get seriously involved with a guy, get some background from mutual acquaintances, or take note. Does he work? Does he pick up the tab at restaurants? Is he interested in you as a person or just as a model?

Each market prefers a specific type of model (although this doesn't mean other types don't stand a chance). In Milan, generally two types of models do well: ones who are curvy yet slim, with natural sex appeal, who are used by designers of sexy clothes, such as Dolce & Gabbana; and girls who are very thin, even boyish, and who have an edgy sort of look and personality that's in demand by clients who want an avant-garde look, such as Giorgio Armani.

If you haven't had any luck finding an agent in the United States, you might want to try going to Milan on your own, to see if you can find an agent there. Before you leave, you'll need to find out what agents are there (check out Appendix C or call a major agency in New York to get a list of referrals). Plan to go for a week or two to investigate the possibilities and get a sense of the market. Check out travel guides, and book a hotel room before you get there.

> **Reality Check**
>
> If you can't find an agent in America, it may be because you're not the right type for New York, but it also may be because you aren't model material. Know that if you don't have what it takes to be a model at home, you may be rejected abroad as well.

Paris

Paris is the epitome of living the life of a model. Paris is the heart of the fashion industry; the industry looks to Paris for innovation and new ideas. The city dictates style and fashion trends and decides the next big models, fashion photographers, and designers.

Paris is less about appealing to the mass-market consumer than working with expensive, luxury brands such as Chanel, Yves Saint Laurent, Louis Vuitton, and Hermès.

If Milan is about establishing yourself as a model, Paris is about building your name and enhancing your prestige: working with the most eminent designers, fashion photographers, and advertising clients. If you can establish your name in Paris, you'll gain prestige and be a part of the pulse of fashion—and your career will be made.

> **Roshumba's Rules**
>
> Plan to go to Milan and Paris in March or October, when the ready-to-wear fashion shows take place. It's a time when lots of models are being hired.

Here you'll build a portfolio's filled with high-class clients and you'll increase your appeal to more well-known fashion designers, fashion photographers, and bigger advertising clients such as Lancôme, Chanel, and L'Oréal.

An abundance of magazines, fashion designers, and advertisers are based in Paris, and all are quite selective about the models they use. They'll use new models, but the girl has to have that something special; she has to be someone whom the French believe represents *la crème de la crème*, with class, elegance, and style.

Another good thing about Paris is that you need to find only one person to open the door for you. If one of the fashion powerhouses accepts you, others will, too. If designer Jean-Paul Gaultier thinks you're a wonderful fresh new talent and hires you for his fashion show, it's a good bet that you'll soon be appearing in the most prestigious magazines and important advertisements.

The models favored by clients in Paris are super-skinny or shapely, as well as fresh and youthful-looking (if a girl is too sophisticated or world-weary, clients feel like she is already developed and there's nothing to work with). Being open-minded and free-spirited is also important because the French abhor narrow-mindedness. Ethnic models have traditionally enjoyed a lot of success in Paris as well.

Model Scoop

When I appeared in an Yves Saint Laurent fashion show in 1987, it said to the rest of the fashion industry, "YSL is using her, she must have something, so let's give her a chance." Right after that, *Elle*, *Marie Claire*, and Benetton all booked me for photo shoots. People from every other fashion market in the world keep an eye on what's happening on the Paris runways and in the French magazines, and that snowball effect rolled me right into New York (my ultimate goal). I worked with the most prestigious fashion designers and appeared on covers and pages of world-famous magazines and in major advertising campaigns.

Living in Paris can be really expensive. The city attracts people from all over the world, including many people involved in the fashion industry. Space is very limited and, therefore, expensive. In the beginning, some girls live in the suburbs, where rent is less expensive, or in model apartments (which are often very crowded). If agencies believe in a girl and feel she has the potential to make it to the top, many will front her the money necessary for living expenses until she starts earning the big bucks necessary to support herself.

Roshumba's Rules

If you spend time in Paris, try to learn some French. Although many people do speak English, the Parisians can be intolerant of people who don't try to speak their language. And speaking French will make your time in Paris much more enjoyable.

As with Milan, it's best if you have an agency in New York that has referred you to an affiliated agent in Paris. Again, plan to go for a short period of time, such as 2 weeks—long enough to meet people and get a sense of the market, but not long enough so you'll need to beg for money. A good time to go is in March and October, when lots of models are hired for the ready-to-wear fashion shows.

New York

New York City is *the* place where models make the biggest bucks. Working in New York is a sign you've really made it. After building your name in Milan and establishing your prestige in Paris, New York is where you come to cash in on all that hard work. In New York, you earn the highest rates for advertisements, plus you're given the longest contracts. There's lots of catalog work, and the pay for catalogs is the highest. (In fact, if you can maintain even one catalog client at a really high day rate, you can live off that for years.) Fashion shows also pay higher rates, but the rates for editorial work are pretty much the same everywhere.

Roshumba's Rules

You need to put in your time in Paris and Milan if you want a successful, big-time career. You may get lucky just staying in New York, but for the most part, you have to pay your dues in the international marketplace to make it big.

New York also offers American models an opportunity to settle down a bit from the frantic modeling lifestyle. It's a good place to build a stable foundation. If you want to get married and start a family, you can still continue to work if you live in New York. (Heidi Klum, Christie Brinkley, and Liya Kebede are all married with children and still continue to work.) You can also further your education in New York, if you decide you want to go back to college. The city offers many opportunities to prepare for a career after modeling, in fields such as acting, broadcasting, and retail sales.

Living in New York can be extremely hectic. Everybody is doing their own thing full throttle, and they don't have time for other people and their issues. Although you're in the midst of millions of people, you can feel very isolated because everyone's going in their own directions. It's also very expensive to live in New York, especially in Manhattan. A bare-minimum, one-room apartment can cost as much as $2,000 a month. On the other hand, New York is incredibly fun and full of cultural events (theater, art exhibits, dance, and music of all kinds).

There's not one specific type of model who's most successful in New York. Because America is a melting pot, home to a variety of different types of people, it's important for the fashion market to appeal to as many cultures as possible. That's why many different types of girls are in demand in NYC. Models who have done the Paris-Milan circuit and established their names are usually the girls who do best in New York. They land the highest-paying catalog gigs and the biggest ad deals, and appear in the top fashion magazines.

Once you've made it in New York, however, a model doesn't just ignore the rest of the world. To stay on top, it's important to maintain an international presence; keep going back to Paris, Milan, and other cities; replenish your tear sheets; keep a presence on the runway circuit; and appear in ads. You can also start to diversify your career, adding movie, TV, books, and charity work to your resumé.

Modeling in London, Tokyo, and Other International Fashion Cities

London is an important fashion market, but even though modeling opportunities there have increased over the past 10 years, it's still not on par with Milan, Paris, and New York. London has long had a fashion industry, but it was known more for its creativity and avant-garde designs than for its viability and commercial appeal.

The increased international visibility of English designers, such as Stella McCartney and Burberry, as well as the many who have been snatched up by old-line French couture houses (John Galliano, Alexander McQueen), has given new credibility and appeal to London's fashion industry. In addition, U.K. models such as Kate Moss, Stella Tennant, and Kirsty Hume have given an English accent to the modeling scene.

The best reason to consider modeling in London is for the editorial work, which is innovative and cutting edge. If, for example, you're *overexposed* in other markets or your career has stalled, go to London to update your look, work with people who may see you in a new light, and get tear sheets from sessions with photographers who have a different vision of you than people in other markets. Tear sheets from magazines such as British *Vogue*, British *Elle*, and British *Marie Claire* could enhance any portfolio.

Another reason to head to London is for a direct booking (meaning a job that's arranged before your arrival) or to start to establish your presence on the London

Catwalk Talk

A model is said to be **overexposed** when she's been working too much in one market—she's appeared in every fashion show, magazine, and ad. Clients get bored with looking at her face and stop hiring her.

runway shows. The models whose looks sell best in London are quirky, Oddball types, along with Classic English Beauties.

If you haven't had much success in Paris, Milan, or New York; you are experiencing a work slowdown; or you just want to make some quick money, try Tokyo. You go there mainly to make money. The Japanese love Western culture, so models from Western countries are in high demand. You may get some tear sheets, but they're not that valuable in other places; in fact, they may make you look like you couldn't get work anywhere else.

Generally, models don't go to Tokyo on their own, and you probably wouldn't want to. The language barrier is nearly impossible to break. All the directions, menus, and other signs are written in Japanese. The society is very closed and isolated, which is why models usually come over under a contract that has been arranged by their mother agency in the United States. Usually, the contract is for a specific period for a certain amount of money ($20,000 for 1 or 2 months' work is a common amount). The agent also arranges for housing, a driver, and a guide so girls don't have to deal with the problems of living there on their own. If you do accept a contract to work in Japan, be prepared to work harder than you ever have before. The Japanese are known for their meticulous preparation: for one fashion show, you could have three fittings and three rehearsals. (One fitting and one rehearsal is the norm elsewhere.)

While in Tokyo, you'll gain exposure to a fascinating culture. The nightclubs are fun, and Tokyo is home to some incredible places to shop. And I suggest taking any opportunity that arises (maybe after you've finished your job) to get out of the city and travel around the beautiful countryside. It's breathtaking.

Reality Check

Even though they're based in one of the fashion capitals, big-time models travel all the time. For example, if you have clients based in Texas, such as Neiman Marcus, the photo shoots may be in different locations, and you'll have to travel to do all of them. Or you may work with a specific designer on an ongoing basis. Maybe she's doing a fashion show to benefit AIDS research in Los Angeles and then showing a special collection of cashmere in Paris. You would need to travel with her. Life on the road may sound like fun, but it can be lonely and exhausting. Also, you may not get to see your family and friends for months on end.

Other emerging fashion locales include Moscow; Singapore; São Paolo, Brazil; and Sydney, Australia. Each of these is home to a growing number of fashion-conscious women, so many designers from the fashion capitals rerun their runway shows for local fashionistas. All also have an emerging cadre of local fashion designers. While the hottest editorial models are often imported for each city's version of Fashion Week, unknown models can find work doing runway and showroom modeling for local designers, editorial work for local publications, and some advertising work.

Are You Ready for the Big Time?

You'll know when you're ready to give big-time modeling a shot. You'll have a portfolio of agency-directed test shots and tear sheets from professional jobs in secondary and local markets that show you at your best, and you'll feel confident and knowledgeable enough to make the move.

When you come from secondary markets, agents and clients aren't looking for who you worked with; to them, it doesn't matter if you haven't worked in New York, Paris, or Milan. They'll be looking at your portfolio to see your potential in a major market. Who you would appeal to? Would you be able to star in a major hair campaign? Are you right for the latest Versace fashion show? Are you able to handle the pressure and responsibility of working with high-paying, demanding clients?

Obviously, another way to know you're ready is if an agency in a fashion capital recruits you. Maybe they spotted you in a local publication or catalog, at a model convention or search, or just walking down the street, and they feel your look is right for their clients.

Why You Should Wait to Make Your Move

Unless you get an offer too good to refuse, such as a lucrative advertising contract, I caution you against moving into the big-time modeling stage too early, before you're 17 or 18. Until then, you're going through a number of changes that will influence your life: your hormones are changing, your menstrual cycle may still be irregular, you're meeting your first boyfriends. Your relationship with your family is changing, and school is becoming more intense.

At 18, you're more mature and better able to handle things that come up. At 18, you can arrive as a finished "product," instead of a 14-year-old work in progress.

Supporting Yourself Until Your Career Takes Off

It's important to keep in mind that even after you've taken the plunge, moved away from home, and acquired an agent, there's no guarantee you'll be earning $100,000 a year right away, or even enough money to support yourself. You'll need to be able to pay your rent, telephone, gas, electric, and cable bills, and buy food, clothes, and toiletries—you name it—because now you are living in an adult world.

A Second Job

You may need to supplement your income with another, nonmodeling job. Many models get jobs waitressing or hostessing in restaurants, bars, and clubs (in fact, some hot spots hire only models); doing temporary work; working in retail (I recently saw two young models I know spritzing perfume at the Henri Bendel department store in New York); working as receptionists in beauty salons; or even walking dogs.

If you need to find a job to supplement your income, focus on getting a position that leaves your weekdays open. Most of your go and sees, test shoots, and other modeling-related appointments are set up during business hours Monday through Friday.

It's also key to find a job that allows you some flexibility in your schedule so when you do book a job, you can take the time off to do it, or in case you need to travel. It's best if the job you find also somehow keeps you exposed to the fashion industry. That's why so many models end up working at major departments stores; in boutiques; and at fashionable clubs, bars, and restaurants.

Model Apartments

Many larger agencies provide "model apartments" for young models. These apartments are owned or rented by the various modeling agencies for use by their models in the fashion capitals. "Usually they are models who are starting out in the business," explains Karen Lee, director of scouting at Elite Model Management and the house mother of an Elite model apartment in New York City. "They are usually girls [who] have no housing, who are going to be here anywhere from a week to several months. They are girls we ask to come to New York, who we want to work with. They come from all over world."

Model apartments aren't just for underage models. "Some are under 18; some are over 18," says Lee. The thing the models have in common is that they haven't yet found a place to live. Girls stay at the model apartment anywhere from a week to several months before they move out on their own. "We help them with finding their own housing after they start to get on their feet a little," adds Lee.

Many of the apartments have a dormlike feel. You share living spaces like bathrooms, kitchens, living rooms, and often bedrooms. Sometimes as many as five or six girls can live in one apartment.

Before you sign with an agency, ask its representatives about the availability of model apartments if you think you might want a place to stay when you first arrive.

Reality Check

Don't think living in a model apartment is going to be like living a wild bachelorette life. Many model apartments have chaperones, usually a scout or booker from the agency. There are house rules, and your behavior is monitored. The Elite model apartment in New York has a curfew and a "no boys, no booze, and no drugs" policy.

Moving to a Fashion Capital Without an Agent

Maybe you've done the model search/convention/model school route and still haven't found an agent. If you're adventurous and don't have a problem packing up and moving to a strange new city, and you don't mind working a part-time job on the side (if necessary) to pay the bills until your modeling career gets going, you might consider moving to a fashion capital without acquiring an agent beforehand. This is especially worth considering if you're 18 and you think or you've been told that you have a look that's more desirable in one of the other fashion capitals. I, for instance, went to Paris because I had been told that ethnic models had an easier time breaking in there. But make no bones about it, this is a very risky move.

Before you take off, you need to deal with the fact that although you may do everything possible to break into the business, be extremely beautiful and incredibly professional, and have a great attitude and a portfolio full of pictures from a secondary market, your look may not be appealing to clients in the fashion capitals. There are no guarantees in modeling, and you may still be waitressing full-time 5 years down the road. But if you're determined to be a model, this might be a worthwhile risk.

Roshumba's Rules

If you're going to take on a fashion capital on your own—you're moving there without having acquired an agent beforehand—consider visiting for a week or two first to get a feel for the city and its opportunities.

The Least You Need to Know

- ◆ Milan, Paris, and New York are the fashion capitals of the world, and each city offers unique opportunities.

- ◆ London, Tokyo, and other international cities also present opportunities for modeling.

- ◆ American models generally acquire an agent in New York, who directs them to the other fashion capitals.

- ◆ It's best to wait until you're 18 to move to a fashion capital.

- ◆ Be prepared to take a second job until your modeling career takes off.

- ◆ Moving to a fashion capital is a risky move, but sometimes it's a risk worth taking.

Chapter 10

Advice for Parents

In This Chapter

◆ Is your teen ready to model?

◆ Helping your teen pursue a modeling career

◆ Finding a reputable agent

◆ Everything you need to know about potential scams

◆ Advice from the Federal Trade Commission and Better Business Bureau

If you're the parent of a teen who's interested in modeling, this chapter is for you. Here, I give you information for guiding your teen who wants to be a model. Parents want the best for their children, and there's no doubt that modeling offers some great opportunities: to make a lot of money at a young age; travel; meet interesting people; and be exposed to art, culture, and people from around the world. At the same time, you've no doubt heard about all the pitfalls of modeling: the drugs, the predatory men, the eating disorders, the con artists, the warped values.

Even if these things don't come true, it's still scary putting a child, especially a girl, on a plane to a big city where she doesn't know anyone and doesn't know her way around. She may need to find a place to live and a job to support her before her career gets started. And of course, to you, she's still a baby.

So while letting go is never easy, in this chapter, I share advice and tips for helping make things go more smoothly. I offer my own advice; I asked an expert—my mother, LaVonne Joslin—for her thoughts; and I also asked an agent, Karen Lee, director of scouting at Elite Model Management in New York, for her advice to parents from an agent's perspective.

Finally, because there are so many scams and swindles out there, I've also included information from the Better Business Bureau (BBB) and the Federal Trade Commission (FTC) on avoiding scams and rip-offs.

Advice from a Mother Who's Been There

First, I thought it would be a good idea to talk to the ultimate expert: my mother, LaVonne Joslin, who has stood in your shoes and knows exactly all the things you're thinking and feeling. In the following sections, she offers her expert advice.

Roshumba's Mom on How You Can Help Your Teen

"A parent can help her child who is interested in pursuing a modeling career by encouraging the child to follow her dreams, by letting her know it's okay to do so, by believing in her, and by having faith in her talents and abilities. Acknowledge her by listening when she talks about her goals and dreams, and don't stand in her way as she sets out to pursue her career. Let her go—but monitor her activities.

"Accompany her as she goes to modeling schools, searches, contests, and other events, if you decide these are a good idea for her—and if the family budget permits it. Help her organize transportation and arrange for someone to accompany her if you're not available. Ask her the results of these events, and listen when she talks about participating in them. I kept close tabs on all of Roshumba's activities, especially when she was first starting out."

Model Scoop _____

My mom says: "I first realized Roshumba was interested in modeling when she was about 16. We were living in Peoria, Illinois, and she heard that the Ebony Fashion Fair, a fashion show sponsored by *Ebony* magazine and Fashion Fair Cosmetics, was coming to town. She saved her money and purchased two tickets to the fair, one for me and one for her. At the event, many people stopped us and asked if she was a model. During the show, I noticed that Roshumba was fixated on the models. After seeing the response of the people at the Fashion Fair to her, and watching how mesmerized she was by the whole scene, I began to take her desire more seriously."

Be Wary, Be Wise

"Be alert when you accompany your child on appointments with modeling agents, scouts, or photographers, or to modeling events. Be on the lookout for any people who seem sleazy, who want you to spend a lot of money, or who make what seem like unrealistic promises.

"If a modeling agency offers to represent your child, read the contract carefully to make sure your child is not signing anything that would tie her life up for longer than a year or two at a time. Make sure it's not going to cost her significant sums of money [a legitimate agency will not charge to represent a model, though there may be fees for test shoots, but they shouldn't be more than $300] and that she is not required to pose nude or be in pornographic movies. Also be aware if drugs are present.

"Google the company to see if there are any complaints about the agency, convention, or search. Also check with the local consumer protection agency [look in the government section of your phone book] and the *Better Business Bureau* [*BBB;* www.bbb. org]. You can find the number of your local BBB online or in the White Pages of the phone book. Or check with the *Federal Trade Commission* [*FTC;* www.ftc.gov] to make sure the company or person you're signing with has a clean reputation, hasn't been involved with any rip-offs, and doesn't have a lot of disgruntled customers. Also make sure they're not running the same scam that is described in complaints [many rip-off artists change their names and start playing the same old games again]."

(Also, check out the BBB's and the FTC's advice for avoiding modeling scams, coming up a little later in this chapter.)

"The best places to get referrals to established, legitimate modeling agencies are fashion-related companies, local advertising agencies, other models, and big New York agencies such as IMG, Next, Elite, and Ford.

"If someone is suggesting that you or your child pay a large sum of money—$500 or $1,000, say—to join the agency, to take pictures, or to have their photos posted on a website, take heed—this is probably a scam. Legitimate agencies work on commission and make money by booking models for modeling jobs; they don't make money from collecting large registration fees. Although most major agencies will arrange for test

> **Catwalk Talk**
>
> The **Better Business Bureau** (**BBB**) is a private, nonprofit organization with offices around the country that provides reports on local businesses. The **Federal Trade Commission** (**FTC**) is a government agency headquartered in Washington, D.C., that enforces consumer-protection laws.

shoots for models, the fees are more nominal [Elite's test shoots average $300, and the agency will often pay for it up front]." (See Chapter 12 for more information.)

Is Your Child Ready for the Catwalk?

"Besides knowing that your child is getting involved with people who can launch an actual modeling career and have her best interests at heart, it's important to know whether your child is ready on a personal level to start a professional career. A few ways to tell whether your child is ready to move away from home and start a modeling career is if she is self-sufficient: she can take care of her body and hygiene, she can prepare meals for herself, she can eat well and take vitamins, she's confident in public and respectful of others. Observe whether she can do these things on her own.

"Other ways to tell if she's ready is that she knows right from wrong: she doesn't take drugs or drink, she doesn't get into trouble at school or with the law, and she stays away from kids who do. She wakes herself up on time for school; gets good grades; and is respectful to siblings, classmates, and authority figures. She obeys school rules and is aware of the consequences of bad behavior.

"It's also possible to tell if your child is *not* mature enough to leave home and start a career. If she cuts school, takes drugs and drinks, is mean or abusive to siblings, gets in trouble with the law, or hangs around with other kids who are known troublemakers, she will only get into worse trouble if she becomes a model. Other signs are: she can't get up in the morning for school on her own, doesn't do her homework, fails classes, and doesn't do household chores without being threatened or punished. Another indication: when she is caught doing something wrong, she always blames the other person."

Model Scoop

Gia Carangi is one of the tragic casualties of modeling, a story told in Stephen M. Fried's book, *Thing of Beauty* (Pocket Books, 1994) and in the HBO movie *Gia*, starring Angelina Jolie. Soon after quitting her job in her father's hoagie restaurant in Philadelphia, Gia was appearing on the covers of *Vogue* and *Cosmopolitan*. Even though she was constantly late and unreliable at photo shoots, Gia became one of the most popular models of the late 1970s. But her behavior became increasingly bizarre: after a fashion team had spent hours preparing her and getting her dressed, Gia jumped into a nearby pool, wrecking their efforts. It soon became apparent that she had a serious heroin problem. Despite efforts to get clean, Gia died of AIDS at age 26.

Some Final Words of Advice from My Mother

"Support and encourage your daughter's dreams and efforts; watch out for pitfalls like drugs, sex, being forced into nude modeling, or signing bad contracts that will tie up her career or take all her money. But equally important, don't stand in the way of her pursuing her career and realizing her dreams."

Roshumba's Advice to Parents

My advice to parents is based on my own personal experience with my parent, as well as my observations of others whose careers grew along with mine and younger models whom I worked with once my career as a model was established.

Modeling is a great career for young people in both the short and long term because it offers many advantages. Some models make a lot of money in a short period of time; they can be exposed to other countries, people, and cultures; and modeling can open the door to other careers in television, in film, and behind the scenes in the fashion industry. Because self-discipline, determination, intuition, patience, and self-reliance are the key components to being successful as a model, these qualities can prepare a young person for success in a variety of fields.

The Good, the Bad, and the Ugly

As with everything else in life, modeling has its good aspects and its bad aspects. Drugs are easily accessible in the fashion industry. Sex is everywhere. Scam and con artists are waiting to take advantage of naive young women at every step of a model's evolution, from beginner to supermodel.

I've seen young, aspiring models who are just starting out get scammed into spending hundreds and even thousands of dollars on unnecessary photos. I've seen models with great careers ahead of them get sidelined by too much partying. I've also witnessed established models lose everything because they got strung out on drugs, while others lost their hard-earned money because of greedy, conniving people.

Reality Check

Some people may feel it's okay to take drugs occasionally or recreationally, and that it's possible to take them without getting addicted, but why even take the chance? It has been proven over and over again by musicians, actors, comedians, models, and the everyday person that indulging in drugs is a quick trip down a dead-end street. Don't do it!

That's why it's important for models to view modeling as a business opportunity and a way to open the door to a positive future, to know the risks of the fashion industry and to avoid them. When models start veering too far off track from these goals, they often find themselves in trouble.

Parents can help their children succeed by encouraging them to follow their dreams, supporting their efforts, and monitoring their actions so they don't get hurt or taken advantage of.

Keeping Them Close When They're Far Away

When your child's career has taken off, you may not be spending as much time with her because she's busy working. The best way to help out at this point is to accept that your child's life has changed and not make her feel guilty. Keep in close contact with her by phone. Listen to her when she needs to talk. Instead of lecturing her, share positive advice on how to handle difficult situations. If problems arise that neither you nor she is equipped to handle, find another adult or professional who can help.

It's a good idea to set aside a special time each week to talk to your daughter once she's embarked on her modeling career to keep abreast of everything she's up to.

Help her manage and make the most of her career by making sure she has a legitimate, knowledgeable accountant to handle her money; sets up savings accounts, trust funds, and retirement funds; and makes sound investments. (Many models have lost their entire nest eggs because they let friends, boyfriends, or other nonprofessionals manage their money.) Help her find a competent lawyer to look over work-related contracts so she doesn't sign anything that's detrimental to her career and well-being. Also encourage her to plan for a future outside of modeling.

Handling Sibling Rivalry

Another issue that may surface after a child's modeling career has geared up is sibling rivalry. This can be tough, especially if one child is famous and the others are not. I'm close to my immediate family, so I was able to observe how my mother handled minor envious outbreaks. If someone felt left out or less important, my mother would explain to my sibling that God blessed everyone with a special gift and we all must find that gift and develop it. She supported and encouraged my siblings' efforts with their education and respective careers as well. Overall, it's best to be a wise friend and confidante whose primary interest is to be sure all your children are happy, healthy, and safe from harm, and to encourage and support them on their individual journeys.

Advice from an Agent

A good, reputable agent is essential to getting the most out of a modeling career, according to Karen Lee, director of scouting at Elite Model Management in New York. It's key that an aspiring model find not only a reputable agent, but one who will help her carve out the most successful career possible.

Finding the Right Agent for Your Teen

"Models need to have an agent because that agent is there to guide them, to help them make decisions regarding which jobs to take, to negotiate money for them," explains Lee. "To be an agent basically [means being] a manager of their career. It's important that the girl looks for a reputable agent. Parents should not be afraid to ask questions and find out if an agency is reputable.

"How do you find that out? You know that by going through the BBB. A better way would be to really see who that agency represents, the caliber of models they represent, and the kinds of work their girls get. Those are things that are all very important in knowing how good and reputable an agency is. If you go into a place and you see no one on the walls you've heard of or know of, or the jobs they're getting for the girls are not great work, you'd better think about that several times."

The Importance of Family Values

Besides making sure your child is signed with a reputable agent, it helps a model's career if she has a good relationship with her parents. "We find, many times, when the girls have supportive, positive families, it's a lot better for the girls," says Lee. "I think you have to, as a parent, be there for your child, be supportive of your child, and be there to communicate with her, so she has a family that loves and supports her, that she can talk to."

Lee also recommends that, time and money permitting, a parent go with her daughter to the city where she will be starting her modeling career. "A lot of times, if a parent can and has the money to come with the girl the first time to New York, it's always nice. That way the parent gets to see what the daughter is doing, and the daughter knows the parent is there for her."

Lee warns, however, against parents who are too overprotective or who get too involved in the daughter's modeling career. "If a parent is too involved and overprotective, then the model can't really do her job well." The model may not feel free to express herself at a photo shoot because the parent is interfering too much, or her career may not be progressing as well as it could because the parent is trying to take over the agent's job and manage every aspect of her daughter's career.

> **Roshumba's Rules**
>
> Agents are the ones who "sell" a model. They want to be sure your look is marketable and appealing to clients. So when they offer you advice, take it. This will greatly increase your chances of having a great career.

Parents Beware: Scams Are Everywhere

Parents must also be on the lookout for scams of all kinds. Because young models don't have much experience with the world in general and the business world in particular, it's important that their parents or guardians be involved with their careers from the beginning. Parents are essential for asking questions, scrutinizing the situation, and reading between the lines. Trust your instincts!

> **Reality Check**
>
> A young aspiring model's desire to launch her career may sometimes overshadow her logic, and she may find herself in a situation she isn't equipped to handle. Or she may not realize she's being ripped off. This is why it's essential for parents to stay involved at every step of their daughter's career, especially when she's starting out.

In fact, modeling agency scams are so prevalent that both the BBB and FTC have released warnings about unscrupulous modeling agencies and modeling scams. I've included their reports on fraudulent modeling-agency practices in this chapter so you'll know the kinds of things you need to be on the lookout for.

Tips from the Federal Trade Commission

The FTC has issued a report for consumers on modeling-agency rip-offs that offers some guidelines about scams. This report, called "If You've Got the Look, Look Out! Avoiding Modeling Scams," gives aspiring models great advice about the many potential rip-off schemes out there (from the FTC's website at www.ftc.gov/bcp/conline/ pubs/services/model.htm):

> Someone approaches you at the mall and says, "You could be a model. You've got the 'look' we're after. Here's my card. Give me a call to set up an appointment." People have always said you're good looking. Now visions of glamour, travel, and money flash before your eyes.
>
> It's true that some successful models have been discovered in everyday places like malls, boutiques, clubs, and airports. But the vast majority of would-be models knock on door after agency door before work comes their way.
>
> **It's All an Act**   If and when you make that follow-up appointment, you'll probably find yourself in an office filled with lots of other model and actor hopefuls. Then the spiel starts. What you thought was a job interview with a talent agency turns into a high-pressure sales pitch for modeling or acting classes, or for "screen tests" or "photo shoots" that can range in price from several hundred to several thousand dollars.
>
> Man, woman, or child—it makes no difference to bogus model and talent scouts. Often these scouts are after one thing—your money—and will say just about anything to get it. But what they say isn't always what they mean.
>
> Unscrupulous model and talent scouts have their acts down pat. Listen carefully to read between their lines.

What They Say vs. What They Mean

What They Say	What They Mean
We're scouting for people with your "look" to model and act.	I need to sign up as many people as possible. My commission depends on it.
Your deposit is totally refundable.	Your deposit is refundable only if you meet very strict refund conditions.

continues

What They Say vs. What They Mean   (continued)

What They Say	What They Mean
Our talent experts will carefully evaluate your chances at success in the field and will only accept a few people into our program.	We take almost everyone.
There's a guaranteed refund if you're not accepted into the program.	Everyone's accepted into the program. Forget the refund.
You can't afford our fees? No problem. You can work them off with the high-paying jobs we'll get you.	We demand payment, whether or not you get work.

Agencies and schools offer separate and distinct services. Make sure you know the difference.

Modeling (or talent) agencies secure employment for experienced models and actors. Some agents require that you sign up exclusively with them; others may allow you to register with them as well as with other agencies in town.

Modeling and acting schools claim to provide instruction—for a fee—in poise, posture, diction, skin care, makeup application, the proper walk, and more. Modeling schools do not necessarily act as agents or find work for you—after you take their classes, you may be on your own.

Talent Tips   Steer clear of modeling companies that require you to use a specific photographer. Compare fees and the work quality of several photographers.

Be suspicious if a company requires an up-front fee to serve as your agent.

Be cautious if the school has a special referral relationship with a specific modeling agency. The two could be splitting your fees, or the agency may not be suited to your needs.

Avoiding a Model Rip-Off   Ask yourself, "Why me?" Don't let your emotions—and the company's flattery—take control. Think carefully and critically about how you were approached: if it was in a crowded mall, think how many others also may have been approached.

Avoid high-pressure sales tactics. Never sign a document without reading and understanding it first. In fact, ask for a blank copy of the contract to take home and review with someone you trust. If the company refuses, walk away.

Be leery of companies that only accept payment in cash or by money order. Read it as a strong signal that the company is more interested in your money than your career.

Be wary of claims about high salaries. Successful models in small markets can earn $75 to $150 an hour, but the work is irregular.

Ask for the names, addresses and phone numbers of models and actors who have secured successful work—recently—based on the company's training.

Roshumba's Rules

Even if an agent says you have what it takes to be a model, it's smart to evaluate yourself to be sure you're not being scammed. Check out Chapter 3 to find out if you have the basic qualifications.

Check out client claims. If an agency says it has placed models and actors in specific jobs, contact the companies to verify that they've hired models and actors from the agency.

Be skeptical of local companies claiming to be the "biggest" agency or a "major player" in the industry, especially if you live in a smaller city or town.

Realize that different parts of the country have different needs. For example, New York is recognized for fashion modeling; the Washington/Baltimore area is known for industrial or training films.

Ask if the company/school is licensed or bonded, if that's required by your state. Verify this information with the appropriate authorities, such as your local consumer protection agency or state Attorney General. Make sure the license is current.

Ask your local Better Business Bureau, consumer protection agency, and state Attorney General if there are any unresolved consumer complaints on file about the company.

Get everything in writing, including any promises that have been made orally.

Keep copies of all important papers, such as your contract and company literature, in a safe place.

Reality Check _____

Keep copies of all important papers, such as your contract and agency literature. You may need these if you have a dispute with the agency. And be sure to get all promises in writing!

If you've been scammed by a bogus model scout or agency, contact your local consumer protection agency, state Attorney General, or Better Business Bureau. [You can find the numbers in the telephone book or online.]

The FTC works to prevent consumer fraud and to provide information to help consumers spot, stop, and avoid them. To file a complaint or to get free information on consumer issues, visit www.ftc.gov or call toll-free 1-877-FTC-HELP (1-877-382-4357).

Advice from the Better Business Bureau

The BBB advises caution when dealing with modeling agencies. Although ethical and legitimate modeling agencies exist, the BBB warns that "far too often, consumers are victimized by unscrupulous talent and modeling agencies promising money, exposure, and stardom" (www.bbb.org/Alerts/article.asp?ID=477).

Further, the BBB advises this:

> Before you become involved with an agency, know exactly what the agency should be doing for you. An agency should be engaged in the marketing and booking of talent. Usually a state license is required to book work for a fee. The agent's role is to promote the talent [in this case, a model] who has contracted them for their marketing services, negotiate the most favorable contract for the talent, and collect a commission from the talent.

Also in its 2003 report, the BBB gives the following advice:

> Do you think you have what it takes to be a model or actor? Many unscrupulous talent and modeling agencies will lead you to believe so. However, far too often, consumers are victimized by fraudulent agencies promising money, exposure and stardom.

> There are ethical and legitimate talent and modeling agencies in the entertainment business. Before becoming involved with an agency, know exactly what they should be doing for you. An agency should be engaged in the marketing and booking of talent. Usually a state license is required to book work for a fee. The agent's role is to promote the talent who has contracted for their marketing services, negotiate the most favorable contract for the talent and collect a commission from the talent. You should interview your agent as thoroughly as

you would interview your doctor, lawyer, or CPA. Remember, the agent will be working for you, not vice versa. Carefully review your contract with your agent. This is your agreement regarding what the agent will do to earn the commission you pay.

To help you detect fraudulent opportunities, the Better Business Bureau warns that disreputable agencies often:

- ◆ Ask for up-front money, which may be called "registration," "consultation," or "administrative" fees. Legitimate agents work on a commission. They don't get any money until you get paid for doing the work they have obtained for you.

- ◆ Pressure you to leave a check or cash deposit or sign a contract immediately. The agent may insist that you take acting lessons at a particular school or from a particular teacher; or may try to get you to buy expensive photographs, audition tapes, or other services or materials sold by someone he or she suggests. An agent's time should be spent finding work for his or her client, not selling products and services.

- ◆ Display pictures of famous models or celebrities on the walls to make you believe they are represented by that agency, although they're not.

- ◆ Use names which sound similar to well-known agencies. Fraudulent companies will sometimes do this to give the incorrect impression that they are connected to a legitimate entity.

- ◆ Place phony ads in the help wanted section of newspapers that say something like, "new faces wanted" for commercials, movies or modeling or claim that "no experience is necessary."

Problems or complaints about an agent or an agency may be referred to the BBB, state Department of Licensing and Regulation or consumer protection agency in the city where the company is located. To obtain helpful consumer information on a particular agency, you will need to contact the local BBB that serves that particular city.

If you have a problem or complaint about an agent or an agency, call the Better Business Bureau in the city where the company is located.

For the BBB nearest you or to obtain helpful consumer information, visit www.bbb.org.

Ten Questions Parents Should Ask Potential Agents

Here are 10 questions a parent should ask the agent before signing a modeling contract for her child:

- What kind of work do you think you'll be able to get my daughter?

- What other models have you represented?

- May I talk to other models you represent?

- What fees will we be responsible for paying?

- Who are some of the clients who have booked your models in the past?

- How long is the term of the contract?

- What individual will be supervising my daughter's career?

- Is that person used to dealing with novice models?

- What percentage of my daughter's earnings will you take as commission?

- Will my daughter be able to work part-time, or do you expect her to drop out of school to work?

My overall advice to parents is to be involved with your child's career. Be especially vigilant when it comes to signing up for an agent, a school, or any other modeling-related conventions. Again, the basic rule of thumb is you shouldn't have to pay more than the most modest fees upfront (with the exceptions of modeling schools and conventions).

The Least You Need to Know

- Parents need to scrutinize all their child's modeling activities to protect her from rip-offs, con artists, and other dangers.

- Carefully check out any modeling agency that wants to represent your child.

- Be sure your child is mature and responsible enough for a modeling career.

Part 3

Now That Your Foot's in the Door, What's Next?

Finding an agent is a model's first big hurdle. But it's only the first step on a long road to success. No need to panic, though! Everything you need to know about getting started in modeling is right here. First, I take you inside a modeling agency, explaining who everyone is and what they do so you can make the most of their services. Next, I explain what test shots and portfolios are, and I give you some great tips for making sure yours really stand out.

Then I cover everything you need to know about those "modeling musts," the essential items a professional model can't live without. Finally, I tell you how to shine at go and sees (job interviews for models) so you'll be one step ahead of the competition when it comes time for you to start booking professional modeling jobs!

Chapter 11

How an Agency Works

In This Chapter

- ◆ Understanding how an agency operates and what an agent does
- ◆ A look at the various departments of an agency
- ◆ Advantages and disadvantages of large and small agencies
- ◆ Tips for switching agencies

It's important to know how an agency works and who does what so you get the most out of the agency's personnel in terms of managing your career. Knowing who's who also helps you when you go to open calls and other meetings when you're in the process of finding an agent. Modeling agencies have their own hierarchy, and staff members tend to be very protective of their duties and titles. You need to know the chain of command and follow it, or you can cause problems.

In this chapter, I give you a guided tour of a modeling agency. I cover the advantages and disadvantages of small and large agencies and tell you the right way to switch agencies if you find that you need to.

The Booker: A Model's Best Friend

The *model managers* (also called agents or bookers) are the people at an agency who manage every aspect of your career in the short and long term. When you're just starting out, model managers direct you to the testing photographers you should work with, decide what photos you should be taking, and determine what aspects of yourself you should be focusing on to sell.

Catwalk Talk

An agent is also called a **model manager** because he or she manages and oversees your whole career, from your first test pictures until the day you decide to retire.

An agent really manages the models' careers, explains Karen Lee, director of scouting at Elite Model Management. "Once we find a girl and decide we want to represent her and she decides she wants to be with Elite, we work on getting the girl's book together by sending her to good, reputable photographers who will take test pictures of her. Then we put a test book together, which shows her in various ways—beauty, fashion, interesting photos, black and white, and/or color. We then send her to various clients."

All the bookers in a department traditionally sit at one table, which makes it easier for them to communicate about the models they're working with.

Developing the Model's Look

"You work on each individual girl," says Lee. "Maybe one girl needs a haircut, maybe one girl needs to learn to dress a little differently, maybe another girl needs to work on her body a little. You work on her presence, her style, her hair, her look, her book.

You want a girl to look great in person—that means very natural, very much in shape, very healthy, not too skinny, not overweight."

When you're ready to start working, the agent decides what clients you should work for. She sends you out to see a variety of clients and then interprets their reactions to you and directs you from there. The agent will soon realize that maybe you don't appeal to fashion designers booking their runway shows, but that your look is attractive to magazine editors and catalogs. An agent will quickly realize your strengths and where you are in your career, and build on that.

Roshumba's Rules

In addition to being reputable (honest, businesslike, not a scammer), it's key that the booker be an expert at doing her job. If she isn't, it could have a negative impact on your career—or you may not have as successful a career as you could.

Your booker chooses the photos that will appear in your portfolio and arranges them in a certain order to "sell" you to the client.

The Daily Details

Your booker also handles the day-to-day details of your life. She schedules all your go and sees (see Chapter 14) and jobs. Clients call the booker directly, and she lets them know when you're available to work. Unless you tell her specifically that you're not available (say you need to go home and see your family, go to the doctor, or go on vacation), she will book jobs for you every day. Try to give your booker as much advance notice as possible when you need days off.

The booker also lets you know when and where a job will be, how long it will last, who the client is, how much you will be paid, and what's expected of you. For example, if it's a lingerie shoot, she'll let you know that you need to shave and get a pedicure beforehand.

Bookers often handle some personal things as well. They can put you in touch with doctors, therapists, nutritionists, or personal trainers. They can help you find housing. They can also refer you to lawyers and accountants and any other professionals you might need.

Model Scoop _____

It's not unusual for me to talk to my booker at least three times a day because things change constantly during the course of a day. Bookers are in touch with American, European, Midwestern, and West Coast clients. I might be scheduled to do a shoot the next day in a studio 2 blocks from my house and suddenly, instead, I'm on a plane to Paris for a shoot for French _Elle_. Depending on what's going on, if the booker is trying to reconcile a double booking (when two clients want me for the same time period), or if it's a particularly busy week, like during the runway show season, I could talk to my booker up to 10 times in 1 day!

The Major Booking Departments

In a small agency, the various types of models are not divided up; one set of bookers works for everyone. In large agencies, however, the agents/bookers work in several different divisions, each specializing in a different type of model:

- New faces
- Model management
- Supermodels/celebrity models
- Catalog and advertising
- Runway
- Television commercials

The New Faces Department

This department is in charge of developing new recruits into full-fledged models and booking all their jobs in the first couple years of their careers. The agents/bookers in the new faces department meet with the girls who come to the agency's open calls. They help choose the models the agency will represent. They help develop a brand-new model so she has a marketable look, giving her advice on bringing out her best qualities. They also help new models set up test shoots with the best photographers and put together their portfolios.

They also introduce the model to the fashion industry and send her on her first go and sees to magazine editors, photographers, and advertisers. They are responsible for helping a girl make living arrangements if she's had to relocate, familiarize herself with the city, learn about public transportation and how to get around, and set up a bank account.

A girl is considered a new face and will stay in the new faces department until she establishes steady clientele and becomes known to industry professionals.

Your booker gives you advice on ways you can make yourself more marketable to clients, including changing your hair or shaping up your body.

The Model Management Department

The biggest department in the agency is the model management department because it handles all the models who have established their careers but who aren't yet superstars or specialists (catalog, advertising, or runway models, for example).

After a model leaves the new faces department, she progresses to the model management department. The bookers/agents in the model management department expand on that foundation to see what type of clients are interested in her and decide how she should focus her career and what she should do next.

Overall, model management's responsibility is to help the model build a well-balanced career, with a range of editorial, fashion show, and ad clients in a variety of markets. They are responsible for figuring out what clients you *should* be working with and creating opportunities for you to meet those clients. If you haven't done any ads, for example, they may send you to see an ad agency to get feedback on what they think of you.

Many models stay with the model management department their whole careers, unless they reach supermodel status or become specialists.

Reality Check _____

Having a well-balanced career is more important than you might think: it's the best way to get the most out of your modeling career, have the most work, and make the most money. Editorial modeling is great for exposure and creating a name for yourself, but it doesn't pay well. In fact, you might not be able to live off of editorial fees alone. Catalog modeling is great for making money, but it's not as well regarded, so your image and status might suffer if you do too much. Modeling in fashion shows offers fairly good money and prestige, but not as much exposure. This is why you want to balance your work.

The Supermodel/Celebrity Model Department

As you can probably guess, the supermodel/celebrity model department handles models who are of supermodel or celebrity status—people who are household names, have multimillion-dollar incomes, and are involved in projects outside modeling, such as producing their own calendars, books, TV shows, exercise videos, and other merchandise.

Because of the high profile of the models in the supermodel/celebrity model department and the caliber of their clientele, this is handled by a separate department. The clients are as famous as the models and include Victoria's Secret, *Sports Illustrated*, *Vogue*, *Harper's Bazaar*, and *Elle*, along with prestigious fashion designers such as Calvin Klein, Donna Karan, and Valentino. They may also include high-end catalogs, such as Bergdorf Goodman or the Neiman Marcus Designer Collection.

The bookers/agents in this department also have high profiles in the fashion industry. They often have a direct relationship with the most important photographers, designers, and editors.

Depending on how their careers progress, models can remain in this department until they're ready to move on to do other things or retire.

The Catalog and Advertising Department

This department specializes in booking models for catalog (as well as for websites) and advertising jobs. Catalog and advertising are the highest-paying types of modeling. Models who are nearing the end of their careers tend to do a lot of this type of work because this is where they make the big bucks (and capitalize on all the prestigious editorial and runway work they did earlier in their careers).

The main difference between the catalog and advertising department and model management is that your career will be handled in a different way: to be sure you make as much money as possible, that you work as often as possible, and that you work for the best clients—in other words, to help you get the most out of the years you put in. The focus isn't so much on getting a variety of work or building clientele.

This department books models for the major catalogs, including Saks Fifth Avenue, Neiman Marcus, Lord & Taylor, Bloomingdale's, and J. Crew. It also books models to appear in print ads in magazines and newspapers for clients such as Oil of Olay, Nine West, Hanes Hosiery, Clairol, The Gap, L'Oréal, Colgate, and Secret.

The Runway Department

The runway department, as the name suggests, handles the scheduling and booking of models for runway and related work, including fittings, trunk shows, and boutique showings.

This department handles runway bookings for *all* the models in the agency, as well as the careers of models who specialize in runway work. During the collections, it submits the composite cards of all the girls interested in doing the shows, including models from the new faces and supermodel/celebrity model departments, to the fashion designers presenting shows. The runway department does all the necessary negotiating and scheduling for all the agency models chosen.

The Television Commercial Department

Most modeling agencies partner with an outside agency that specializes in booking talent on TV commercials to handle all its models' television bookings. Usually one booker serves as the liaison between the outside agency and the modeling agency. This person coordinates the bookings for all the models in the agency who are hired to do television commercials—for instance, TV ads for cars (Ford, Mercedes, Lexus), beverage companies (Coke, Pepsi, Red Bull), and beauty products (Revlon, Finesse). He also handles related work, such as guest appearances on TV shows or even movie appearances.

Specialty Departments

Many large agencies have departments that handle specialty models. These might include but are not limited to the following:

- Plus-size models
- Elegant (older) models
- Parts models
- Male models

In Chapter 20, I cover specialty modeling, but for now, let's take a look at some of these departments.

The Plus-Size Department

Plus-size models are an increasingly busy category of models. The average American woman is a size 14 and cannot identify with a size 2 or 4 model, and designers are finally catching on to this fact. Advertisers and catalogs are trying to appeal to this growing market by using plus-size models.

Catwalk Talk

Plus size refers to women's clothing sizes 12 or 14 and larger. More and more American women wear plus-size clothing, which has gotten more fashionable and better made in the last few years. Today nearly all department and mass merchandise stores (such as Macy's, Saks Fifth Avenue, Target, and K-Mart) carry plus-size lines.

Plus-size models are larger than regular models, but they're healthy, tall (at least 5'8" or 5'10"), and toned. They may be large-boned, with broad shoulders, full hips, and full breasts, and maybe a bit of a tummy. They wear a woman's size 12 to 18. Plus-size models usually have beautiful, classic facial features and exude warmth and appeal. They're true proof that beauty comes in all sizes.

Plus-size models are booked to model absolutely everything, including lingerie, bathing suits, sportswear, and evening dresses. They appear in magazines, catalogs, and advertisements.

The Elegant Department

Elegant models are usually older models; the minimum age to enter this department is about 35. A model might work through this department for the rest of her life.

Elegant models have become very popular over the last few years. As baby boomers and even Gen Xers have aged, designers want to use models who appeal to this huge group of consumers, and they've found that 40- and 50-year-old consumers just don't identify with 14-year-old models.

Elegant models used to work only part-time, but now some model full-time. They have a range of clients, including runway, advertising, and editorial. Most of their work, however, is modeling for catalogs.

The Parts Department

Many large agencies have parts departments that represent models who specialize in leg, hand, and foot modeling. These women probably would not be regular model material—maybe they're not tall enough—but they have at least one standout "part," such as beautiful hands, gorgeous legs, or perfect size 6 feet.

Hand models model jewelry and nail products—anything where an advertiser would want to focus attention on the hand. Leg models model hosiery, footwear, shaving products, and body creams. They need to have long, lean, toned legs with no scars, bruises, tattoos, or scratches. Foot models model shoes, socks, foot-care products, and toenail polish. They wear size 5½ to 7 medium-width shoes and have a medium to high arch, without any bunions, toenail fungus, crooked toes, badly proportioned toes, or calluses.

The Men's Department

Some small agencies handle men exclusively, while some larger agencies have a separate men's department. In either case, a men's agency or department specifically focuses on the development and marketing of male models, from beginners to established models.

Male models walk the runway for major menswear designers, including Joseph Abboud, Paul Smith, Prada, Gucci, Ralph Lauren, and Calvin Klein. They also appear in men's magazines, such as *GQ* and *Esquire*. They model for such catalogs and websites as J. Crew, Benetton, Saks Fifth Avenue, and Macy's. They also appear in ads for soft drinks, men's clothing, cars, men's grooming products, and sports products.

Other Agency Departments

Modeling agencies have other departments that are common to many other types of businesses:

- ◆ Accounting
- ◆ Promotions and publicity
- ◆ Administration
- ◆ Receptionist(s)

It's important to know what each department is and does because all will have an effect on your career as a model.

The accounting department deals with all money, both incoming (from clients) and outgoing (to you, among others). When you work a job, you need to have the client sign a special voucher acknowledging that you did indeed work. (Every model is issued her own voucher book with the agency logo on it.) Then you turn that voucher in to the accounting department, and it bills the client for the work you did. The bill includes the model's fee, the agent's fee, and any other negotiated fees.

Promotions and publicity is in charge of promoting the agency's name and image in the advertising and business community. It ties the agency's name in with charity events by providing models for the event for the sake of name exposure. This department also handles press inquiries about the agency and, often, individual models.

The administration includes the presidents, vice presidents, and department directors of the agency. They run the agency, hire and fire bookers and other personnel, and rent and remodel the agency's office. They plan for the agency's future and troubleshoot any internal or external problems.

> **Roshumba's Rules**
>
> Make friends with your agency's receptionist because your portfolio will be passing through her hands on a daily basis as it's sent out to various clients.

One of the key people in the agency, and someone you'll have a lot of contact with, is the receptionist. She greets all visitors and routes callers to the correct department. She answers general questions about the agency and deals with all the messengers who are constantly dropping off and delivering packages.

What Size Agency Is Right for You?

When you're first starting out, working with a small agency has several advantages. There's a lot less internal competition, so you're not competing with so many girls in your own agency. The bookers in a small agency may work harder for you when you're getting started because they may not have as many high-profile models bringing in the big bucks. They may need to get you jobs to ensure a steady stream of income and keep the agency going. Also, many agents/bookers in a small agency may have a personal financial stake in the company, so they have a vested interest in making sure you succeed.

One of the downsides of being with a small agency is that each individual model manager has a lot more responsibility than someone at a larger agency. The manager may be responsible for scouting new models, developing them, organizing their books, sending them to see clients, booking the models, and following up. She may be doing everything involved with managing the models, promoting and running the agency, and even balancing the checkbook, which may take away from the time she's able to devote to you.

Reality Check

Smaller agencies are much more vulnerable to going out of business than larger ones. Their volume of business is lower, so they don't have the same financial stability as a larger agency. In fact, two of the smaller agencies I was represented by at different points in my career have since gone out of business. Unfortunately, sometimes models don't get paid when agencies go bankrupt.

In addition, if you want to focus on one area—say, building a strong editorial career—a small agency may not have contacts with all the editorial clients because the agency is also trying to service advertising, catalog, and fashion-designer clients.

The reason a large agency might be a good option when you're starting your career is that has the manpower to take care of all your individual needs. You can also grow with a larger agency, starting your career with the new faces department, which develops new models. New faces typically has more knowledge of model development and have special relationships with the clients who tend to hire new faces.

Roshumba's Rules

If you're new to modeling or very young, a small agency might be the best choice for you. It's less intimidating for girls who need a lot of attention, hand-holding, and confidence building.

Also, more than one person is looking out for you at a larger agency, in addition to your own personal booker. Even if you're not working with a particular booker directly, if a request comes in to her for someone who looks like you, she'll recommend you.

Once you've developed, grown, had a full career, and decide you want to focus on a specific area, such as runway or catalogs, a large agency has a special department to meet your needs, and you'll be able to move there without switching agencies.

Larger agencies have the financial and manpower capacities to hire in-house as well as freelance model scouts, and most large agencies also sponsor model searches and other scouting events. All this may make it easier for you to get signed by a larger agency in the first place; finding a smaller agency to represent you may take a little more legwork on your part. Larger agencies may also be able to provide a place for you to live because a big company has the money available to afford model apartments.

Although large agencies employ a lot more bookers who specialize in what they do, they also work with a lot more models. As a result, you end up competing not only with models from other agencies, but also with your own agency-mates. And if your career isn't progressing the way the agency had hoped, you may get lost in the shuffle because they have so many other girls to think about. They might not take the time to focus on your weak areas and help you improve.

Is This a Match Made in Heaven?

An agent shouldn't look at you as a commodity only—something that can be marketed and sold. The agent should be interested in you as a person. Whether the agency is large or small, you should get the feeling that it's interested in representing you. You also want an agent who maintains a certain level of professionalism, has ethics, and treats you with respect.

You want an agent who won't lose interest in you, one who will work hard to sell you. At some point, everyone needs an extra push. You may have difficulty getting started in the business and have trouble landing those first jobs. Or maybe you start off well, but things slow down a year or two later. You want an agent who looks at you as a human being first and a client second. You have to have a personal relationship so you know the agent won't give up on you as soon as you hit a rough spot in your career.

The best way to tell if an agency is right for you is if, after about 3 to 6 months, the agency has booked some jobs for you. If you're not working after 6 months, either you're not marketable or your agency doesn't know how to market you.

Switching Agencies, Staying Friends

Many relationships end, and your relationship with your agency might be one of them. Before you switch agencies, though, find out if there's something you need to improve first. If you leave an agency and *you* are the problem, you're going to run into the same situation at the next agency. So start by asking your booker if there's something you need to improve either physically or mentally.

But if you've been with the agency for 3 to 6 months and you feel like you're not being handled properly, the agency may be the problem.

Other reasons to switch agencies include …

◆ You're having problems getting paid for the jobs you do.

◆ You're not being sent out to see clients.

◆ You're not being pushed or marketed.

◆ You don't get along with your booker.

If these problems can't be resolved and the agency can't find anyone else for you to work with, it may be time to move on.

Before you head for the door, however, be sure you've made all the personal improvements the booker has asked you to make. Then talk to her and let her know you're not satisfied with what's happening with your career. You've gone on appointments, and still nothing is happening. Or maybe she's not sending you on go and sees at all. Whatever the reason, your career has stalled. Let her know you're not happy. After you've had this talk, give her about a month to make changes and show you she's making an effort to improve the situation. If she doesn't do anything, you'll probably want to move on.

You should have two or three other agencies lined up before you leave your current one. You can find out about other agencies by word of mouth from other models or by

> **Reality Check**
>
> If someone is making threats, saying you'll never get work if you don't have sex with them, don't believe it. No professional agency conducts business like that, so this person probably couldn't help your career anyway. Tell the supervisor of the person who threatened you, or if the harasser is the big boss, leave that agency immediately.

looking at various agencies' websites to see what models they handle. When you've narrowed it down to two or three agencies, call each one, introduce yourself, and ask for a meeting.

At the appointment, explain what you want to do, the problems you're having with your current agency, and why you want to leave. Let the agency know what kind of work you think you should be doing. Meet with two or three agencies so you can compare them, gauge their reactions, and see how enthusiastic they are about you. If they listen intently to what you're saying, study your book, study you, and get a feel for your potential, these are strong signs they're interested in you.

Reality Check

Before you leave one agency, be sure you've contacted another agency.

When you have two or three strong possibilities, let your current agency know you want to change. Approach your booker and tell her you've really thought about it but you think a change will be best for everyone involved. Tell her what date you will be changing, and ask her if she will have all your pictures, composites, and portfolios ready to give to you (after all, you paid for and own these). Also be sure you get your final paychecks.

Although you may be tempted to tell the agency staff exactly what you think of them, it's better to leave as friends, not as enemies. Be respectful and polite—even though you didn't get what you wanted out of the relationship, they did make time for you. It's not a good idea to burn bridges because the agency might try to alienate your clients. Instead of telling clients you switched agencies, they might tell your clients that you're pregnant and quit modeling, or the same booker might later be at your new agency!

Roshumba's Rules

In addition to telling your agent in person or on the phone that you're switching agencies, it's good to put it in writing for legal protection. Just write her a letter and mail or fax it to her.

Most of the time, agencies will give you the money they owe you. But it's always a good idea to have it set up so you get paid on a regular basis—say, every 2 weeks—so they never owe you a lot of money. If you owe money to the agency for composites, portfolios, or Federal Express or messenger expenses, the agency may hold on to your paycheck until you've paid them back. The agency pays these fees in advance for you. When your client pays for a job you've done, the agency deducts from your paycheck monies they've paid in advance for you.

The agency will be at the center of your life as long as you're a model. The more you know about how an agency works and the better you cultivate relationships with the agency staff, the easier your career will flow.

The Least You Need to Know

- ◆ Your agent/booker is responsible for all aspects of your career, including development and day-to-day management.

- ◆ Depending on the stage of your career, you may be handled by the new faces, model management, or supermodel/celebrity model department, or by another specialty department.

- ◆ Many behind the scenes people will play a key role in your career.

12

Testing, Testing, 1, 2, 3: Test Shoots

In This Chapter

◆ Familiarizing yourself with the camera: test shoots for experience

◆ Getting the shots you want

◆ Practice (posing) makes perfect

◆ Your calling card: test shoots for your book

Test shoots are special photo shoots models do throughout their career, but mainly when they're getting started in the business. There are three different kinds:

◆ Test shoots for experience

◆ Test shoots for your book

◆ Test shoots to show a new look

Models who don't yet have an agent do test shoots for experience. These photos are usually done with novice photographers who want to gain experience working with models and perfecting their craft. These are not pictures you want to show to agents; you just want to study them and learn from them.

When an agency has agreed to represent you, your agent/booker will arrange for you to have a photo session with a reputable photographer to do test shoots for your book. The agency usually pays for these photos up front (the cost is deducted from your first paychecks) and the photos from the session are arranged in your book (which is also called a portfolio, a photo album you bring to clients that contains your best pictures).

Other test shots can be done at any time during a model's career. They can show off a new look (a hair cut, weight loss or gain) or restart the career of a model who has taken time off (for instance, to have a baby) and is now getting back to the industry.

In this chapter, I discuss all three types of test shoots in depth, what you should expect from each, and how you can make the most of them.

Your Camera Debut: Test Shoots for Experience

As the name suggests, *test shoots for experience* are done for the experience. They don't help you get an agent, and they don't help you get clients. But they do help you learn how to pose and move naturally in front of the camera so you don't look uncomfortable, stiff, afraid, or like you're "modeling."

These test shoots help you figure out the best angles of your body and face, get comfortable in the environment of a photo studio, and learn to take directions from a photographer.

The Price of Experience

Test shoots for experience should cost you very little (no more than $50 to $100 for film, processing, and prints) or nothing. Paying more is a waste of money because the only purpose of these photos is for you to see how you photograph and to learn from looking at the pictures.

If someone wants to charge you more than that for a test shoot for experience, just say no. Either he's not the right photographer for your needs (you don't need an experienced pro) or he's trying to scam you.

It's also not worth it to hire a makeup artist and hairstylist for a test shoot (unless they want to test, too, and are willing to work for free). Forcing you to pay for hair and makeup is another common scam. If you're really not confident about your ability to style your own hair, get your hair done at your local salon; it will be a lot cheaper than having a stylist come to the shoot. If you're not handy with makeup, go to a department store and get a free makeover at the cosmetics counter.

> **Roshumba's Rules**
>
> Don't spend a lot of money on test photos for experience, even though hundreds of rip-off artists out there will tell you that you have to. They are a waste of money! When you get an agent, he or she will set up professional test shoots with experienced photographers. You shouldn't spend more than the cost of photo development—$50 to $100 tops.

Finding the Right Photographer

To find a photographer to do a test shoot for experience with you, inquire at local hair salons or stores. They may be connected with the local fashion scene and know some beginning photographers.

Another great place to check is the photo club or yearbook staff at school. Often aspiring student photographers are eager to find models to shoot. You could also sign up for a photography class yourself, where you're likely to meet other novice photographers—and it's not a bad idea to gain some behind-the-camera experience.

Giving It Your Best Shot

Before you begin the test shoot, talk to the photographer to get an idea of the image he's trying to capture. (Because it's *your* test shoot, you may want to work on a concept together, whether it's a spring day in the park or a studio shoot with special props.) Let him know what you want to accomplish—maybe you want to imitate a fashion story you saw in a magazine—but also open yourself up to his ideas so he can help you make the most of the session.

Find Your Best Look

Before you do a test shoot for experience, practice posing in a mirror at your house. This sounds silly, but it's a great technique for figuring out your best angles, whether you look better smiling or pouting, and which stance best hides a figure flaw.

Roshumba's Rules _____

Looking at your reflection in the mirror is also a good way to try to figure out which model type you are (see Chapter 5). Start by putting on your favorite music and posing and dancing around.

Reality Check _____

Don't worry if you can't pull off every single look you see professional models doing. Even professional models don't do every look. Rebecca Romijn, for instance, is almost always pictured smiling and would probably be much less appealing with Kate Moss's trademark pout. Figuring out what works on you gives you a big head start once you're in front of the camera.

Try out some of the poses you see in catalogs and fashion magazines. See if you can imitate the poses and expressions of some of your favorite models. Imitate the sexy pout of Victoria's Secret model Heidi Klum. Do you look like you're pouting, or do you look like your lips are chapped?

Next you might want to try the intense, animalistic stare of supermodel Adriana Lima. In photos, her gaze is so unwavering it seems like she's looking right through you. See if you can do that stare, and critique yourself. Do you look like your eyes are looking through someone's soul, or does it look like you're about to tear up?

If you have long hair, play with it. Flip it back and forth. Work your hands through it. See what kind of creative hair poses you can come up with. Look at a magazine, and you'll see that professional models are often asked to play with their hair. If your hair is a selling point, learn how to make it move so it attracts attention. Models with beautiful hair luck out because they are often selected to appear in lucrative advertisements for hair-care products.

Also check how you look in different mirrors in different rooms throughout your house. Notice how you look in different kinds of light and which light you look best in.

See how your body looks in various poses in front of the mirror as well. Look at the models in lingerie or bathing suit catalogs, and try to mimic their poses. Stand with your hands on your hips, or try lying on your side, supporting the weight of your head with your hands. Does your body look similar to the models in the catalog? If not, look for ways to disguise any flaws.

Shot by Shot: Photos You'll Want

As I mentioned earlier, you'll want three basic types of shots: pictures of your face, pictures of your body, and shots that show your personality. Here are the photos you'll want to capture in your test shoot for experience.

Face/Beauty/Head Shots

First you'll want to focus on beauty or head shots—close-ups of your face. In these photos, experiment with different facial expressions—happy, pouty, sexy, intense, aloof—to get an idea of what you look like with a smile, with a soft and sultry look, or with an intense stare. Trying different expressions gives you an idea of the range of emotions you can project and which expressions best suit your personality and facial features.

> **Catwalk Talk**
>
> When a photographer wants your head or body to face the camera, that's called a **straight-on** shot. A **profile** shot is a photo of the side of your face or body. Another popular shot is the **three-quarters angle**, which means you're facing slightly off to the side, halfway between the straight-on and profile shots.

Also take pictures of your face at different angles: *straight-on* and in *profile*. Throw your head back and laugh, tilt your head up, tilt your head down, and thrust out your jaw.

Even though the pictures will focus on your face, you want to move your body as well to see how that affects the way your face looks. Turn your body sideways, but move your head to look straight at the camera. Lie on your back to see how the weight of your face shifts when you're prone. Turn your body straight to the camera, poke out one hip, and then turn your head to the *three-quarters angle* but look straight at the camera and make big doe eyes.

You'll want to have three different kinds of head shots taken:

◆ Natural—wearing very little makeup

◆ Enhanced—wearing a medium amount of makeup

◆ Glamour—wearing a lot of makeup

For the natural photos, don't wear a lot of makeup because these shots are meant to give you an idea of how your skin and facial features look in their natural state. At most, you'll want to apply just a little liquid foundation, brow powder, mascara, and lipstick in a natural color. (For more information on applying makeup, see Chapter 21.) Also pull your hair back off your face.

When you're doing test shoots for experience, try out three makeup looks (from left to right): natural (with very little makeup), enhanced (with just enough makeup to make your features stand out), and glamour (the to-the-max Miss America look). Also try out a variety of expressions—pensive, happy, pouty—to see which ones suit you best.

(Photographer: Kwame Brathwaite; model: Laura McLafferty)

Enhanced Beauty Shots

In the second set of photos, wear a medium amount of makeup—just enough to enhance your natural features and a little more than you wore in the natural shots. Apply some more blush to your cheeks, line your upper lash line with an eye pencil, line your lips with a lip pencil before applying lipstick, and/or use a powder eye shadow to enhance your brows. Your eyes will stand out more if you add a darker-colored shadow in the crease of your eye. You may also want to experiment with slightly darker or more dramatic makeup colors. Your hair can be worn parted straight down, slicked back, or in any other simple style.

> **Roshumba's Rules**
>
> If your nose is broad, avoid poses in which your head is tilted down looking straight at the camera. Instead, turn your head to the three-quarters angle and use your eyes expressively to attract attention away from your nose.

For these shots, you'll again want to see how you look with a range of expressions on your face: happy, sultry, serious, intense. Try moving your head and body in a variety of positions as well.

Dramatic Test Photos

These are the glamour shots. You'll be wearing intense, dramatic makeup (bright red lips, smoky eyes, deep blush), and your hair will be done up (now's the time to try out a bouffant or other dramatic style). All in all, you'll look like you're going to the red-carpet event of the year.

These shots give you an idea of how you look wearing a lot of makeup, how you feel with it on, and how your skin reacts. Some people look like the most gorgeous super-models in the world wearing a lot of makeup; others look like they've been playing with their mom's cosmetics kit.

For this look, apply foundation all over your face for a smooth canvas on which to work. Next, dust on loose powder to set the makeup. You'll definitely want to apply dramatic eye makeup—a smoky eye shadow on the lid, a darker color in the crease of the eye, liner along the upper lash line, at least three coats of mascara, and/or false eyelashes (if you know how to apply them).

Accentuate your cheekbones by applying blush on the apples of your cheeks and along your cheekbones. Choose a bold lip color; first line your lips in a matching color and then use a lipstick brush to fill in. You might even want to put a gloss over your lipstick for a more dramatic look.

Your hair can be a true 'do. Try teasing it, spraying it, putting it in a French twist or pin curls, blowing it up into a bouffant—whatever suits your hair. And don't forget the jewelry: earrings, necklaces, and bracelets.

Again, try a range of poses to see what your features look like when you're soft and pouty looking, are sultry and sexy looking, or have a big, broad laugh or pleasant smile. Take a few shots in profile, in three-quarters, while looking straight at the camera, and with your head tilted up and down.

Body Shots

Body shots help you familiarize yourself with what your body looks like without a lot of clothes on so you can clearly see your body in the photographs and learn about your body's lines, proportions, and best (and worst) features. Do you have long, bony arms, or a long, elegant neck? Do you have a rounded tummy or wide shoulders? Test pictures can help you learn how to pose in ways that enhance your best features and disguise your worst. For instance, by arching your back and pushing out your chest and butt, you can accentuate a sexy, curvy body.

Roshumba's Rules

Even though many women's hips are larger than their shoulders, you don't want the photograph to show this. One way models often disguise this imbalance and make their shoulders and hips seem like they're actually the same width is to turn their hips to the three-quarters angle but keep their shoulders and head facing straight ahead to the camera.

For body shots, pose in a simple one- or two-piece bathing suit. You can also wear a unitard, shorts and a tank top, panties and a T-shirt, or body-conscious lingerie. Wear whichever style of makeup most complements your face—natural, enhanced, or dramatic.

When you're posing for body shots, be sure your whole body is working. You don't want to have a big, brilliant smile while the rest of your body looks limp. A good example of this is the advertisement for the Clinique fragrance Happy. In both the print ads and the TV commercials, every part of the models' bodies expresses happiness—from their beaming smiles to their energized body positions and kinetic movements—their whole bodies look happy!

Here are some body poses you'll want to capture in your shots:

◆ The T-leg, the classic beauty pageant pose, with your feet together, one pointing straight ahead, and the other pointing outward

◆ Facing the camera with your hands on your hips

◆ Hips facing three-quarters, and your shoulders and head facing the camera straight on

◆ Full profile, with your body and head turned sideways

◆ Sitting on the floor sideways with your legs bent and your arms behind you, supporting your weight

◆ Kneeling on the floor sideways with your hands on your knees and your head facing the camera

◆ Lying on your side, with your arm bent and your head propped up with your hand

During your test shoots for experience, practice the T-leg pose, with one foot in front of the other. (Turning your hips to the three-quarters angle while facing the camera with your shoulders and head is a great way to camouflage wide hips and thighs.) You'll also want to move around as much as possible. Try turning your body to the side for a full profile shot, as well as sitting and kneeling on the floor.

(Photographer: Kwame Brathwaite; model: Laura McLafferty)

Personality Shots

The third type of photo you'll want to take during a test shoot for experience is a personality shot. When you look at the *contact sheets* of these shots, you'll be able to discover what you're capable of in front of the camera, which helps you figure out what type of model you are and what moods you're best able to project.

> **Catwalk Talk**
>
> Although most photographers download the pictures they take and work with them directly on the computer, often they'll have a **contact sheet** printed as well. This is a large sheet of photographic paper that contains mini prints of all the pictures captured by the photographer during the session.

For these photos, experiment with different types of clothing, makeup, even wigs—let your imagination guide you. Most likely you'll collaborate with the photographer on the looks you want to use. Some ideas: an elegant evening dress, a punk rock look (tight black jeans, leather jacket), or business wear (suit and stockings). You may also want to try playing with different types of wigs, high heels, fishnet stockings, and other fun, costume-y items that allow you to create a character.

For your personality photos, try a variety of poses: in motion, standing completely still, and sitting down.

Reviewing Contact Sheets

Usually, a photographer gets contact sheets on a disc, via e-mail, or printed on a sheet, not individual prints. When you get them, study them closely and evaluate each one. Look at your facial expression in every photo. Do you look fake and stiff in certain poses, comfortable and natural in others? In which photos do you look best: with natural, minimal makeup or dramatic, intense makeup? In which pictures does your hair look its best? At what angle does your face look its best: straight-on, in profile, tilted up, or tilted down? Does your nose look broad when you face the camera? Do you have a gorgeous profile? Do you look better smiling, pouting, or being serious?

Study how your body looks in the body shots. What poses best complement your body? Which body parts look big, and which look slim? Does your body look comparable to the models in the Victoria's Secret catalog, *Sports Illustrated*, or *Fitness* magazine? If not, you'll want to figure out poses that better complement your figure, or you may need to work on your body to get it in better shape.

In all three categories (head, body, and personality shots), critique yourself and learn from the mistakes you made in the test shoot. Also have someone else critique you—parent, friend, boyfriend—for an objective viewpoint. When you move on to the next step of modeling—professional test shoots for your book, or even a real photo shoot—you'll have a big headstart on learning what to avoid and what to play up.

> **Reality Check** _____
>
> In general, you don't want to show your test shoots for experience to an agent. Perhaps you didn't photograph well because of bad lighting, or you look 5 pounds heavier in the pictures because you weren't familiar with the best poses for your body. But an agent might think it's because you don't photograph well, when, in fact, it's because you were working with an inexperienced photographer.

Picture Time

You may want—although it's not necessary—to have some of your favorite photos printed. But remember, this is just for fun, not to help advance your modeling career. Having more than two photos printed of each different category is really not necessary unless you want to give them away as Christmas presents. You're just learning from these photos; they're not something you're going to be showing or giving away to a professional modeling agent. Also there's no need to purchase an expensive portfolio. An inexpensive photo album is all you need now because when you get an agent, he or she will provide you with an agency portfolio.

Test Shoots for Your Professional Portfolio/Book

The second type of test shoots are test shoots for your professional portfolio, which are usually referred to as *test shoots for your book*. These are very different from test shoots for experience. You won't do test shoots for your book until you have an agent, who will set them up for you.

Your Calling Card

Test shoots for your book give you experience in front of the camera, but that's not their primary purpose. The real reason you do them is to have photos to put in your portfolio, or book. When your agency is booking a magazine shoot, fashion show, or

> **Catwalk Talk** _____
>
> Test shoots for your book, as the name suggests, are done so you'll have photos to put in your portfolio, which you take to potential employers to give them an idea of your look and personality in pictures.

advertisement, they show potential clients your book. It gives clients an idea of what you look like and how well you photograph.

Unlike test shoots for experience, test shoots for your book won't require much of your input. You don't have to find the photographer or decide which photos to take. Your agent arranges all this. Most agencies have *testing photographers* they work with all the time. Your agent will confer with the photographer before the shoot to determine the type of look they'd like to see you try—whether it's fresh-faced girl next door or something very glamorous. The agent and photographer will set up the time and place of the shoot. Afterward, the photographer will e-mail the photos to the agent, who will pick the best ones to be printed and put in your portfolio.

> **Catwalk Talk**
>
> **Testing photographers** often have day jobs as assistants to major working photographers. They are aspiring to become working photographers in their own right.

At What Cost Beauty?

The aspiring model is responsible for paying for the test shoot. But in most cases, the agency pays for it in advance and then deducts the money from your first paycheck. Elite's testing photographers are paid $300 for each test, which covers the photographer's time, the location, processing, and prints.

Shooting on Location

Most test shoots for your book take place on location, which means they are not shot in a studio. They can take place just about anywhere: in a park, in a café, or at the beach. Inexperienced models often don't know how to move in front of the camera, especially in a bare studio setting, so often the photographer will move the shoot to an outdoor setting, where the model will be inspired to move more naturally.

The photographer may also bring props (or ask you to bring them), such as in-line skates, a dog, or a bike because these are good ways of helping inexperienced models pose more spontaneously.

No Advance Preparation Necessary

Unfortunately, there's not too much a model can do beforehand to ensure that her test shoot is a success. Do find out where the test shoot will take place, and think about how people act in that setting. Also practice a bunch of expressions and poses in front of the mirror.

The best thing you can do is go in with an enthusiastic attitude and a spirit of collaboration with the photographer. Even if you don't like his or her vision at first, an open outlook can help you make the most of the opportunity.

Reality Check

Legitimate agencies will send aspiring models to photo shoots with specific photographers they have selected. Unfortunately, this is very similar to a scam many unscrupulous agencies and con artists use on new models. They tell a girl that before they can represent her, she first needs to set up a photo session with a specific photographer who charges an exorbitant fee. The unscrupulous agent, meanwhile, gets a big kickback.

Hit Me with Your Best Shot

After the test shoot, the photographer looks over the pictures, usually on the computer, and picks out the best shots. He discards any that aren't top-notch—maybe the lighting is poor, the pictures are out of focus, the model's hair is hiding her face, or she's just not looking her best. Then the photographer sends the photos to the agent, who picks the ones he wants to include in the girl's book. The girl is generally not involved in deciding which pictures will be chosen. When it comes to knowing what pictures are best for selling you to clients, agents are the experts. So defer to their judgment when it comes to the photos that will be included in your portfolio—even if you don't like them.

When your book has some great test shots in it, you're ready to get the rest of your modeling materials together, which I discuss in the next chapter.

The Least You Need to Know

◆ Test shoots for experience help you get experience in front of the camera.

◆ Practice posing in front of the mirror—it will come in very handy when you step in front of the camera.

◆ You'll want to capture several standard poses at your shoot.

◆ Your agent arranges test shoots for your book. These serve as your calling card when you start to go on interviews for modeling jobs.

Chapter 13

Tools of the Modeling Trade

In This Chapter

◆ Your portfolio and composite card

◆ Getting paid: how vouchers work

◆ Keeping track and staying in touch

◆ Other promotional materials

Writers have their laptops; tennis players have their racquets; ballerinas have their toe shoes. Like all these other professionals, models have certain things that are absolute necessities for their careers. When you've found an agent, you need to acquire these model must-haves: photos, tear sheets, composites, and portfolios. These items show clients the work you've done and the work you're capable of doing. You'll also need vouchers, which are how you get paid, and a date book or PDA, a cell phone, voicemail, and access to e-mail to let you know when and where you need to be at any given time.

In this chapter, I explain everything you need for a modeling career.

Shooting Stars: Photos and Tear Sheets

A model needs photos of herself for her portfolio, for composite cards (two-sided cards with several pictures of one model on them), and for the agency's website. (I discuss portfolios, composite cards, and agency head sheets later in this chapter.) Depending on the stage of your career, photos for your portfolio, photos for composite cards, and the agency head sheet come from two major sources: they're taken at a test shoot for your portfolio, or they're *tear sheets* from an advertisement or editorial photo shoot you appeared in.

Whenever a model does a job, she or her agent removes tear sheets from the magazine or catalog for which she worked and places these in her book.

Catwalk Talk

Tear sheets are pages torn from a magazine, newspaper, or other periodical. A model tears out any pages on which she's pictured and puts them in her portfolio.

If you're just starting out and haven't worked yet, you could use the photos from your test shots in your portfolio (see Chapter 12 for more information). Once you start working, however, your test shots are gradually replaced by examples of your professional work, or tear sheets.

Your agency will get tear sheets for all the work you do. Often the magazine or catalog company will send them copies, or the agency may subscribe to the publications themselves. It's also a good idea for the model to have her own copies of her tear sheets. Your agency may be able to give them to you, or you may want to buy one or two copies of the magazine. It's also acceptable to scan and print color copies or make color copies of your tear sheets and test photos for your portfolio.

Roshumba's Rules

Keep at least five copies of all your tear sheets. When your career gets going, you may find that you have acquired agencies in several different cities, so you'll need extras so you can keep a current portfolio in every market. Also, if you decide you want to change agencies and something gets lost in the shuffle, you have your own archives to fall back on.

Beauty Book: Your Professional Portfolio

Your portfolio or book is basically a photo album that contains select test shots and tear sheets. The portfolio is a leather- or quality vinyl-bound album that holds see-through sleeves. It can vary in size, but averages are around 12×15 inches. Your agency provides portfolios to all its models with the agency's name, address, phone number, and logo on the cover.

Portfolios have pockets on the inside covers where you can store composites and extra photos. (See the section on composites later in this chapter.) You keep one copy of your portfolio and take it with you on all your go and sees at magazines or with advertisers, fashion designers, and photographers. Your agency keeps two or three copies that can be sent out when requested by clients.

A portfolio keeps your photographs neat and organized, tells your individual "story," and gives clients a sense of your best features and your personality. Your portfolio may open with a head shot, followed by a lovely body shot on the next page, followed by shots that reveal your personality. Other photos may spotlight your best features, such as your hair, legs, or skin.

You may be wondering why you need to bring a portfolio with you to a go and see. After all, you're standing in front of the clients, so why do they need to look at photos of you as well? The client also needs to know how well you photograph, whether your features are enhanced or lost in photos, what kind of personality you project, and how you move in pictures. That's why a portfolio full of great photos is so important.

Roshumba's Rules

When you're first starting out, your portfolio may contain from 6 to 10 photos; more will be added as your career progresses. An established model's portfolio could have up to 20 shots. But you don't want to include too many pictures as that can overwhelm the client.

Here are a couple pages from my portfolio. As a model gets more experience, her test shoot photos are replaced by tear sheets like these from actual jobs.

Your agent selects the pictures to be used in your book and arranges them in a particular order that best markets your individual assets. Although you might not like the pictures she's chosen or the order they appear in, don't change the pictures on your own without at least discussing it with your agent first. Often the agent has spoken with and sold you to the client in a certain way, and she wants your book to show you in that same way.

Reality Check

Your book is your calling card to the client; it represents who you are. If it's messy, is littered with old slips of paper, or has appointments or phone numbers scrawled on it, it's annoying for the client and reflects badly on you. A clean, organized book sends the positive message to a client that you are reliable and professional. To keep the inside sleeves clean, moisten a cotton ball with water and wipe off each sleeve. Also be sure all the photos are neatly aligned.

How often your portfolio is updated will depend on your progress as a model. If you have five magazines stories coming out, your entire book may change practically overnight. On the other hand, if one image is a classic, it might remain in your book for 10 years.

Even supermodels need to have up-to-date portfolios. Although people in the fashion industry may be up on all your most recent accomplishments, you may get a call from a client who's not necessarily familiar with your most recent appearance in the pages of *Vogue*. It's best if your portfolio contains your most recent work.

It's also key to update your portfolio whenever you undergo a significant physical change—for example, if you cut your hair or after you've had a baby. A supermodel may also have a separate portfolio containing all the magazine covers on which she's appeared, as well as a separate publicity or press clippings book containing all the interviews she's done.

Model Scoop

I have three different portfolios, which is common for models who have worked as much as I have. I have a regular fashion portfolio, with images of my magazine and advertisement work. It contains beauty, fashion, and personality shots and is sent to editorial, advertising, catalog, and fashion designer clients. I also have a cover book, which contains all the magazine covers on which I've appeared. So if someone wants to do a documentary on my career, my cover book, which documents my evolutions as a model, would be more useful than my fashion book. I also have a book of my press clippings, which includes all the interviews I've done.

A Picture's Worth a 1,000 Words: Your Composite Card

A *composite card*, or *comp card*, is an $8^1/_2 \times 6$-inch card. Each agency has its own trademark style of comp card it uses for all its models, so the size may be larger or smaller, depending on the style the agency has chosen. The comp card contains an arrangement of up to six photos of the model in different poses. The front of the card usually contains one or two pictures (usually at least one is a head shot). The back holds three or four more photos, including a body shot, a personality shot, and one showing some of the model's outstanding attributes: beautiful hair, a lovely smile, or incredible legs. The comp card also lists the model's measurements, including height; weight; bust, waist, and hip measurements; dress and shoe sizes; and the agency's logo, name, address, phone, and fax numbers.

Catwalk Talk

A **composite card**, also known as a **comp card**, is a card that features several different shots of a model. It is given out to clients so they can get an idea of the model's look.

You will need to take your comp cards with you when you go on go and sees, auditions, and castings. Clients use them to refresh their memories when they're selecting models for fashion shows, advertisements, magazine shoots, and TV commercials.

Sometimes a client may see hundreds of faces in one afternoon, which is why they need comp cards to remind them of all the people they've met. A comp card is like a sales brochure for the model's look and style.

Your comp card includes photos from the best of your test shoots and tear sheets. Your agent puts together your comp card and decides which photos go where, adds the necessary statistical information, and arranges for the comp cards to be printed. (There's never any reason for a model to have a comp card before she finds an agent, so don't let anyone try to talk you into paying for them before you have an agent.) You can be a part of this process if you like, but it's not mandatory. I suggest that you do take part in the selection and arrangement of your photos, however, because it helps you become involved with the management of your career. You can also learn a lot about how the agency sees you, how it's marketing you, and what's currently in fashion.

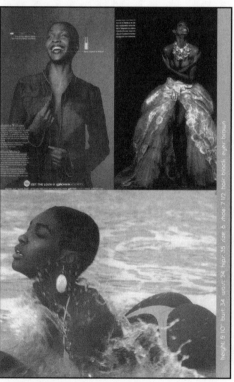

Comp cards are given out to clients to give them a quick idea of a model's look and image.

As a model, you'll try out many different makeup looks to see which ones suit you best. This photo shows a minimum of makeup—some foundation, mascara, and a little lipstick—just enough to look good on camera.

This photo shows a medium makeup look. I'm wearing some blush, eyeliner, and lip liner, yet I don't look too "done."

This photo shows a glamour makeup look. My eyes are done up to the max; my lips are a vivid, bold pink; and my cheekbones have been contoured. A dramatic accessory, like this shawl, heightens the illusion of sophistication.

A big part (an hour and a half, at least) of any model's day is getting her hair and makeup done, as I am here, before going onstage to host the Elite Model Look model search. Sitting in that chair a couple hours a day is not as fun as it sounds at first!

I'm demonstrating the classic T-stance pose in this photo taken of me at the Emmy Awards.

As the name suggests, a headshot is a close-up of a model's face and head. A photo like this can be your official headshot in your modeling portfolio.

(Photo courtesy of Antoine Verglas)

ROSHUMBA

This photo shoot took place on the warm, sunny beaches of Jamaica. Because the trend right now for magazines, advertisements, and catalogs is for outdoor photography, many shoots happen in sunny climates, to take advantage of the beautiful weather; this means models must travel continuously from shoot to shoot.

(Roshumba's personal archives)

This shot, which was taken for a calendar, really plays up my image as an Amazon, one of the seven distinct model types.

In this shot, taken for a calendar, I'm walking toward the camera, creating the illusion of an action shot.

As a model, it's up to you to make every kind of outfit— even a classic business suit— look interesting. Notice that you can still see the clothes clearly in this shot.

(Photo courtesy of Rodney Ray)

This is a classic editorial pose. Note the creative, interesting way they shot me wearing this suit.

Nylon multi-colored 70's print
shirt by Hamnett Active
London
Lime Green Suede boot-cut
pant. by Katharine Hamnett
Denim
Brown suede four pocket with
saddle stitching trim jacket by
Dimitri
Caramel suede hi-cut-ups by
Stephane Kelian

(Roshumba's personal archives)

This shot is a great example of how to pose for catalogs. You can clearly see the outfit and how it fits, and I have a huge smile on my face (which, hopefully, the viewer will read as "she's so happy in that dress" and then be inspired to order it from the catalog).

(Photo courtesy of Charles Tracy)

This photo is for an editorial fashion spread. The picture is more about creating an image of glamour and allure than it is about showing the outfit—which is typical of editorial work.

(Photo courtesy of Charles Tracy)

Here I'm posing at a U.S. Open tennis event I hosted called Arthur Ashe Kids Day. Doing a variety of extracurricular activities adds longevity to your career.

After judging and hosting the Sports Illustrated *Swimsuit Model Search, I posed with the contestants.*

(Roshumba's personal archives)

This was from one of my favorite photos shoots, an ad for the Elizabeth Glaser Pediatric AIDS Foundation event.

Generally, an agency has 100 to 200 composite cards printed at one time. You, not the agency, pay for your comp cards. The cost is often deducted from your salary once you start to work. Usually, you're charged anywhere from $150 to $175 for 100 comps (the price depends somewhat on how many photos are included).

Comp cards need to be updated and changed on a regular basis, at least once a year, and sometimes as frequently as every 3 months. In the first 5 years of my career, I was doing so many magazine shoots that I was changing my comp card every season (every 3 months). Later, when my career was established, I would go for up to a year without changing my card. Still, if a comp is more than a year old, clients may get the feeling that you're not in demand, that you're not doing anything new. As with your portfolio, you'll need to update your comp card whenever your appearance changes. Old, outdated photos may cause a client to think your new look is not selling. Evaluate your comp card on a regular basis, and discuss it with your agent periodically to ensure that all the photos are current and reflect what you look like at the moment.

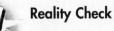

Reality Check

Although it's a good idea to get involved with selecting pictures for your comp card, don't be too adamant about your likes and dislikes. If you're just starting out, your agent may see you differently from the way you see yourself, and it may be that a photo you don't like may be crucial for promoting a certain image of you to the industry.

Model Scoop

Another use for comp cards is to label the rack holding all the garments a model will be wearing in a fashion show. This helps the designers and stylists at a fashion show keep the clothing organized. Clients may also use comp cards for inspiration for a photo shoot. If a client has a new collection of clothing and they haven't figured out a creative way to shoot it, they may look at comp cards for ideas. Say there's an energetic shot of you on a trampoline on your comp card; that could be a great inspiration for the client in finding a way to shoot their collection.

Because you need to take them with you whenever you go on job interviews, keep your comp cards in a pocket on the inside cover of your portfolio. It's customary to keep about 10 composites in the pocket of your portfolio. You may want to keep about 20 more at home so you can replenish your supply as necessary. The agency keeps the rest and sends them out to clients who request to see a specific model or a particular type of model. Whenever you run out, stop by the agency and pick up some more, or ask your agent to send you more.

She Works Hard for the Money: Model Vouchers

Instead of punching time cards, models are paid through a *voucher* system. Agencies issue vouchers to their models, usually in books of 20 or so vouchers. The model takes the voucher with her to the job, where it's signed by the client, confirming that she worked. Then the model submits the signed copy to her agency's accounting department, which bills the client and pays the model.

> **Catwalk Talk**
>
> **Vouchers** are model time sheets. Agencies give these special forms to their models. At the end of a shoot, the client signs the voucher verifying that the model worked and should be paid.

The vouchers have your agency's name and address printed on them along with blank spaces the client is responsible for filling in, including his or her name, the name of the company, the address and phone number, the photographer's name, the contact person in the client's billing department, and the client's signature.

The model fills in her name, the date the work was performed, the amount of the modeling fee, any extra costs such as travel fees (if the model is to be paid for flying to a location), and miscellaneous fees for such things as special haircuts, manicures, pedicures, or bikini waxes, and overtime fees.

Each voucher form has an original and two copies. The model tears off and gives the client his copy at the end of the shoot. She also tears off the agency's copy and mails, hand delivers, or faxes it to the agency's accounting department. The model's copy stays in the voucher book. It should be retained until full payment has been received for the job done.

> **Reality Check**
>
> Many models don't bother with getting vouchers signed and instead leave their finances up to the agency. But I'm a stickler about getting vouchers signed. If any problems arise after the shoot is over, that piece of paper is concrete documentation of the time you worked and the amount you're owed.

Take your voucher book with you to every job. You should have the vouchers signed on the spot because they are your only legal document proving that you worked and should be paid. The voucher states the legal and binding terms of the relationship between the client, the model, and the agency. Once it's signed by a client, it legally binds them to the stated terms and rates. Whenever a problem arises regarding payment, terms, or fees for a specific job, consult with the agent who booked the job.

Keeping in Touch with Your Agent and Clients

As a model, so much of your time is spent running around going on go and sees or working away from home, and it can be almost impossible for your agent to keep in touch with you. She may need to talk to you several times a day to let you know about newly scheduled go and sees and jobs.

That's why having a cell phone and voicemail that you can check regularly is so important. You'll be using your voicemail for work as well as personal messages, so keep your outgoing message short, sweet, and professional. Simply state your name and ask the caller to leave a message. Access to e-mail is also a great extra for the model on the go.

Roshumba's Rules

Models chatting endlessly on their cell phones on go and sees, jobs, and other appointments is extremely unprofessional. While a brief check with your agent is acceptable, don't have lengthy conversations in waiting areas or when you're seeing a client or agent. Definitely don't talk on (or answer) your phone while you're in an interview or a client is looking at your book. At a photo shoot, talk (but keep it brief) in the model's dressing room, not in the studio.

The Essential Date Book or PDA

Models rely on their date book and PDA to keep their lives organized. If you can't afford a PDA, a date book is fine; the best type is the kind in which each day has its own page. You need room to write down as many as 15 appointments per day, all the details about each one, as well as any personal engagements, which is why the day-per-page format is preferable. Try to select one that's not too bulky because you'll be carrying it around a lot, and if it's too heavy, it can be a pain—literally. A good size is 5×7 inches.

Your date book or PDA is also good for keeping track of how much you're owed for jobs, which helps you be sure you're getting paid the right amount for the work you're doing. Also it can help you be sure you're getting the same amount when clients hire you again. If I worked for J. Crew 6 months ago and they paid $5,000, and this week they want to pay me $4,000, I'll know they're cutting my rate and I'll be able to ask my agent to check into it.

Whether you go the date book or PDA route, be sure to get one that has an address book section where you can keep track of addresses and phone numbers of your bookers, photographers, and clients, as well as other important names and numbers. Plus, at the end of the year, if you want to send out holiday cards to all the clients you've worked with that year (I always think this is a nice idea for showing clients how much you appreciate their hiring you), you have all the addresses right there in your PDA or date book!

Calling All Models: Agency Promotional Materials

Although agencies used to have their own portfolio of all their models they'd send to clients, now everything is online. Every agency has its own website, with pictures of all the models it represents. Anyone can access a few basic pictures, but clients and potential clients are usually given a password, which allows them to look at even more pictures. Clients can log on to the website and look at new faces; search for a particular type of model they need for a story, catalog shoot, or advertisement; or search the whole site for inspiration.

When an agency agrees to represent you, it'll put your photo on its website. At first, it will probably be one of your test photos; later, it'll be replaced by a photo from one of your professional jobs.

All of these tools of the trade are necessary to keep your modeling career running smoothly and efficiently. Although they may seem foreign to you now, when your career gets going, they'll become must-haves.

The Least You Need to Know

◆ A model's portfolio and composite card are used to help sell her and her look to clients.

◆ Model vouchers, which are signed by the client, allow models to get paid.

◆ Date books or PDAs are essential for helping models keep track of their appointments.

◆ Cell phones, voicemail, and e-mail help models keep in touch with their agents and new job developments.

14

Go and Sees

In This Chapter

◆ Go and sees explained

◆ It's all in the preparation

◆ Overcoming a case of the jitters

◆ What to expect at a go and see

◆ How to stand out: tips from an expert

You've come a long way, baby! You've found an agent, you've done your test shoots, and you've assembled all your model materials. Now it's time to go out and find a job. Unfortunately, legitimate modeling jobs aren't listed in the want ads, and landing a modeling job involves more than filling out an application.

Getting a modeling job involves a lot of legwork—literally. Your agent will set up job interviews, which in the modeling business are referred to as "go and sees." You can go on as many as 15 go and sees in a day.

Although a lot of your success at go and sees depends on your physical attributes, your personality and demeanor also count a great deal. That's why it's important to know what goes on at a go and see, so you can be prepared. Your preparation will enable you to stand out—in a positive way—from the dozens of other models the client may be meeting.

I also asked Nikki Suero-O'Brien, a long-time model editor for many major magazines, for her expert, insider tips on succeeding at a go and see. I share these with you later in this chapter.

Go, Girl: What Are Go and Sees?

When a model's portfolio and composite card are ready, her agent/booker sets up appointments for her to go on go and sees and *castings*. You may meet with any number of people on a go and see: the model editor and/or the fashion editor of a magazine, photographers, catalog clients, advertising clients, and/or executives from advertising agencies.

> **Catwalk Talk** _____
>
> **Castings** is another word for go and sees. In America, a casting usually refers to a go and see for a TV commercial. In Europe, the term is used more often for all types of go and sees.

Although some go and sees are for specific jobs, they're also for you to introduce yourself to the fashion industry and get to know as many people as possible—any one of whom could be a possible future employer. You may be sent to meet with a photographer, who then may refer you to a model editor trying to book a job, or maybe the photographer himself will keep you in mind for a future job. You may see a fashion designer who's not hiring any models at the present time but whom your agent wanted you to meet so she'd consider you for future runway shows.

One of the most important aspects of go and sees is for clients to see you up close and personal. Although a model may have a book full of wonderful test shots, clients want to know what she's like in person. Sometimes models photograph different from how they look in person due to the lighting, the makeup, the pose, or just some intangible quality that makes them photogenic.

> **Roshumba's Rules** _____
>
> Be sure you write down all the facts regarding your appointments in your date book or PDA (such as a BlackBerry) so you don't lose them. It's annoying for agents to have to repeat information about appointments.

During a go and see, clients are looking for a model's unique, individual qualities. Is she at ease with strangers? Does she come off as a haughty princess, a gregarious best friend, or a sweet and naive little girl? Is she fun and bubbly, sexy and sultry, or quiet and moody?

Your agent will set up your go and sees as much as a week or as little as a day in advance. Every evening you must call the agency to find out all your go and see appointments for the following day, including the client's name, street address, suite or floor number, and any special requests the client has.

The Model Maze

I won't sugarcoat it: go and sees can be a draining, depressing experience. I've had to go on up to 15 a day, so I know how hard it can be: you're running from place to place all day long, getting on and off the subway, often getting lost or getting caught in bad weather. Also, you're undergoing that nerve-wracking experience of meeting people for the first time all day long, so you're constantly feeling tense and fearful. On top of all that, you know in advance that your chances of being rejected are high.

Despite all these obstacles, the most important thing is to stay cheerful, always be yourself, and let your natural personality shine through because every client is looking for something unique and individual in each model.

My First Go and See

My first go and see came just one day after I had gotten my agent in Paris. My booker assembled a temporary composite card for me (which is common when you're first starting out, especially in Europe, where business practices tend to be more informal). When I stopped by the agency to pick up my temporary composites, the agents told me they were going to send me to see a few clients.

The haute couture runway collection shows were coming up, and they hoped I would be able to find a job doing fittings for the shows or maybe book a show. I was sent to several design houses. One of them happened to be Yves Saint Laurent, who needed a *fittings model*.

Walking into the mansion where Saint Laurent's design business is housed was overwhelming. It was so large and elegant, it felt like something from a grand old movie. I rang the bell and was buzzed into a marble entryway with a golden staircase. The receptionist was an extremely elegant, utterly intimidating French woman.

Catwalk Talk

Fittings models work in a designer's studio. They try on the unfinished clothes; the designer then makes necessary adjustments to the garment so it fits perfectly.

She directed me to the room where all the models were waiting to meet with Saint Laurent. He has a lot of unique rules for the models he works with, so I was required to put on a special white coatdress, black sheer stockings, and high heels before an assistant came out to get me. He led me into Yves's workroom, where I was dressed in a garment that was being prepared for the upcoming couture show.

Finally, I was brought in to stand in front of Yves and was asked to walk back and forth. He looked at me in the clothes and then simply said "Thank you." I had no idea what he thought—whether he loved, hated, or didn't care about me. Later that day, however, one of his assistants called my agent and told him Yves wanted to book me. (Usually, a client won't give you any clues as to what he thinks of you, although you can usually get an idea from the amount of time he spends with you and his general reaction to you.)

> **Model Scoop** _____
>
> On some go and sees, the client will reject you before you even get all the way in the door. The worst reaction I ever got was during a season when the designers were using only blondes. I had barely gotten my foot in the door of one designer's offices when the people at the front desk yelled, "No black girls!" It wasn't a racist thing; it was just the way fashion was at that moment. In fact, the very next season, exotic girls were hot. The very same client called and requested me. I said to my agent, "I thought they didn't work with black models." His reply was: "That was just last season!"

Go and Sees Never Go Out of Style

Models at all stages of their careers do go and sees—even models who have been working for 7 or 8 years and have established clientele. A model's appearance might change: she might gain or lose weight, cut her hair or grow it out, go from brunette to blond and back again. A go and see gives the client the chance to see what the model looks like at that moment.

Fashion—and the "it" models—change as well. What was in style last season may not be in this season, so a client who wouldn't give you a second glance 3 months ago can be suddenly booking you every day.

Also, the people who hire the models are always changing jobs and new people take their places. For instance, even though I had worked for *Sports Illustrated* for 4 years, when a new model editor was hired, I still had to meet her so she could get to know me. (It's true, however, that the number of go and sees a model goes on decreases as her career becomes more established. For one thing, you'll already have met many clients, and for another, you may be so busy working, you won't have the time.)

What Should I Wear?

It's totally acceptable to wear casual clothes on a go and see, and they're preferable from a comfort point of view. Jeans, a short skirt, a T-shirt, a sweater or denim jacket, and comfortable shoes (even sneakers) are perfect. Avoid wearing clothes that are too tight or baggy. Makeup should be clean and simple or none at all. Remember, agents and clients want to see what can be done to you, not what you've done to yourself.

This model is wearing the ideal clothes for a go and see. She looks comfortable and casual, yet her figure is evident under the slim-fitting T-shirt and jeans.

With her oversized top, baggy pants, and messy hair, this model might have a difficult time getting booked because she's hiding her assets.

Don't wear high heels if you're spending your day doing go and sees. You're going to be on your feet a lot, and high heels will just add to your misery. For runway go and sees, you might want to put a pair of high heels in your bag in case the client wants to see you walk in heels.

Countdown to a Successful Go and See

The night before a go and see, figure out how you're going to get there (whether you can walk or whether you need to take public transportation and, if so, what subways or buses you'll need to take). Also plan what you're going to wear. You may also want to think of a few topics you can chat about with the client (but leave room for spontaneous conversation).

Be sure to get a good night's sleep. Take a shower or bath the night before or that morning. Try to eat some breakfast or at least drink some juice before you leave for the day.

A lot of models carry backpacks or tote bags when they have a day full of go and sees. When you're spending that much time away from home, you'll need to bring a lot of things with you, and it's just easier and more comfortable to carry them in a backpack.

Here are some things you'll want to bring with you on go and sees:

◆ Your date book or PDA (of course!)

◆ Your portfolio

◆ A stack of comp cards (see Chapter 13)

◆ A subway, bus, and/or street map

◆ Snacks

◆ A bottle of water

◆ A sweater or jacket, in case it gets cold

◆ Any toiletries or medications you may need, such as contact lens solution or allergy medicine

◆ Makeup, if you wear it, such as light liquid foundation, powder, lip balm, or natural-colored lipstick

◆ A magazine or book to read while you wait, or an iPod to listen to

◆ A cell phone

◆ High heels, if you're going to see runway clients

Overcoming Nervousness

It's only natural to feel insecure at go and sees. So that my attention isn't so focused on everything that can go wrong, I always bring something with me to read, such as a magazine or book. Reading serves the dual purpose of giving me something to do besides stare into space and think about how scared I am, and showing the client I have interests outside modeling, that I'm into learning and bettering myself, and that there's more to me than meets the eye.

Another way to keep yourself feeling calm during a go and see is to ask the receptionist if you may use the bathroom while you're waiting for the client to come out and meet with you. In the bathroom, drink some water and splash some on your face. Another good trick is to take 10 deep breaths, exhaling fully from your diaphragm each time. Sometimes if I'm really jittery, I'll go into the stall and run in place to get rid of all my nervous energy.

I also keep repeating some positive affirmations to myself while I wait. For instance, if there are many other beautiful girls in the room, I might repeat to myself "Beauty is only skin deep" over and over to keep my confidence up.

Roshumba's Rules

A great book can be a useful conversation piece when you're meeting with the client. For example, if you're reading a best-seller, you can ask the client, "I'm reading this great book—have you checked it out?"

The most important thing about go and sees is to just do them—do your best at each one and keep your focus on moving ahead and booking jobs. Don't get caught up in clients' negative reactions because the client who rejects you because your look is not right for her today might turn around and book you for a major ad campaign when the look of fashion changes 6 months down the road.

The Early Bird Catches the Worm

Try to arrive at the go and see at least 5 to 10 minutes early. Give the receptionist at the client's office your name and ask her to tell the contact person you're there. Depending on the layout of the offices, the client may ask you to come into his private office or may come out and talk to you in the reception area.

The client will definitely want to look at your portfolio. He will also probably ask you various questions: whether you've modeled before, what type of modeling you like best, what you see yourself doing in the future. *What* you say isn't as important as saying *something*. The client just wants to get an idea of your personality and how confident and self-assured you are. Be yourself and allow your personality to shine through. Avoid giving one- or two-word answers to every question you're asked. Instead, be friendly and talkative, and try to share some (positive) personal things with the interviewer. That's the only way your personality will come through—if you open up and share some part of yourself.

Roshumba's Rules

As clients look at your portfolio, study their faces to try to judge their response to the various photos. Their reactions can help you get an idea of how good your portfolio is.

Show the client you're interested in their work by asking about the job you're being considered for or about any upcoming projects. Many of the people you'll be meeting interview models all day long and are friendly and easy to talk to. Many (especially at magazines, clothing companies, and advertising agencies) are young, artistic, and interested in meeting with other young, artistic people.

In addition to chatting with you to get a feel for your personality, the client might ask you to walk or move around, and you may also be asked to try on a garment. From start to finish, a go and see can last anywhere from 15 to 30 minutes.

Insider Tips from a Magazine Model Editor

Nikki Suero-O'Brien, who has been a model editor for nearly two decades, explains the go and see process from her perspective and what *model editors* are looking for:

"Once I see what the story is about, whether it's about little black dresses or bathing suits, I then work with the fashion editor and the photographer, and together we come up with ideas for models for the shoot," says Suero-O'Brien. "I'll have my input of girls I've seen that I thought were great and sometimes the photographer may request a specific girl.

> **Catwalk Talk**
>
> A **model editor** books all the models featured in a magazine, including those used in fashion stories, beauty pieces, and all the other features in the magazine.

"Every single day, I see 5 to 20 girls. Sometimes it's a general go see, [meaning] the modeling agency calls and says, 'We'd love you to meet this girl.' Sometimes it's us calling them saying, 'I'm looking for a girl with great hair for a hair story—a brunette with curly hair.' We deal with all the agencies, from the mega to the tiny. You never know where you can find your little superstar. She can be with a little agency.

"I do go and sees by appointment. The models come in and sit down, and I take a look at their book, see what their pictures look like, see what they look like in person. I ask them questions, where they come from, a little about their background, schooling, how long they've been in the business, how they like the business, how they like New York, just to get a feeling as to what they're all about.

"From there, I take Polaroids of her. I have thousands of them. They help me in casting. It's hard to remember all those girls! Sometimes a model will come back four to five times before she gets booked on a specific job.

"I prefer to see them in a short little skirt—in winter it's obviously difficult. That way you can see what her legs look like. Also something formfitting, where you can see her stature, the structure of her shoulders, her legs. The worst thing a model can do is walk in wearing a huge skirt, a wide balloony dress, or the hip-hop look.

"Once I see a girl who is the magazine's type, I introduce her to the fashion editor, the editor in chief, and the creative director of the magazine (who's in charge of the visual look of the magazine).

"Personality is also critical. I've had so many beautiful girls come here, and they'll sit in my office and not say a word. You're looking at their portfolio, and their eyes are just roaming around. They'd rather be anywhere than there. You have to get a certain energy because if I'm not getting it here [in the office], then she's not going to do it in the studio with a photographer in front of a camera.

"Confidence really comes into play. It comes through in the way she expresses herself, in the way she communicates, in her stature when she walks through the door. Even if she's petrified, at least she gives the illusion—and it's all illusion, all image in this business—that she's happy to be there, she loves what she's doing, she feels great about herself. She communicates that in her style, her language, her wardrobe.

The good news is, the more go and sees you do over the years, the more comfortable you'll become with them. You'll learn what to expect and develop a technique or routine for getting through them successfully.

> **Reality Check**
>
> According to Nikki Suero-O'Brien, turnoffs about models include: "Someone who's obnoxious—you have to be confident but nice, not obnoxious; someone who's not friendly; someone who's not well-kept (in the sense of grooming)."

But all the hassle and tension will seem worth it when your agent tells you: "The magazine has finally confirmed: you'll be doing an eight-page fashion story about the best new clothes for fall!"

The Least You Need to Know

- Go and sees are interviews for modeling jobs.

- Wear simple, comfortable clothes on go and sees.

- Prepare the night before for go and sees, and bring your portfolio and your composite cards with you.

- It's important that you can converse with the client. Your personality could be the deciding factor in helping you get a job.

Part 4

Oh My God, I've Booked a Job, Now What?!

Booking your first modeling job is equal cause for excitement and panic. But don't worry. You'll be calm, cool, and collected once you've read all the information and tips I have for you in Part 4.

First I tell you, step by step, everything you need to do to prepare for the job. To ensure that you'll be comfortable when you arrive at the photo studio, I explain who's who at the shoot, including the photographer, client, hairstylist, makeup artist, fashion stylist, and various assistants.

Finally, I take you through a day of shooting in a photo studio versus a day of shooting on location outdoors. When you know the advantages and disadvantages of both, you'll be able to give it your best shot!

Preparing for Your First Modeling Job

In This Chapter

◆ The who, what, where, and when of your first job

◆ The ABCs of high maintenance

◆ Getting photo-ready

◆ Beauty and grooming countdown

◆ Staying cool, calm, and collected

Booking your first modeling job can be the most exciting day of your life, the most frightening day of your life, or most likely both. Whatever you feel, there are certain things you'll need to know to make your day go as smoothly as possible. As always, knowledge and preparation are key to ensuring that your first day on the job is a success.

In this chapter, I talk about what you need to do to get ready for that first shoot: what you should do the day before the shoot, the night before, and that morning so when you walk into the studio, you can be confident and ready to give it your best shot.

What You Need to Know Before the Shoot

Whether it's your first job or your thousandth, it's a good idea to make certain preparations the day before the day of the shoot. The first thing you want to do is get all the necessary details from your booker about the job:

- The location of the shoot (be sure to get the exact street address, the cross streets, and the floor or suite number)

- The *call time* (the time you're required to arrive)

- How long the shoot will last

- The client's name

- The name and phone number of the contact person for the shoot

- How much you'll be paid

> **Catwalk Talk**
>
> The **call time** is the time a shoot starts. If the call time is 9, you need to be walking through the door at 9.

You'll also want to know any special requests the client has. If it's a lingerie or bathing-suit shoot, for example, you may need to get a bikini wax or the client may ask that you get a manicure or pedicure.

Write down all this important information in your date book or PDA, not on a little piece of paper or the back of an envelope that can easily get lost. Agents hate it when they have to repeatedly give job information to a model. Writing down all your appointments is a good habit to get into. That way, you'll always know where you're supposed to be, when you're supposed to be there, and what you need to do to prepare for it.

Writing appointments in your date book or PDA also helps you plan ahead. Say you look in your date book or PDA and see you're booked for a bathing-suit shoot on Friday, and 2 days before then, you have an afternoon free. You'll know you should go get a bikini wax as long as you have some free time. Or maybe you realize from looking at your date book or PDA that you're flying to the Caribbean for a shoot in a week; you'll have plenty of time to make any necessary preparations, such as packing your summer clothes and buying sunscreen and other necessary toiletries. If all your appointments are written on sticky notes crumpled in the bottom of your backpack, you won't be able to plan ahead with the same

> **Roshumba's Rules**
>
> Writing down all your appointments in your date book or PDA helps you at the end of the year, too, when you want to send Christmas cards to all your clients. You'll have all the names right at your fingertips.

efficiency. Also writing appointments in your date book or PDA helps you keep track of how much you're owed for the work you've done.

In addition to getting the where, who, what, and when from your agent, you'll want to get as many details as possible about the shoot. Find out who the client is and what they do, what type of shoot it will be (whether it's a fashion shoot, in which case the focus will be on clothing, or whether it's a beauty shoot, which may concentrate on the skin, the hair, makeup, or the body). This will give you an idea of what you're getting yourself into and what the client is expecting from you so you can get into the mood of the shoot beforehand.

Also ask your agent for any feedback, comments, or compliments the client offered about you when she met you, or about work you've done in the past. Maybe the client loved a particular shot in which you resembled a certain actress. This will give you a good clue to what the client liked about you, which, in turn, will allow you to give them what they want at the shoot. Or if they liked a particular picture in your book of you running on the beach, you'll know they want to promote an image of health and athleticism. You can apply this information at the shoot.

> **Roshumba's Rules**
>
> If the client says they're looking for a certain look, such as an Audrey Hepburn spirit or Sophia Loren sultriness, do your homework. Rent some of the actress's movies before the shoot.

Are You Photo-Ready? The Day Before the Shoot

The evening before your first big shoot is not the time to start thinking about getting your hair trimmed, your legs waxed, and a manicure and a pedicure. Good grooming is an essential part of your job as a model. You'll want to stay on top of these things so you don't need to panic and try to fit everything in the evening before a shoot.

Regular Maintenance

You should get your hair trimmed every 2 to 4 weeks, depending on how fast it grows. You should get a manicure and pedicure on a weekly or biweekly basis. Your legs, bikini area, and underarms (some people prefer shaving their underarms) should be waxed as often as necessary (it's a good idea to get this done several days in advance, as waxing can cause breakouts). Some models also like to get a facial or a massage every couple months.

Well-manicured nails are a model must.

Clean-shaven legs are mandatory because you never know when you'll have to model a skirt, shorts, or a bathing suit.

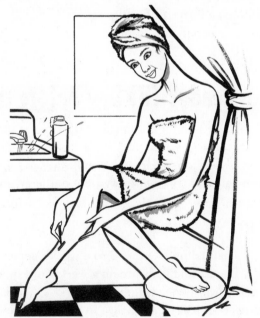

If you color your hair, be sure your roots don't need a touch-up or, in the case of African American models, that your roots don't need to be straightened.

If you don't know a good salon in your city, ask your agent to recommend one. Many agencies have arrangements with certain salons, allowing their models to get discounts on beauty services.

A Little Light Housecleaning

Either the night before the shoot or the morning of, be sure to shower or bathe so your body is clean and odor-free. Applying deodorant is also essential. The hairstylist and makeup artist will be working close to your body, and the fashion stylist will be pinning you and helping you take clothes on and off. You don't want them to be exposed to anything unpleasant, including body odors and armpit hair. (Believe it or not, some models go to work with bad body odor!)

Another reason that it's so important to shower and apply deodorant is so you don't perspire in the clothes and leave any odors or stains on them. The garments used in a fashion shoot for a magazine (and sometimes for ads and television commercials) are generally borrowed from the designer in return for a *fashion credit* in the magazine. The clothes are lent with the understanding that they will be returned clean and odor-free.

> **Catwalk Talk**
>
> In return for being allowed to borrow clothes from designers for fashions shoots, the magazine identifies the designer in the magazine's **fashion credits** (for example, "Ralph Lauren linen skirt in black, $275"). This is great PR for a designer's newest collection.

Apply your favorite body lotion after showering, whatever makes your skin look and feel good. But avoid wearing strong perfume and really greasy or heavily scented body lotions. These also stain and leave odors that could ruin clothes. Instead, try using fragrance-free or nongreasy products.

Good Hair, Bad Hair

Your legs and underarms should always be freshly shaved or waxed whenever you're shooting. You may get to the studio and discover you have to shoot in a tank top; the client won't appreciate it if you have a jungle growing under your arms. That's why it's best to be clean and well groomed at all times, even if the client doesn't specifically request it.

You also want to have clean hair when you arrive at the shoot. The hairstylist won't take too kindly to greasy, dirty hair; hair that's full of dandruff; or hair that's not well maintained. Before the shoot, you should shampoo and condition your hair—but skip the styling products; the hairstylist will apply any that are needed.

Ready, Steady, Go!

It's also a good idea to pack what you'll need the night before so you're not rushing around in the morning and forgetting important things. You'll want to bring your voucher book, an iPod or a book to read during any downtime, any special makeup requirements (for instance, if you have sensitive skin and need special foundation), any prescriptions you need, contact lens solution, your date book or PDA, and your cell phone. Pack it all together in a backpack, tote bag, or large purse.

If you want to listen to music, be sure you have earphones with the tiny earplugs that fit inside your ears (not the bulky kind that sit on your head). Big earphones interfere with the hairstylist's and makeup artist's work. In any case, it's always a good idea to ask the hair and makeup artists if it's okay if you listen to music.

Another night-before-the-shoot essential: plan the easiest and fastest route to take to the shoot. Check out a street map or public-transportation map, or plot your course via one of the many online mapping sites to be sure you know where you're going and the best way to get there. If you're not sure or are new to the city, ask your agent for suggestions.

I also suggest that before you go to sleep, you practice your poses and facial expressions in the mirror so they'll feel natural to you when you step in front of the camera. It might be a good idea to spend some time looking through your portfolio so you can get a feel for why the client may have booked you for the job. If your agent told you the client liked a specific picture, study it and try to figure out what they liked about it.

Dress for Success

You should also plan what you're going to wear, check it to see how it looks, and lay it out for quick dressing in the morning. Try to keep it simple—clean and neat jeans, a T-shirt, and sneakers are fine.

It's smart to dress simply when you're just starting out because right now, your focus should be more on learning how to make your image more marketable. Dressing up could be distracting—for you and for the client.

Reality Check

Don't think you have to run out and buy an expensive designer outfit for your first shoot. As your career progresses and you start to make money, your wardrobe can become more elaborate. Also you'll no doubt start to develop a personal sense of style from being around people in the fashion industry so much. But in the beginning, it's best to keep your dress simple.

But if you're the type of model (a Chameleon or an Oddball, for instance) who has a strong personality and a strong sense of personal style that contributes to your image as a model, by all means, let it shine through in your choice of outfit.

Goodnight Moon, Hello Star!

You'll also want to get a good night's sleep so that when you arrive at work you'll feel rested and energetic, without any bags under your eyes and with fresh, glowing skin and the necessary energy to get the job done. Don't celebrate your first job by going out for a big night on the town the evening before the shoot. Lack of sleep can make a model cranky, irritable, and less enthusiastic than normal—in other words, the sort of model no one wants to hire.

Remember, models are selected for the sexy, healthful image they project; that tired and worn look doesn't sell very well. If you're feeling tired, the pictures will reflect that.

The Best Way of Waking Up: The Morning of the Shoot

On the morning of the shoot, be sure you eat a good meal before you leave for the job. Breakfast is usually served at the shoot, but if you think you may be too nervous to eat in front on a bunch of strangers, eat something beforehand. (Otherwise, it's fine to eat at the studio, where breakfast is usually provided by the client.) You don't want to eat something too heavy, but you want something substantial enough to give you the energy necessary to help you stay alert and focused, which will allow you to do the best job possible.

If you're hungry, chances are, you'll be concentrating on your empty stomach, not on how to do your best job as a debut model. If you're not accustomed to eating in the morning, at least try to drink a glass of fruit juice so you'll be able to perform at work. A rumbling stomach is embarrassing—especially when people are working so close to you!

Roshumba's Rules _____

> Definitely have a cup of coffee if you always drink it, but this isn't the morning to drink your first-ever cup of java. It may totally throw your body's chemistry off and make you feel extrahyper.

Skipping breakfast is not a good way to keep your weight under control. You won't have enough energy to get through the day, and you'll be a lot more likely to overeat later in the day.

The morning of the shoot, you should also shower (if you didn't the night before) and wash your face as usual. You should apply a light moisturizer as well, if you're shooting indoors. If you're working outdoors and there is a possibility of your getting sunburned, apply a moisturizer with sunscreen.

Also be sure you brush your teeth the morning of the shoot. Remember, you will be spending the day in an environment where you will be in very close and intimate contact with people you are probably meeting for the first time. The makeup artist will be working on your face, and bad breath won't be appreciated. Also, as a model, you want to take care of your teeth; a winning smile will play a large part in the success of your career.

First-Job Checklist

Here's a quick checklist to help keep you organized—and calm!—before your first shoot.

The day before:

- ❏ Be sure hair, nails, and toenails are photo-ready.
- ❏ Get a bikini wax, if necessary.
- ❏ Write all the details about the shoot in your date book or PDA.
- ❏ Exercise or take a yoga class to relax.

The night before:

- ❏ Call your parents for moral support.
- ❏ Shave your underarms and legs.
- ❏ Plan what you're going to wear.
- ❏ Pack your bag.
- ❏ Figure out the best route to the shoot.

❏ Practice your modeling poses.

❏ Get a good night's sleep.

The morning of the shoot:

❏ Take a shower or bath.

❏ Wash your hair.

❏ Apply deodorant.

❏ Brush your teeth.

❏ Apply moisturizer or sunscreen.

❏ Eat a light breakfast.

Building Confidence and Reducing Stress

Now that we've talked about your body, let's talk about your mind. It's normal if you're a little bit nervous or excited about your big debut. Here are some tried-and-true tips for staying calm.

The night before, call your parents for some much-needed moral support, to hear some encouraging words, and to build your confidence. I would wait to call your friends, however. You'll probably be nervous enough, and you don't want to add to that tension by chatting with friends, who, although they may have the best of intentions, may increase your expectations—and your nervousness—with their enthusiasm.

Reality Check _____

Before you tell people about your first shoot, you should know that many things can happen to prevent the photos from being published. Sometimes it may be due to bad weather, or maybe the clothes didn't photograph well, or perhaps the model wasn't quite right for the image the client was after. Other times, the client just changes her mind. I usually wait until I know a photo will definitely be published before I tell people.

If you're feeling minor jitters, relax and find your center. When I'm nervous or feeling off-balance, I read my yoga books on the way to the shoot or take a yoga class the evening before. Other times, I take an aerobic class or do some other physical activity to release excess energy and tension. Meditating is another way to calm your nerves.

Taking a relaxing bath, watching your favorite television show, or listening to some mellow music can help, too.

Finally, try to keep everything in perspective. Although your first job is important, know that it's just one step on the ladder of success, not the whole ladder, so treat it as such and keep minor mishaps in perspective.

One job, no matter how glamorous, does not make a modeling career. Just because you may be working with one of the most famous photographers in the world or are being paid a large sum of money to pose for an advertisement, doesn't mean you've got it made and that now it's time to act like a diva. Be humble and grateful that you're being given a chance to work. Try to make friends and build relationships with the entire team, including the client, photographer, hairstylist, makeup artist, fashion stylist, assistants, and other models on the shoot. These relationships may come in handy in building and maintaining your career.

On the other hand, if things *don't* go well at your first shoot, if you can't seem to figure out what the photographer wants you to do, or if it seems like no matter how hard you try, you're not giving the client what he or she wants, don't freak out—it doesn't mean you'll never work again. Keep a positive attitude and keep trying for the duration of the shoot to do what's required of you. Keep asking the photographer, the fashion editor, or the advertising client questions about what they're looking for, and try your best to give it to them.

> **Reality Check**
>
> Don't give anyone at the shoot attitude, and try not to break down crying. If there's a break, call your agent and tell her about the situation; he or she may be able to intervene or give you some good advice.

> **Catwalk Talk**
>
> A **panic attack** is an extreme reaction to a situation that wouldn't be cause for abnormal distress for most people. It's characterized by an extreme sense of anxiety, fear, and stress.

Panic Attacks

Minor jitters are natural before your first job. But if you find that the thought of your first job gives you a *panic attack*—a feeling of extreme anxiety, fear, and stress—and makes you want to throw up, or makes you so nervous you break out in hives, you're experiencing way more anxiety than is normal in this situation. If it's at all possible, try to get through the job to protect your professional reputation. But know that you will need to seek help immediately if you want to continue modeling.

Although these extreme reactions might stop after you've worked your first few jobs, you're better off trying to work through them with a medical professional as soon as possible. The first step is to let your parents and your agent know what's going on. Your agent will appreciate your candor and professionalism in dealing with this problem. She may also be able to refer you to a doctor who can help you deal with it. (Your best bet is to talk to your regular doctor first, who will probably refer you to a psychologist or psychiatrist.) Don't be embarrassed; you're not the first model to suffer from this problem!

Even if your career gets a shaky start due to your anxiety, it's not the end of your career. When your condition is straightened out, you may go on to work at the top of the fashion heap.

Hopefully, though, panic attacks won't be a problem for you. If they are, hopefully you can decrease the tension and anxiety level by preparing thoroughly for your first shoot, following the advice I've given in this chapter.

The Least You Need to Know

- ◆ Write down all the details of the shoot in your date book or PDA.
- ◆ Be sure your hair, skin, and body are photo-ready.
- ◆ Get a good night's sleep before the shoot and eat breakfast before you leave.
- ◆ Stress is normal; try to find positive ways to deal with it, such as exercising, listening to mellow music, or meditating.
- ◆ If you suffer from extreme anxiety before a shoot, get professional help to deal with the problem.

Chapter 16

Who's Who at the Shoot

In This Chapter

- ◆ Wooing the client
- ◆ Wowing the photographer
- ◆ Working with the creative team

You're about to walk in the door of the photo shoot to begin your modeling career. You've done all your homework, you're freshly showered and shampooed, and you're eager to get started and make a splendid debut in front of the cameras.

Your first day will be even more successful if you know and understand who's who at a photo shoot. In this chapter, I explain who all the people at a shoot are and what their roles are, and give you special tips on how to woo them, establish a solid working relationship with them, and make them want to work with you again and again. A client is more likely to hire again a team (photographer, model, hairstylist, and makeup artist) that works well together to produce outstanding images.

Impressing the Boss: The Client

Clients come in all different shapes and sizes and work in all different aspects of the business. The type you encounter depends on the type of shoot you're doing—whether it's for a magazine, a catalog, or an advertisement. The client can range from the young, superchic *fashion editor* at a top magazine, to a businesslike catalog client, to a hip advertising agency executive.

On a magazine shoot, the client is the fashion editor. On a catalog shoot, the client is the art director, an in-house representative of the catalog company, or a freelance person who's been hired to produce the catalog. At an advertising shoot, the client is the person who works for the company that produces the product being advertised. The advertising agency that came up with the idea for the shoot and is responsible for producing the ad also will usually have at least one representative on the *set*.

> **Catwalk Talk**
>
> The **fashion editor** (or fashion stylist or sittings editor) selects the clothes to be photographed, arranges the shoots, and makes sure the magazine's vision is being captured during the shoot.
>
> The area in a photo shoot where the pictures are actually taken is called the **set**. The cameras, lighting, and any necessary backdrops or props are positioned on the set.

A client's job on the set is to oversee the entire shoot itself, making sure the team is there and accomplishing what they need to get done. The client also has final approval of the hair, makeup, clothes, lighting, and poses.

The important thing to know about clients is this: no matter who they are, you want to get on their good side by being polite, friendly, and attuned and responsive to their needs and personality. Above all, no matter who the client is, be professional and respectful.

Magazine Clients

The client on a magazine shoot is the fashion editor. She's usually very fashion-savvy and well dressed. She probably worked very hard to rise through the ranks of the magazine, from intern, to assistant, to associate, to senior fashion editor. She may attend international fashion shows every season, or she may have worked directly with fashion designers at one time or another. Sometimes, however, her natural fashion savoir-faire has been the key to her progress up the ladder.

This type of person is really into the who's who of the fashion industry. She may own all the newest clothes—the latest Prada bag, the coolest Gucci shoes. Compliment her on the way she looks and how she dresses, and share your own personal likes.

Fashion editors appreciate being acknowledged for the work they do, so to get on her good side, acknowledge her talent and respect her power. You can compliment her on her work by saying something like, "I loved your dress piece in the June issue." Also be sure to thank her for giving you the chance to appear in the magazine.

Catalog Clients

Catalog shoots tend to be businesslike and no-nonsense compared with magazine shoots because a catalog is more interested in selling clothes than in creating illusions. They have a strict schedule of what they have to get done and how many pieces they need to shoot in a day. The format of a catalog shoot is a lot more rigid, a lot more garments are shot, and the days are busier and more pressed than with other shoots. Catalogs are usually catering to an audience that's a bit more down-to-earth than a fashion magazine's audience.

When it comes to work, catalog clients tend to be more low-key and business-oriented than some of the other people you might work with. Their primary focus is on the business of the day. They want to work with models who know what they're doing, who are grounded, and who have a strong sense of self.

Roshumba's Rules

When you're dealing with the representatives from a catalog, be professional and mature. You don't want to be as chit-chatty and informal as you would be with a magazine editor.

Advertising Clients

Advertising clients are trying to appeal to the world at large. The atmosphere in the studio might reflect that excitement and creative energy. You want to tune into the mood of the shoot and help keep that excitement alive. To do this, get as much information as possible in advance from your agent about the product, the image the client's trying to create, and what they're looking for from the model. Advertising shoots tend to be a little looser and more casual than catalog shoots. Because people in advertising tend to be very creative, hip, and modern, you, too, can showcase your creative, humorous, or artistic side.

Scenes from Behind the Camera: The Photographer

The photographer is the person with the camera, but he's not there to just mindlessly snap pictures. He has a lot of input on the format, imaging, and story behind the photo shoot. Often a photographer is selected because of his style of photography, whether it's realistic, fantasy based, or somewhere in between.

For instance, if *Vogue* wants to do a photo shoot featuring the latest swimsuits for the May issue, they don't just call in a random photographer and say, "We want to shoot swimwear. Come on down and bring your camera." The magazine's editors and art director sit down and discuss with the photographer the story they want to tell and the look the photos should have.

The photographer might suggest different types of locations, such as models in bikinis on motorcycles in a small town in California for biker-inspired bathing suits, or a shoot in the middle of a remote Moroccan town with models in bikinis on donkeys. The photographer might also suggest the poses that can be used and the hair and makeup styles.

The photographer and the model must communicate throughout the photo shoot. The photographer might offer advice, yet the model must also know how to move.

The photographer must also inspire the model and be open to inspiration by the model. That's why the relationship between the photographer and the model is so important, and why they really have to be in sync.

Many times, if a model has never worked with a photographer, he might want to meet the model before the shoot to get a feeling for her temperament and personality, and to explain the concept he has in mind for the shoot. Even if a photographer has seen pictures of you, he won't have a true sense of what you really look like until he sees you in person.

Model Scoop

Linda Evangelista did several famous photo shoots with photographer Steven Meisel in which she changed her appearance drastically in each picture, going from a blonde, Marilyn Monroe–inspired starlet in one, to a dark-haired Spanish flamenco dancer in another, to a redheaded Eva Perón diva in a third. This was a classic example of model and photographer inspiring each other, of a model acting as a muse for a photographer. Meisel was able to envision Linda in each of those guises, and she was able to fulfill his vision through her poses. Their working relationship, which was also a close personal friendship, spanned many years and resulted in many indelible images.

It takes a while for a model to develop posing techniques, so your best bet until then is to listen to the photographer's directions. That might mean putting your ego in check so you can understand and learn what he's asking you to do. Sometimes when a girl is working with a photographer and he's telling her to move her arm a bit to the left, tilt her head down, or move her feet closer together, it can be tedious and annoying, especially if you feel like you already know what you're doing. Just know he's not picking on you and trying to imply that you're a bad model. Rather, the photographer's trying to capture you at the best angles and in the best light, depending on the lens and lighting he's using. His main goal is to get the best pictures possible.

When you're working with a photographer, be polite at all times, even when things don't go as planned or the shoot starts to get hairy. Sometimes everything on a shoot can start getting out of whack, especially if it's at an outdoor location. You might be scheduled to shoot at a gorgeous beach location on the island of Bermuda, but then it starts to rain and the shoot is spoiled! You can help the situation by being open to the idea that the concept of the shoot might need to change. Have a sense of humor and try to enjoy yourself. Just look at each shoot as a learning experience.

Model Scoop

I remember one shoot that was especially harrowing. *Sports Illustrated* was in Barcelona, where they had rented a huge stadium for a night shoot. Three other girls and I were being shot in gold bikinis. We were shooting in November, when Barcelona is still pretty warm—a light sweater is all you usually need. But that night, there was a freezing sleet storm. We could use the stadium for only one night, the photographer had rented all sorts of special equipment, and the other models were leaving the next morning. So we went out and posed in a sleet storm. That was a true test of my professionalism.

All in all, you want to try to make the photographer your friend. One photographer could make your whole career if the two of you get along well and inspire each other. During the first 3 years of my career, I worked with Oliviero Toscani nearly every single day, shooting magazine stories for *Elle* and *Grazia*, and advertisements for Benetton, Sisley, and Esprit. Working with this one photographer paid my rent (and more) for years.

Backstage with the Creative Team

When you're working with any member of the creative team, whether it be the hairstylist, makeup artist, or fashion stylist, you want to be friendly, polite, open to her ideas, and cautious about expressing your personal dislikes. At all times, you need to remember that you're there so these people can create an image with you. Your physical self is a canvas they'll be using to create the illusion needed for the particular photograph. Ultimately, your personal likes and dislikes about hair, makeup, and clothes don't matter. Avoid expressing any negative opinions, unless someone wants to do something that can physically harm you.

Reality Check

Feuding with any member of the team on a shoot could have negative repercussions for a model's career. The same team might have worked with the client for years, and you might be the new kid on the block. If the (trusted) hairstylist or makeup artist tells the client that you're difficult, there's a good chance the client won't book you again.

The fashion industry is relatively small, and more likely than not, you will be working with these people again. If you leave on a good note, you'll start on a good note at the next shoot. You want to start to form strong relationships, which will contribute to the workings of a great team.

The Hairstylist

On most shoots, your hair is done first, before your makeup and before the fashion stylist gets you dressed. The hairstylist usually has a special, separate room in the photo studio (which she may share with the makeup artist). The stylist may wet your hair and apply various hair products to it to give it the texture she wants it to have. Then she may blow-dry it straight, curl it with a curling iron, or put hot curlers in it; decorate your hair with jewels or hair accessories; or create any other look the client and photographer have decided they want. It often takes 45 minutes to 1½ hours for your hair to be done.

The hairstylist might restyle your hair every time you change clothes, too. For one photo, she may blow it straight; for another, she may curl it; for a third, she may put it up in a chignon.

The hairstylist also comes with you onto the set to make sure your hair always looks its best. For example, if your hair starts to fall in your face, she pulls it back. She might brush your hair periodically to keep it looking freshly styled. She might also direct you to work your hair so it looks its best, say, by telling you to run your fingers through it.

Roshumba's Rules

Often hairstylists are very sensitive, especially when it comes to their work. You don't want to offend them or deflate their egos. Just sit back, relax, and let them do their thing. Look at it as an opportunity for you to experiment and see how different styles look on you!

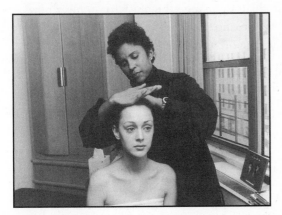 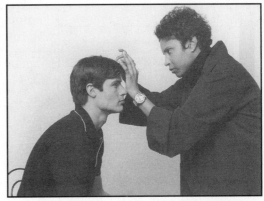

Patience is a virtue for models. They'll spend up to an hour and a half being prepped by the hairstylist before a shoot.

(Photographer: Kwame Brathwaite; models: Laura McLafferty and Ryan Kopko; makeup artist: Andrea Fairweather)

If a hairstylist asks you, you can suggest hairstyles that make you feel comfortable—but only if she asks. The only time you should speak up is if the hairstylist is doing something that can damage your hair—for instance, if she applies gel to your hair and then wants to use a curling iron on it. But instead of freaking out, try to offer a positive alternative that will protect your hair and allow her to pursue her vision. You can say, "My hair's very fragile at the moment. I love your idea, but if you could use curlers instead of curling iron, I'd really appreciate it." When it comes to her actual artistic expression, however, you should let her do her thing.

The Makeup Artist

When the hairstylist has finished with your hair, the makeup artist will apply your makeup. She'll prepare your skin with toners and/or moisturizers and then apply all the necessary makeup to your face. Foundation goes on first, followed by concealer, any necessary *contouring*, and loose powder. Then she begins to "paint" with eye liner, eye shadow, brow enhancer, blush, lipstick, and mascara. If body makeup is called for, she'll apply that as well. Depending on how elaborate the makeup look is, it can take the makeup artist anywhere from 45 minutes to 1 1/2 hours to do her job.

> **Catwalk Talk**
>
> Contouring means shading a model's face with darker or lighter foundation to enhance her facial features, by creating the illusion of high cheekbones or a slender nose, for example.

If different makeup looks are required for subsequent photos, the makeup artist will redo the makeup each time. Generally, though, once your foundation is on, the basic makeup is set for the day. But with the various changes of clothing, the makeup artist might add some eye shadow, change the blush, or apply a new lipstick. When an entirely different look is called for, she might take off all the makeup and start over.

Even if the basic look doesn't change, the makeup artist checks your face before every picture to be sure your makeup looks fresh and beautiful. She also watches you as you work on the set, and if touchups are needed (for example, if you're sweating), she will blot your skin or apply some powder.

Makeup artists are just that—artists—so respect their talent and artistry. They tend to be a bit receptive to your input, especially when it comes to your skin and how it reacts to various products. Even as you make suggestions, always be respectful of their talent and of the time they have taken to create a beautiful makeup look. You don't want to insult them or hurt their egos. They want to make you look as good as possible—within the confines of the shoot.

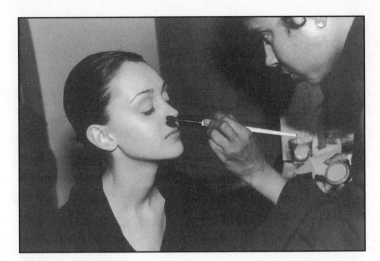

Here, the makeup artist applies the finishing touches to the model's makeup.

(Photographer: Kwame Brathwaite; model: Laura McLafferty; makeup artist: Andrea Fairweather)

The Fashion Stylist

The fashion stylist is in charge of all the clothes that will be used in the photos. Her job might include visiting all the clothing designers' showrooms and selecting the clothing, shoes, and accessories that will be used for the shoot. (At larger magazines, other editors, called market editors, go to the shows and keep track of the newest items in designers' showrooms.)

The fashion stylist is also responsible for all the logistics of borrowing the clothes from the designer, arranging for their transportation from the showroom to the photo studio, and making sure they're all returned to the right place. She also must be sure all garments and accessories are returned in the same condition in which they were borrowed, which means they are clean and fresh, with no stains, dirt, body odors, rips, or tears.

When the model has the garment on, the stylist will pin the clothes if they don't fit properly, make any other necessary adjustments, and accessorize the outfit as needed.

The best thing a model can do to make the fashion stylist her friend is to do everything she can to respect the clothes and keep them clean, unwrinkled, and properly hung up. A model should always arrive at a shoot freshly showered so body odors aren't transferred to the clothes. (See Chapter 15 for more information on preparing for a shoot.)

Here are some other wardrobe do's and don'ts to keep in mind:

◆ Be extra careful when putting clothes on and taking them off so makeup doesn't rub off on the clothes.

◆ Don't smoke when you're dressed in the clothes for the shoot. You don't want to burn them or leave them with a smoky smell.

◆ Don't spray perfume once you're dressed. You'll leave the scent on the clothes.

◆ Don't eat with the clothes on. Stains can happen.

◆ Avoid any body movements that can wrinkle the clothes. Don't sit down, and be very careful about folding or bending your arms.

◆ When you take off the clothes, hang them up neatly.

> **Reality Check**
>
> Even though the garment might not appeal to your personal taste, any negative remarks about the clothing or outright refusal to wear something reflects very badly on you. Remember, it's not your job to like the clothes; it's your job to wear them. Don't complain about what you have to wear.

It's a good idea to talk to the fashion stylist to get any information about what's special about the garment, why the client is featuring it, or whether it's part of a larger fashion trend. She might also give you some clues to how you can best show off the garment's special features.

You should also chat up the fashion stylist to get to know her better on a personal level. You can talk about fashion trends (stylists are often very interested in fashion) or share other personal stories.

The Assistants

Often the professionals at a shoot—the client, photographer, hairstylist, makeup artist, and fashion stylist—bring along assistants to help them. Many of these assistants are aspiring professionals themselves; they take care of some of the more mundane aspects of the professionals' jobs. It's important that you establish good working relationships with them to ensure a smooth shoot—and because they are the photographers, hairstylists, and makeup artists you may be working with in the future.

While you want to acknowledge the assistants' presence and treat them politely and cordially, you don't want to be overly friendly or extremely personal. As a model, you need to do a tightrope walk between being friendly to the assistants and being overly intimate. The lion's share of the attention must be directed to the head people—the client, photographer, hairstylist, makeup artist, and fashion stylist.

Now that you know all the people on the shoot, you'll have the confidence to make an auspicious debut. Good luck!

The Least You Need to Know

- ◆ Your relationship with the client may vary, depending on whether you're shooting for a magazine, a catalog, or an advertisement. Whatever the job, though, treat all of them with professionalism and respect.

- ◆ The photographer is in charge of every aspect of the photo shoot, so it behooves a model to cooperate with him.

- ◆ The creative team—the hairstylist, makeup artist, and fashion stylist, as well as their assistants—is there to make you look your best and everyone deserves your respect and cooperation.

Chapter 17

In the Studio and on Location

In This Chapter

◆ Working in a photo studio

◆ Shooting on location, in town and out of town

◆ Leaving on a jet plane: supermodel travel tips

In Chapter 16, I talked about all the essential people at a photo shoot and the role each of them plays. Now that you know who the key players are, you're probably wondering what a day at a shoot is *really* like.

There are two basic types of photo shoots: indoor shoots at a photo studio and location shoots. A location shoot refers to any shoot that takes place outside a photo studio: in a park, on a beach, in a café, in a bank, or wherever. The kind of shoot you're doing determines what your day on the set is like.

In this chapter, I take you through a typical day shooting in the studio and a day shooting on location and explain the pros and cons of each one. Along the way, I give you some tips about shoot etiquette that ensure you're a success no matter where you're shooting.

Behind the Scenes at a Photo Studio

A studio photo shoot takes place in a rented photo studio. (Occasionally, photographers have their own personal studios, but more often a studio is rented for the day of the shoot.) The call time for most photo shoots is 9 A.M. (most end at 5 P.M.). You are expected to be there on time. Most of the other professionals on the set (hairstylist, makeup artist, fashion stylist) also arrive at 9 A.M., although some may come earlier to prepare for the day. I always try to arrive at the studio 5 to 10 minutes early. Arriving early also shows the client that you take your work seriously.

The client may also come in early to be sure everything that needs to be there is there, such as the clothes and any props, and that the team is there on time. The photographers' assistants may also come in early to start setting up the lights and camera.

The photographer, however, may come in from 1 to 2 hours later because he's not needed until then. The model will be getting her hair and makeup done, and the assistants will be setting up the lighting, camera, and set.

The client almost always provides breakfast. Usually it consists of coffee, juice, bagels, muffins, fruit, smoked salmon, cream cheese, and preserves. It's usually laid out buffet-style; feel free to help yourself.

Your First Stop: Hair, Makeup, and Wardrobe

Eat your breakfast quickly because the hair and makeup people will be waiting for you to finish so they can get started. Makeup and hair are most often done in the same room, which is usually separate from the shooting area. Usually music is playing in the hair and makeup room.

> **Reality Check**
>
> Although it's acceptable to eat and drink in the hair chair, it's considered rude to eat and drink while you're in the makeup chair. The makeup artist needs to focus on your face, and chewing is very distracting for her.

The hair and makeup chairs are often set up side by side facing a big mirror. The makeup chair is usually a high director's chair, while the hair chair is lower, like the ones in a hair salon.

Hair is usually styled first so the various gels and spritzes the hairstylist applies don't ruin the makeup. Unless you're otherwise instructed, you should arrive at the shoot with clean, shampooed hair that's neatly trimmed. Don't glop lots of products on your hair or try to style it yourself. It should just be clean and ready to work with.

When your hair is finished, it's time to move over to the makeup chair, where the makeup artist works her magic. This is when the look starts to come alive and the studio starts to buzz with energy. Often the team starts chatting, telling stories, maybe reminiscing about another shoot, or talking about the future. If the team hasn't worked together before, everyone gets to know each other.

When your hair and makeup are done, you'll often have a 5- or 10-minute break. This is a great time to go to the bathroom because you might not be able to go after you're dressed.

Next, it's time to go into *wardrobe*. In some studios, this can be in the same room as hair and makeup, but usually it's a separate room to give the model some privacy when she changes.

The fashion stylist's assistant will give you everything you need to wear, from any special undergarments to shoes, and show you where to get dressed. She may help you put on a garment to make sure you don't get makeup on it.

The stylist will check you after you're dressed to be sure everything fits; that the color looks good on you; that all the buttons are buttoned; and that there are no rips, tears, or stains. If something doesn't fit, she'll clip or pin it (in the back, or wherever it won't show in the photo) so it looks like it fits perfectly. She might have you try different shoes, or another color hose, or another pair of earrings.

> **Catwalk Talk**
>
> **Wardrobe** refers to both the clothes you'll be wearing and the area where you get dressed. It's where the fashion stylist works and where the model changes from her street clothes into the clothes for the shoot.

> **Roshumba's Rules**
>
> I suggest you wear a flesh-color thong panty and a flesh-color bra to a photo shoot. These are versatile enough to work with most garments.

Although most models have pierced ears, it's not a problem if you don't. Most stylists have special attachments that convert pierced earrings to clip-ons. (If you don't have pierced ears, it's not a bad idea for you to buy a couple pairs just in case—you can find them at jewelry stores.)

When you're dressed, don't sit down, don't eat, don't smoke—don't do anything that will wrinkle, stain, or damage the clothes. Also try to avoid bending your arms, which can crease the sleeves. To avoid leaving footprints on the set, often you won't put on the shoes you'll be wearing for the shot until you get on the set itself. In the meantime, you might be given temporary shoes so you don't have to walk around barefoot.

Lights, Camera, Action: On the Set

When you go out on the set, usually the entire team will accompany you—the head hairstylist, makeup artist, and fashion stylist. The photographer and the client will also be there to do the final touchups. The hairstylist might rebrush your hair; the makeup artist might apply more powder and touch up your lipstick; the fashion stylist might adjust your clothing.

After that, you'll probably be asked to practice a few poses to give the team an idea of what you plan to do. You might also pose for a Polaroid so the photographer can check the lighting and the other professionals can check your hair, makeup, and clothes to be sure everything looks perfect. At this preliminary stage in the shoot, the photographer and client will probably start talking about the image they're looking to capture.

The hairstylist and makeup artist accompany the model onto the set so they can touch up her hair and makeup whenever necessary.

Finally, the shoot begins. Despite all your preparations, it's natural to feel unsure and frightened the first time you step in front of the camera. If you've done your homework, studied other models, practiced posing in the mirror, and done test shoots, you should have some ideas of what to do. If it doesn't seem to come naturally, stay calm, don't get frustrated, and try to listen to and follow the photographer's direction as best you can.

Depending on how elaborate the shot is, you could be posing anywhere from 20 minutes to 1 hour in an outfit. Shoots can go more slowly if special details in the clothing need to be captured (maybe they're photographing a garment with a lot of details on the back that need to be shot in a special way) or if problems arise (say, a buttonhole won't stay closed).

Reality Check

Some models have such huge egos that even though the poses they're doing aren't what the client and photographer envisioned, they refuse to take direction from the photographer, much less ask, "Is this what you want?" The question-and-answer process is the best way to get feedback from the photographer and the client. Don't be afraid (or too proud) to ask.

When the garment has been shot to the photographer and client's satisfaction, you'll head back to the dressing room to change clothes. Your hair and makeup will be checked and retouched as needed, you will change into the next outfit, you will return to the set, and the whole process will be repeated.

Midway through the shoot, you'll have a break for lunch. Lunch is generally catered, and there's usually a wide variety of choices. But you're free to order something different or bring your own food if you're on a special diet.

After lunch, the hair and makeup people will again touch you up, and then you'll put on another garment and shoot again.

On an editorial shoot, you'll shoot anywhere from 4 to 10 garments; the average is around 6. On a catalog shoot, the number of garments shot is much higher: I've shot as many as 20 outfits in 1 day. The average, however, is about 12 pieces. Advertising shoots can vary, depending on the type of product.

Catwalk Talk

"We're **wrapped**" is the official word from the photographer or client that the shoot is over, that the work of the day has been completed, and that the model and the team can pack up and go home.

On the last shot of the day when everything is finished, the photographer or the client will say, "We're *wrapped.*"

Before or after you put your own clothes back on, politely ask the client or the client's assistant to sign your voucher. It's also nice if you thank them for the day and tell them you hope everything turns out as they wanted. But don't go overboard and beg for another job: your work and attitude will speak for themselves.

Out-of-Town Studio Shoots

Sometimes you'll be hired to do a studio shoot out of town, in a studio in a city other than your home base. Out-of-town studio shoots are very similar to studio shoots in your home base. The biggest difference may be in the call time, to take into consideration the travel schedules for both the models and the clothes, which may be flown in for the shoot from another location.

When you're shooting out of town, keep in mind that you might not be able to find everything you're used to being able to easily get. If you have special dietary or other needs, plan ahead and bring whatever you need with you.

In-Town Location Shoots

There are two types of location shoots: in town (at your home base) and out of town. In-town location shoots often take place in a picturesque local street, a busy area of town such as Times Square in New York, architecturally significant places such as the Duomo cathedral in Milan, or even a beach. Most, but not all, location shoots take place outdoors. Shooting evening gowns at the Ritz Hotel in Paris or business suits for a catalog in an architect's office in Atlanta is also considered a location shoot.

Often location shoots have odd hours because of the restrictions imposed by shooting permits, which are often necessary for location shoots, especially in big cities. More important, the hours might be affected by the shoot's lighting requirements.

Roshumba's Rules

Because of the logistical problems involved with location shoots, it's especially important that you arrive on time. If you arrive even 15 minutes late, you could inconvenience the whole team and wreck the whole shoot.

Generally, photographers don't like to shoot in the middle of the day, when the bright, glaring midday light looks harsh in photos. Early morning and early evening light is much more complimentary. Often you'll have a 4 or 5 A.M. call time to take advantage of the early morning light.

You might get an odd call time if you're shooting in a busy location, too, such as a grand old railroad station. Because it can be nearly impossible to shoot with huge crowds of people around, you might be asked to come in very early in the morning. Other times, the call time may be 11 P.M. for a night shoot, when the photographer wants to capture a glamorous nighttime look.

For the majority of in-town location shoots, specially outfitted RV trailers are used for all the shoot preparations. The hairstylist and makeup artist work here, the clothes are prepared here, and the model gets dressed here. This is also where you eat, socialize, and wait between shoots, and where the bathroom is.

Whenever you're working in a trailer, know that space is limited. Don't bring a lot of stuff with you, and don't leave what you brought strewn about the whole trailer. When you're ready, you'll wait in the trailer until the photographer or his assistants call you to the set. They are on the set getting ready and keep in contact with you in the trailer via walkie-talkies.

After you've gotten your hair and makeup done, stay out of the way of the team because they need space to work. Try to be extra patient. With such close quarters, it can be tedious and annoying with everyone on top of each other.

Model Scoop

One particularly glamorous night shoot I did was for French *Elle*. We were shooting couture evening gowns, and the editor wanted to shoot them in an especially alluring setting—the magnificent Place de la Concorde in Paris. Special makeup was used that would glisten in the night lights. In addition, the photographer used a special light, a "sun gun," to give the pictures a unique look. The biggest challenge on the shoot was the lighting; we had a much longer wait time than usual between every shot. As odd as it felt to be shooting at that hour, it was fun because there was kind of a party atmosphere at the location.

Normally, the trailer is parked a few yards away from the set, although the location could be a couple blocks away because of parking restrictions. In the latter case, you need to walk from the trailer to the location. If it's any farther than that, a car will probably transport you.

Just as at a studio shoot, an 8-hour day is the norm on location. Despite the more complicated logistics of a location shoot, you can usually get the same amount of work done. As for food, both breakfast and lunch will be catered.

Out-of-Town Location Shoots

The second type of location shoot is an out-of-town location shoot. A client may decide to do a shoot away from home to capture a special ambiance. For example, if the client wants to capture the image of sunny skies and beautiful beaches, they may decide to shoot on a Greek island. Furthermore, because the fashion capitals (Paris, Milan, and New York) have cold, rainy winters, clients often travel to sunnier, warmer locations when they want to shoot outdoors, especially during the winter months.

As with in-town location shoots, the average location photo shoot away from home may have an odd call time. Generally, you'll start very early in the morning to take advantage of the flattering early morning light; it's generally less crowded at this time, too. The location might be available only during certain hours. Often, though, you get a long lunch break (from 1 to 3 hours) during the middle of the day, when the harsh lighting looks the worst on the model's face. You may be shooting later than 5 P.M., however, because the light is also complimentary in the early evening.

Depending on where the shoot is taking place, you'll usually travel from your home base to the location the night or day before the shoot to be sure you arrive in time. The client is responsible for paying for you and your expenses (including hotel, transportation, and food) from the time you arrive for the shoot. However, you are responsible for paying for anything you take from the mini bar, any long-distance telephone charges (some places don't have good cell reception), and any pay television.

Model Scoop

When you're required to travel to a shoot, you'll probably be paid for the time it takes you to get from your home base to the location. Depending on where you're going, your travel fee could be the equivalent of 1 day's pay, half a day's pay, or whatever the agent negotiates. (Sometimes, however, you might not be paid a travel fee at all.)

Days on location tend to be extremely relaxed if everything goes smoothly—the weather cooperates, the sets are all available, and the models and the rest of the team all show up. It can almost seem like you're on vacation! On the other hand, if the elements don't cooperate and things don't go according to schedule, a location shoot can be your worst nightmare! Maybe the clothes, models, or other members of the team don't arrive or are delayed. The weather might not be agreeable, the hotel might not be accommodating, someone might get sick, or someone might be in a bad mood. Maybe there's no crowd control and no real security on the set. The camera might break. The things that can go wrong are endless.

Even though none of these things is the model's fault (assuming her attitude is positive and she doesn't cause any unnecessary disturbances) and no one is blaming her, she may be affected by the tense, pressurized atmosphere of a shoot gone wrong. Just be sure you remain professional, cooperative, and willing to work to the best of your ability at all times.

Another disadvantage of location shoots is that sometimes models might be asked to do things that can cause them some physical discomfort. For example, you might be asked to pose outdoors in a wool suit on a steamy day in July or wear a bathing suit on a beach when it's only 40 degrees. These sorts of discomforts come with the job, and you should do your best to be accommodating.

When shooting on location, especially in a foreign country, people don't always know the etiquette of a photo shoot. Crowds might gather to ogle or harass the models. And even when you have security, it can be an uncomfortable situation that can fray the nerves of everyone on the set.

Model Scoop

I remember one *Sports Illustrated* swimsuit issue shoot in a foreign country where model Paulina Porizkova had to climb up on top of a light tower to pose. When the local guys found out Paulina was actually up there, they circled the set and started screaming her name. Although they probably meant no harm, it was a very scary situation at the time, being surrounded as we were by a threatening, screaming mob. We kind of got the feeling that even though we had a couple security guards, the whole thing could get out of hand and a riot could erupt at any moment.

Super Travel Tips for Supermodels

The number-one rule of traveling for a modeling job is to pack as lightly as possible. Whenever possible, try to carry on your bag. Airlines lose baggage all the time, and it's an awful feeling to arrive at a location and not have the things you need to make you as comfortable as possible. Plus, it's a pain to have to wait for it at baggage claim. Also it makes a model look like a prima donna if she shows up with five suitcases for a week of work.

If you're going to be away for only 2 or 3 days, everything you need can probably fit into a carry-on bag. If your trip is longer than that, however, you'll probably need to check it.

Roshumba's Rules

I advise against using very high-end brand-name luggage (unless it's a carry-on). Expensive luggage is an inviting target for theft. Instead, I recommend good-quality, rugged bags (wheeled bags are the best), but nothing too flashy.

Reality Check

Even in the nicest hotel in the world, you want to take precautions to ensure your personal safety. When you're in your room, lock the door and put the security chain on. As soon as you've checked in, call someone at your home base to say you reached your destination safely, and give that person the phone number of the hotel.

Another reason to pack lightly is that often you will have to leave for the airport directly from the shoot, so you'll need to bring your baggage with you to the location. You'll want to have the smallest amount of luggage possible so you don't have to lug tons of stuff around.

When you're packing, keep in mind that you'll need to bring only the clothes you'll wear from your hotel to the shoot (as well as maybe an outfit or two to wear out at night). At the shoot, you'll take off your own clothes and put on whatever's being photographed.

It's best to keep your wardrobe as simple as possible: jeans, T-shirts, and sweaters are your best choices. Bring a fresh top to wear each day, but it's okay to "recycle" bottoms and wear the same pair of jeans 2 days in a row. Also pack something slightly dressier that you can put on if you go out at night, such as a slip dress or a nice pair of pants and top, or a lightweight sweater.

It's also a good idea to pack clothes you can layer. Although the average temperature may be 80 degrees where you're going, the weather can change suddenly, and it's great if you can slip on a long-sleeve shirt and a sweater over your tank top. Bring a couple pairs of socks and two or three pairs of comfortable shoes (running shoes, sandals or other shoes you can walk in, and a pair you can wear out in the evening are sufficient).

You might also want to bring workout clothes and a swimsuit. Many of the hotels you'll be staying in have gyms and pools, or you might have the opportunity to go running.

I also always suggest bringing your own personal alarm clock because you can't always depend on wake-up calls from the hotel staff. If you have to leave at 5 A.M. for a location that's an hour away, you don't want to inconvenience the client by being late. To be sure I'm up, I like to arrange for a wake-up call *and* set my alarm clock.

Here is a checklist of some other items you might need:

- ❏ Your composites

- ❏ Your portfolio, if it's not too large

- ❏ Your voucher book

- ❏ Your passport, if you'll be traveling to a foreign location

- ❏ Your driver's license or other valid ID (for airport check-in)

- ❏ Makeup, if you like (lip color and mascara are all you'll absolutely need)

- ❏ Body lotion, facial cleansers, hairstyling products, contact lens solution, any other special toiletries you'll need

- ❏ Sunblock

- ❏ Insect repellent (depending on where the shoot is and the time of year you're going)

- ❏ Aspirin or ibuprofen, along with other medicine (such as allergy medicine), if necessary

- ❏ Prescriptions

- ❏ Vitamins

- ❏ Food, if you have special dietary needs

Before you leave home, find out the best way to get from the airport to the hotel at your destination so you'll know if you're being taken on an unrequested sightseeing trip by the cab driver. (Google the hotel, which will have a link with information about arriving from the airport.) Before you get in a taxi, you'll want to know how long it will take and how much you'll have to pay.

The most important thing you can do when you're traveling is to stay aware and alert. Be especially aware of con artists and thieves.

Reality Check

There are many stories of a traveler setting down his bags to make a quick phone call and finding that someone has walked away with them while he's on the phone. Or someone's wallet might be swiped out of an open purse before she's even aware anyone is nearby. Always stay alert and protect yourself and your belongings.

By following these helpful tips, you can ensure that your career will be a successful one, no matter where in the world you're shooting.

The Least You Need to Know

- Studio photo shoots are the most controlled and have the fewest hassles.
- Photo shoots on location are more exciting and creative, but they also come with more logistical problems.
- Models should travel light and always be alert to potential dangers.

Part 5

There's Something for Everyone

As you've no doubt realized by now, there are many different types of modeling, from a walk down the runway in a fashion show, to a photo shoot for a magazine cover, to a television commercial for a consumer product. In Part 5, I discuss in depth print modeling, which includes magazine and catalog work, and the advantages and disadvantages of each. I also talk frankly about nude modeling and why you might—and might not—want to consider it.

I also talk about the exciting world of runway modeling and why it's important for your career, as well as give you some warnings about its drawbacks. I also discuss the big-bucks realm of modeling for advertisements, plus its pros and cons.

Finally, I talk about specialty modeling, which includes nontraditional models such as plus-size models, classic (older) models, male models, and child models. And because not everyone meets the stringent qualifications to be a fashion model, I discuss opportunities for real-people models, including character and parts modeling

Chapter 18

Print and Runway Modeling

In This Chapter

- ◆ The prestige of editorial modeling
- ◆ The lucrative world of catalog modeling
- ◆ Nude modeling: a very personal choice
- ◆ The three categories of designer runway shows: haute couture, ready-to-wear, and resort
- ◆ Fit, in-store, and trunk-show modeling

As you might know by this point in the book, there are many different kinds of modeling work available to models. From runway work to editorial, to in-store modeling, you surely can find the job you're sure to shine in.

Print work, which includes modeling for magazines and catalogs, is the foundation of many models' careers. In this chapter, I discuss its advantages and disadvantages—in terms of the pay, career advancement, and prestige. The ultimate print job is appearing on magazine covers; I talk about how that happens and what it's like here, too. I also discuss runway, one of the most exciting modeling jobs, and other related types of modeling.

Also in this chapter, I touch on a potentially controversial subject: nude modeling. To appear nude is a very personal choice, and in this chapter, I talk about what you need to consider before you take it all off.

Editorial Work and What It Means to Your Career

The most prestigious type of print work is editorial work, or modeling for magazines. As you learned in Chapter 2, editorial work includes fashion stories that showcase the latest style trends—the newest look in coats, the must-have shoes for spring, or the new suits for fall. The other major type of editorial story is beauty-related, which means anything having to do with skin care, hair care, makeup, or cosmetic procedures such as facials and massages.

With editorial fashion shoots, equal emphasis is placed on showing the clothes and creating a beautiful photo, such as this one I did several years ago.

(Photo: Charles Tracy)

Fashion magazines establish the visual standards—the style of photography, the types of models, the graphics—for the fashion industry at large. Because of the creative license they enjoy, magazines are the launch pad for many new and innovative ideas. Magazines are where new fashions and ideas come alive, whether they involve clothing, makeup, hair, or lifestyle trends.

If fashion designers decide that miniskirts should be revived, for instance, that idea won't take hold in consumers' minds until a magazine features them in a story. Minis can be in every store and every catalog, but few people will buy them until they see them on some fabulous model in *Elle* or *Glamour* or *Seventeen*. Once one of these magazines gives minis the stamp of approval, consumers realize that minis are back in fashion and are much more likely to go out and spend their money.

Model Scoop

Each magazine tends to use models who embody its idea of the ideal woman. *Vogue* uses models who exemplify the modern, style-conscious woman. For almost a decade, Christy Turlington, Claudia Schiffer, and Linda Evangelista—three models who exude sophistication, class, worldliness, luxury, and decadence—dominated the pages of *Vogue*. When a recession hit in the early 1990s, however, that image was no longer marketable. Enter Kate Moss and the grunge look, along with the idea of paring down and living a more bohemian lifestyle. When the economy grew stronger, Christy, Claudia, and Linda came back bigger than ever. Today the highest-profile actresses and celebrities have replaced models on *Vogue*'s cover (although the hottest models are still featured in its fashion stories).

Celebrities now share a lot of the editorial work with models, both in traditional fashion magazines and in celebrity magazines. (The latter have become a new, important source of fashion information, chronicling what the stars are wearing.)

Eyes on the Prize: Editorial Modeling

Big-time models in the fashion capitals (New York, Paris, and Milan) do most of the editorial work because that's where the majority of magazines are based. Models in secondary markets (Chicago, Miami, and Los Angeles) may appear in magazines based in those cities, but it's unlikely they would be hired to appear in a well-known magazine in a fashion capital. Because so few magazines are located in those cities, editorial work for models in local markets is very limited. (Your agent is your best source for finding out about opportunities for editorial modeling outside the fashion capitals.)

Even for models who do get lucky and are booked to appear in magazines, this is usually just a phase that happens early in their careers. During this period, they're known as editorial models because they're appearing in so many magazine stories. (Some lucky few are known throughout their careers as editorial models.)

If you're appearing in numerous magazines every month, it says to the fashion industry and to the marketplace at large that you're hot, that your beauty has been accepted as the current standard, and that you embody the look of the moment. It also (usually) sets the stage for a successful career overall. When you've appeared in a magazine, the rest of the industry—fashion designers booking runway shows, advertisers, catalogs, as well as other magazines—will also want to use you because magazines establish the standards that others follow.

Model Scoop

I was very lucky in my career and was able to appear in numerous magazine stories. As is typical of many models, I went through a phase in the first 5 years of my career in which I was considered an editorial model. When one magazine started using me, numerous other magazines soon started calling, wanting to book me. The more work I did for French *Elle*, for instance, the more I was in heavy demand by every other fashion magazine. When I had established my presence in magazines, I soon found myself being booked for advertisements, TV commercials, and fashion shows. This "snowball" effect is very characteristic of the career path of successful editorial models.

Why Editorial Is Important for Your Career

Being a successful editorial model benefits all aspects of a model's career. If a model is featured on the covers and in the pages of numerous magazines, her career is made. She will be able to demand the highest day rates and enjoy the incredible perks that go with a high-flying modeling career.

Editorial itself doesn't pay well, but the payoff comes with the exposure and prestige editorial offers because you'll be in demand by all facets of the fashion industry. As a model's visibility in the editorial arena goes up, so does the demand for her services and her day rate for catalog, advertising, and fashion shows. She could even find herself in line for lucrative endorsement deals.

Roshumba's Rules

If you do editorial work, be sure to keep copies of all the stories from the magazines you appear in. You'll want them for your portfolio, and keeping copies is a great way to remember your career. Some models even frame some of their special stories.

Editorial is the best way to build your portfolio when you're just starting out. It's more creative and daring than other types of work, too. You get to experiment with different types of looks and work with the best people in the industry. Editorial work allows you to demonstrate that you have personality and range, that there's something special about you. A portfolio featuring a lot of editorial tear sheets inspires clients, which helps you land more jobs. Catalog pictures, on the other hand, feature more mundane poses and less interesting hair and makeup, and don't show off the model's personality or range in the same way editorial tear sheets do.

This is a good example of an editorial beauty shot I did, as the focus of the photo is on the makeup and skin (as well as the attitude), not the clothes.

(Photo: Charles Tracy)

The Disadvantages of Editorial

Although overall the advantages of editorial far outweigh the disadvantages, a few cons to doing lots of editorial exist as well. The main disadvantage is that it doesn't pay well. You probably can't pay your rent if you're just doing editorial—the day rate averages $300, even for covers. For many young people, $300 may sound like a lot of money, especially if you live at home with your parents and they take care of all your major expenses. But if you live on your own in a fashion capital and are responsible for paying for everything from rent to lightbulbs, $300 is not a lot of money, even if you work every day.

Another disadvantage is that although an editorial model's career is more prominent on the way up, it's also more noticeable when a model is on her way down. Magazines thrive on change, and eventually they'll start booking someone else—the next hot model. You might find your career shifting from a point that you're in constant demand by all the top magazines to not being booked by them at all. You might find yourself forced to accept less prestigious bookings.

Cover Girl: The Pinnacle of a Model's Career

Appearing on a magazine cover is the icing on the cake for a model. It means that out of all the people in the world who could have been selected to sell that magazine, you were the chosen one! Landing a cover is the industry's way of honoring you as a valuable commodity. Unfortunately, because many magazines prefer to feature celebs on covers these days, the opportunities for models to appear on covers are more limited.

The picture on the cover sells the magazine because often people don't have a chance to look inside the magazine or read any of the articles before they buy it. What motivates them to purchase the magazine might be simply the image on the cover.

A model might be chosen to appear on a cover for a number of reasons. Perhaps you're the new It Girl in town and the magazine wants to feature you. Maybe you embody the look or style prevalent at that moment. Or maybe you are so classically beautiful that some editor fell in love with your face and put you on the cover.

Surprisingly, despite their high visibility, covers don't pay well. Usually a model earns the standard editorial rate, $300 a day, and nothing more. But the benefits are far greater than any day rates. A beautiful cover shot for a well-known magazine can give your career a huge boost.

The major drawback of covers is that if you don't look your best on them—if you look out of shape, tired, or in any way less beautiful than normal—it can have a serious negative impact on your career. The cover photo is highly visible; it's not buried inside the magazine where people might flip past it or part of an eight-page story where the impact of one bad photo is mitigated by seven beautiful ones.

Catwalk Talk

Look books are photo albums clothing companies put together so fashion editors, retail buyers, and customers can see all of that season's styles in one place. Look books can be in-store photo albums or printed brochures mailed out to customers. They can also often be found online

The Lucrative World of Catalog and Website Modeling

Modeling for catalogs and websites is one of the most lucrative types of modeling. Clients might include retailers such as J. Crew, Spiegel, and J. Jill, and department stores such as Neiman Marcus, Saks Fifth Avenue, Filene's, and Dillard's. One department store might do a dozen or so different types of catalogs, including those featuring designer, bridge (midprice lines such as DKNY and Marc by Marc Jacobs), and moderate merchandise, as well as ones with seasonal themes, such as Christmas and Mother's Day. Catalog modeling also includes *look books*, such as those published by fashion designers or fashion companies, such as Esprit, Benetton, and Louis Vuitton.

Catalog and website work is not fancy or creative—I like to call it bread-and-butter work. The purpose of a catalog or website is to sell merchandise, and the purpose of a catalog/website shoot is to show the merchandise at its best. The model, photographer, hairstylist, and makeup artist are all chosen for their ability to make the clothes look appealing and desirable.

The Advantages of Catalogs

Catalogs and websites can offer a very lucrative, steady source of work for a model. Many, many catalogs and websites exist. They also pay very high day rates and can offer a way to make a really good living. The day rate averages about $3,500 but can range from $1,000 up to $50,000 for top models. In addition, they're extremely loyal: you can find yourself working for a single catalog steadily for many years if the client likes you and finds that the garments you model sell very well.

Catalogs are not interested in following the latest trend—they don't want to use only the hottest new girls. The models they choose appeal to the average consumer in the mass market, not just to a small clique of fashion-industry professionals.

Building Your Mass Appeal

Catalog work paid a lot of my bills and also kept me exposed in the international marketplace. My catalog work helped build my clientele and appeal in a way that I wasn't able to do through magazines, even though I had a strong editorial presence.

Model Scoop _____

> I've done a lot of catalog and website work and always will. I've probably appeared in every fashion catalog imaginable, including Neiman Marcus, Saks Fifth Avenue, Filene's, Dillard's, Rich's, JCPenney, and Sears. Catalog companies discovered that whatever I put on, even if it was a hot pink muumuu, would sell. It always made me feel good when clients said something like, "That dress you wore in the spring catalog sold out." It let me know that I was doing a good job.

Whenever clients held focus groups, my image always garnered a strong positive response from customers. I found that by appearing in so many catalogs, my appeal to "real" women grew stronger.

In this picture taken for a catalog, I'm posing in a way that lets the viewer see as many details of the clothes as possible.

(Photo: Charles Tracy)

Catalog modeling increased the number of people who knew my face. It helped me relate more to a mass audience and taught me how to appeal to them. It kept me grounded because I was modeling for real people. And that experience definitely helped me in the next stages of my career. Even when people see me on TV, they always say, "She's so human," and I know that comes from my doing so much catalog modeling. Part of that is because most catalog clothes are real clothes for real women, not size-0 garments only fashionistas and a few celebrities will be wearing.

Keep It On or Take It Off?

Nude modeling is a very sensitive subject. Every individual has her own opinion on what's tasteful, what's vulgar, and what's immoral when it comes to nudity. In the United States, nude modeling is generally considered to be kind of taboo. In Europe, however, the nude human body is considered beautiful, and no one blinks an eye when models appear topless in tasteful magazines, advertisements, and TV commercials.

In ads for body lotions, breast creams, or cellulite treatment, the model may even be completely naked.

If you decide you don't want to model nude, that's absolutely fine. Industry professionals will understand and respect your decision.

If you do decide you want to model nude, that's fine, too. But be very careful about the jobs you accept. Artistic nudes are most acceptable—beautiful, aesthetically pleasing photos that evoke a mood and explore the body's form and line. Most often, these types of photos appear in a women's magazine or advertisement, in an art magazine, or in a photography book or exhibit, more often in Europe.

Also acceptable is nude work for a tasteful men's magazine such as *Playboy*, which is considered more respectable than most of the other men's magazines. Although the models are baring all, they're not shown in a vulgar, exploitative way. *Playboy* also has a history of featuring legitimate models and celebrities in its pages, including Sharon Stone, Carmen Electra, Cindy Crawford, and Elle Macpherson. It's considered the "okay" naughty magazine.

Nude modeling has several advantages: it shows the world that you have a perfect, beautiful body. Doing a feature in a magazine such as *Playboy* can help launch your career in a different direction and lead to high-end gigs for quality clients such as Victoria's Secret.

> **Reality Check**
>
> If you cross the line into the world of actual *pornography*, you'll no longer be looked at as a high-quality, marketable model, and you might find yourself unable to book other types of jobs.

Nude modeling shoots are somewhat different from ordinary ones. Usually, there's a closed set, meaning access to the area where shooting is taking place is strictly limited. The only people who are permitted are those directly involved—the photographer, client, hairstylist, makeup artist. (You can request that only the photographer be present, and that wish will usually be honored.) Also special care is taken to cover you up between shots.

If an opportunity to do a nude photo shoot arises, talk it over with your agent and family to decide if it's something that will benefit—or hamper—your career.

Runway Modeling: Are You Ready to Work It?

You've no doubt seen footage on TV of models strutting up and down a long, narrow stage (called the runway or catwalk) dressed in the newest fashions. Runway shows enable fashion designers to present their latest creations to the press, buyers from clothing stores, and individual customers. For these fashion shows, the designers hire a squadron of models to wear the clothes and present them on the runway for all to see.

At a traditional runway show, the models walk up and down a narrow stage that juts out into the audience.

Other types of fashion shows hire models as well, including local events at malls and stores around the country. These shows are known as *consumer fashion shows*. These shows give local shoppers an idea of the newest design trends and styles; hopefully, the audience will then buy the fashions they see on the runway. Generally, local models are booked for these shows.

When it comes to designer fashion shows, there are three different categories of shows, each featuring a different type of garment:

◆ Haute couture

◆ Ready-to-wear

◆ Resort wear

Haute couture clothes are ultraexpensive clothes custom-made to fit the few women wealthy enough to afford them. They are made of the most expensive, luxurious fabrics, with exquisite details and hand-sewn seams. Unlike couture garments, which are custom-made to fit the client, ready-to-wear clothes are mass-produced in standard sizes. All the clothes you see at the local mall fall into the ready-to-wear category. Resort wear is casual clothing traditionally worn at resorts in warm-weather climates by people escaping cold winters. It includes T-shirts, shorts, skirts, jackets, and swimwear and sports-specific garments (for tennis, golf, and sailing).

The Exclusive World of Haute Couture

Haute couture shows (called *alta moda* in Italy) are the most exclusive and prestigious of all runway shows. They take place in Milan and Paris twice a year. Customers attend a show and then order the garments they want. Couture clients are a very elite group, including movie stars, millionaires, and royalty.

Designers' couture collections focus mainly on evening wear but also include dresses and suits for day. Couture garments start at around $10,000 and can cost up to $500,000, such as the diamond-encrusted wedding dress Christian LaCroix designed for the wife of a sheik. Because few customers buy these types of clothes, and because presenting a couture collection is expensive, only a few design houses do couture, including Armani, Chanel, Christian Dior, Jean Paul Gaultier, Christian LaCroix, and Valentino.

This glamorous ballgown is a classic example of a haute-couture garment.

The High Style of Ready-to-Wear Shows

Ready-to-wear (known in Europe as *prêt-à-porter*) is the largest category of fashion shows. Ready-to-wear includes most types of clothes: shirts, sweaters, jackets, pants, skirts, shorts, suits, dresses, evening wear (fancy dresses, gowns, cocktail dresses), and coats.

Ready-to-wear shows take place twice a year in Milan, Paris, and New York, as well as in secondary markets, such as Germany, Spain, England, and Japan.

This stylish tailored suit is typical of ready-to-wear clothing.

Resort Wear

The third category of garments shown in designer runway shows is *resort wear*. This smaller category features clothing made for warm weather and transitional times of the year. The emphasis is on leisure and casual wear, such as shorts, T-shirts, casual sweaters, jackets, sundresses, and bathing suits. Resort shows are presented mostly in New York but also in some secondary markets.

Tennis, anyone? This sporty outfit is characteristic of resort wear.

Walking the Runway to Fame: The Pros of Runway Modeling

Appearing in a designer runway show is great exposure, whether you're a novice or an established supermodel. All the fashion industry heavy-hitters go to runway shows. They take note of which models are participating because it's a barometer of who's hot at that moment. Many new models' careers have been launched on the runway.

Runway work is also fun because of all the excitement surrounding the *collections* every season. The backstage area is abuzz with a celebratory atmosphere, and you meet a lot of new people there. Special celebrations, such as parties and club openings, are often scheduled around runway shows because all the important people in the fashion industry will be in town.

Models are paid for fittings, rehearsals, and fashion shows or on an hourly basis. Or a flat fee may be negotiated for the model's time. Doing fashion shows in the Milan, Paris, and New York pays well, although the amount varies according to how famous

Catwalk Talk

Collections refers to the collective showing of designers' new fashions in one particular city. The New York collections take place when all the top New York designers show their latest designs for the season.

the model is and who the designer is. Famous designers pay more than lesser-known ones—a top designer might pay a name model up to $20,000 to appear in his show, while some of the models in the Victoria's Secret runway show, for instance, can earn up to $30,000 for a show that lasts less than 30 minutes! Of course, even in the fashion capitals, most models make a lot less than this. A few thousand dollars is more the norm. But if you do many shows within a short period of time, you can end up really making a lot of money doing runway shows.

Even if you're just appearing in a hobby modeling show in the local mall for which you're not being paid, runway modeling is fun. (For more information on runway opportunities for hobby models, see Chapter 8.)

The Fast Track to Exhaustion: The Cons of Runway Modeling

Fashion shows are extremely draining. Every fashion show you do could involve one or more go and sees, up to three fittings, one or more rehearsals, plus the actual show. Even if you're not doing that many shows, you could work more hours than you would the rest of the year. Doing the collections can be so overwhelming that a lot of models get run down physically as well as emotionally. Their skin breaks out, their hair gets fried from being styled so many times, and they get completely exhausted.

One season in my second year of modeling, I did 32 shows in 5 days in Paris. It was great, but to this day, I still cannot believe I managed it. I was doing up to five shows a day, plus fittings, rehearsals, and go and sees. Then I had to repeat the process in New York and Milan.

Runway Shows A to Z

The grueling process of go and sees or castings (as they're called in Europe) for designer runway shows in the fashion capitals generally starts about 10 days to 2 weeks before the shows take place. You often feel like herded cattle at these because so many models are there. During runway season, you could do up to 15 go and sees a day. Often 50 girls are ahead of you, also waiting to be seen. Some of them are dismissed outright because they're just not right for that particular designer. Others are invited in to walk, show their books, maybe try on a few outfits, and meet with the designer. This can take from 20 to 30 minutes per model.

These days, the models who are most likely to get booked for a runway show are those editorial models who have appeared in the pages of *Vogue, Harper's Bazaar,* and *Elle* (although some designers will take a chance on a newcomer).

After the go and see/casting, if a client is interested in you, he or she will call your agent to book you. Then you'll be scheduled to go in for a fitting, which is when all the garments you'll be wearing in the show are altered to fit your body. For ready-to-wear clothes, there's usually just one fitting session. For couture, there may be up to three because the garment is custom-fit to your body.

A fitting can last from $1/2$ hour to 3 hours, depending on how many garments you'll be wearing in the show, how complicated the designs are, and what design problems arise with the clothes. Elaborate designs, such as evening dresses with details like feathers, lace, or embroidery, take longer to fit.

Model Scoop

The average number of garments a single model might wear in a ready-to-wear show is five. The most I've ever seen a model wear—and the most I've ever worn—is 10 outfits.

Couture requires more fittings because the designer must first make a facsimile of the garment in muslin, an inexpensive white cotton fabric. At the first appointment, you try on the muslin so it can be fitted to your body. The muslin is then used as a pattern for the actual garment. At the final fitting, any last-minute adjustments are made to the actual garment, and any necessary accessories—shoes, belts, shawls, capes—are added.

Dress Rehearsals

In addition to fittings, fashion shows generally involve at least one rehearsal, which can take place a day or two before the show or even the morning of the show if it's scheduled in the evening.

At a rehearsal, you'll usually run through the whole show once, albeit with a lot of stops and starts. Any kinks are worked out so everything flows smoothly. Generally, rehearsals can take about an hour, though sometimes they can take up to 2 hours.

It's kind of an unspoken rule that supermodels don't have to attend fashion show rehearsals. Designers know these women are professionals who already know what they're doing—and that likely they're frantically busy with all the other shows they're in, too.

It's Show Time!

Often designers request that you arrive 2 to 3 hours before the show starts to get your hair and makeup done and to get dressed. That way, there's time to be sure everything is perfect—the lost earring can be found, the broken high heel can be mended, the unfinished seam can be sewn.

At the rehearsal, each model is given a clothing rack where all the clothes she'll be wearing in the show are hanging. That way, everything is in one place (including shoes, jewelry, or any other accessories) so she can change quickly. Each model also has her own dresser to help her get out of one garment and into the next. Dressers are people who work at the designer's company, students from a design college, interns who are trying to get into the industry, or professional dressers.

As you've probably seen on various TV shows, backstage at a fashion show is a frenzy of activity. The hair and makeup team, which could number up to 16, are working. Champagne and a buffet table are laid out, and everyone is welcome to something to eat or drink. Models are sitting around chatting or getting their hair and makeup done. People from the design team are making last-minute alterations. TV cameras and TV, newspaper, and magazine journalists are interviewing the designer and the models.

About 15 minutes before the show begins, the models get dressed in the first outfit they're going to wear. The designer makes final adjustments to the clothes, the hair and makeup artists check all the models to be sure everything looks perfect, and the choreographer reminds them one last time about any special things they may need to remember.

All the models line up, the music starts, and the *featured model* walks out in the first outfit, followed down the runway by all the other models.

When you've walked the runway and returned backstage, you have to *run* to your rack because you may have only $1^1/_2$ to 3 minutes to change your outfit, shoes, stockings, accessories, and whatever else goes with it and then look perfect and get back out on the runway. Your dresser will help you slip out of one

> **Roshumba's Rules**
>
> Despite the crazed atmosphere backstage at a fashion show, it's best to stay calm and not get caught up in the craziness. Read a book, listen to music, or chat with friends. This enables you to remain professional and focus on doing a great job.

> **Catwalk Talk**
>
> The **featured model** may be the designer's favorite celeb or a famous supermodel. She's usually the first or the last one to appear, and at the end of the show, she walks down the runway with the designer.

outfit and into the next. When you're dressed, you dash past the fashion designer and the hair and makeup team, who may make quick adjustments or give you little tips.

If you do ever trip mid-catwalk, just pick yourself up with as much grace as possible and continue down the runway. Don't worry, it happens to even the biggest super-model: Naomi Campbell is famous for taking a spill while wearing platforms in a Vivienne Westwood show.

Model Scoop

One of the most outstanding runway models of all time was Pat Cleveland, an African American model who appeared in every major fashion show in every city—Milan, Paris, and New York—for years during the 1960s and 1970s. At that time, the models in fashion shows moved in a more dramatic, theatrical way, not the straightforward, simple moves common in today's shows. Even among the models of her time, Pat moved in a beautifully fluid way that made clothes look their best.

Fashion shows generally last about a half hour, and at the end, all the models file out onto the runway, where the featured model appears on the arm of the designer, who takes a bow.

After the show, models may dash out if they have another show to do, or they may stick around for the post-show celebration. Usually, champagne and hors d'oeuvres are served, and throngs of well-wishers and journalists crowd backstage to congratulate the designer on the collection.

Reality Check

It often happens that you absolutely fall in love with something you wear in a fashion show. But never just take something. For one, it's stealing, and for another, the designer might need it for a photo shoot or to show to store buyers in the showroom. One famous model swiped a pair of shoes from a show, and the incident was reported in the tabloids. If you want something, ask your dresser or the designer if there's any way you can get it.

Beyond the Runway

In addition to fashion shows, several other types of modeling come under the category of "runway," including fit modeling, in-store modeling, and trunk-show modeling.

Sizing Up Fit Models

Fit models work closely with the fashion designer, trying on all the garments so they can be adjusted and fitted correctly.

The first type of model is the sample model. A sample model must be a perfect size 6. Although she generally won't appear in the designer's fashion show, all the garments the other models in a designer's runway show wear are fit on her. Sample models usually work for several designers, and in the weeks leading up to the collections, they can be frantically busy.

After the show has taken place, another fitting is done, which is called the duplicate fitting. At a duplicate fitting, all the size 6 garments worn in the fashion show are resized and remade into a size 8. The duplicate model must be a perfect size 8 because the size 6 garment will be remade to fit her body. This is necessary for the manufacturing process because this duplicate sample serves as the standard from which all the other sizes are made.

Showroom models work in the designer or manufacturer's showroom, modeling the garments for visiting clients such as department store buyers so they can see how the clothes look on the body.

Sample, duplicate, and showroom models don't gain the fame and recognition other models do, but their careers last much longer than other models'—some work up to the ages of 35 or 40. And although the rates they earn aren't that high, they get a lot of work, so this can be a very lucrative type of modeling.

This is an area where size, shape, and proportion are more important than anything else, however sample models must have a perfect size-6 body, and duplicate models must be a perfect size 8. They must keep their bodies in perfect shape and cannot gain or lose weight.

In-Store Modeling

With in-store modeling (also called informal modeling), the models are dressed in the clothes from the store and walk around to let the customers see the clothes up close as they shop. Hobby model, as well as models in secondary and local markets and the fashion capitals, handle most of the in-store modeling. In fact, one of my first jobs was doing in-store modeling at a boutique in Peoria, Illinois.

In-store modeling is a great way for hobby models to get experience. It's also great if you're the type of model who enjoys meeting people. The pay scale depends on the caliber and location of the store and can range from nothing to several hundred dollars.

Trunk-Show Modeling

Trunk shows allow designers to take their designs directly to consumers all over the country. For instance, a department store might invite designer Michael Kors to do a trunk show. He'd bring his newest collection to the store to do a fashion show. Locally hired models would try on the clothes for the customers, who can then try them on themselves when the show is over. Trunk shows tend to be informal, as opposed to grand, staged presentations.

Trunk-show modeling opportunities are available in all large, many medium, and some small markets. Sometimes the designer attends personally; other times a member of the design team or some other company employee attends, depending on the size of the market and how important that market is to the company.

The pay scale for trunk-show modeling is generally middle of the road—approximately several hundred dollars per day.

It's fortunate that trunk-show modeling is available in almost all areas of the country, as well as in the fashion capitals, because it really is one of the most fun and most exciting types of modeling.

The Least You Need to Know

- ◆ Modeling for magazines is the most prestigious type of modeling, and models who are lucky enough to do it end up having the most successful careers.

- ◆ Modeling for catalogs can be a lucrative and steady (if less than thrilling) source of work.

- ◆ Nude modeling offers advantages, but it is a very personal choice.

- ◆ Designer runway shows come in three categories: haute couture, ready-to-wear, and resort. A different type of clothing is shown at each one.

- ◆ Fit models are a specialized category of runway models; this can be a lucrative specialty for a model with a perfect size 6 or size 8 body.

- ◆ Trunk shows and in-store modeling take place all over the country and offer great opportunities for live modeling.

Chapter 19

Advertisements, Endorsements, and TV Commercials

In This Chapter

- Modeling in print advertisements
- Landing an endorsement deal
- Lights, camera, action: modeling in TV commercials

Advertisements, endorsements, and TV commercials are some of the most lucrative jobs a model can land. Although you can make a lot of money working for catalogs and doing fashion shows, modeling for advertisements, endorsements, and TV commercials enables you to make money in a much shorter period of time. In addition, it can help you extend and broaden your career by introducing you to new, large audiences and showing you in a whole different light to clients.

In this chapter, I explain how modeling for advertisements, endorsements, and TV commercials works. I also tell you the types of models who get booked for them and how you can maximize your chances to cash in on these great opportunities.

Modeling for Advertisements

Doing advertisements is extremely important to your career because it says—not only to the fashion industry, but to all of corporate America—that you are a marketable product, that you have the power to inspire people to buy the products you represent. Ads represent a whole level of power different from editorial work. You may appear in fashion magazines because you embody the hot new look, but that says nothing about your marketability, your ability to sell things.

Doing advertisements can take your career into the realm of being a viable, marketable product. It can give your career longevity because clients realize you're not just the flavor of the month, but a force to be reckoned with.

> **Model Scoop**
>
> Advertisements took me from being an exciting, exotic fashion girl into being a viable, marketable product. Major corporations put time, energy, and money into me because they believed I could sell products. Over the years, I've done tons of ads for clients such as Oil of Olay, Maybelline, The Gap, Anne Klein, Benetton, Esprit, Yves Saint Laurent, Paco Rabonne, Samsung, Sprite, and Hanes.

If your face and image can sell an everyday product like a bar of soap, that's an incredible talent. If you're smart and your agent is smart, you could really rack up substantial sums doing ads for a variety of clients.

> **Catwalk Talk**
>
> **Conflict of interest** is when a model appears in two advertisements for similar products, thus undermining her ability to sell either one. An example is a model who appears in cosmetic ads for both Revlon and Maybelline ads.

Advertising work includes print ads (TV commercials are covered separately, later in this chapter) that will appear in magazines, in newspapers, on billboards, and/or in brochures. The contract with the client specifies the amount of time the ad can run (3 months is common) and in what format (such as magazine ads and billboards, among others). If the client wants to use the ad for a longer period of time or in any other format, they have to pay an additional fee.

It's rare that one model will be booked to appear in ads for more than one company that makes the same product. Once you've done an ad for Colgate, for example, it's extremely unlikely you'll be hired to do an ad for Crest because it's seen as a *conflict of interest*. Often, in fact, the contract will state that during the term of the contract, you can't appear in ads for a similar product. You can, however, do ads for different products, even if they're running simultaneously.

The Types of Models Who Get Ad Work

Models who land advertisement bookings often have physical attributes that relate to the product. This is particularly true of beauty ads, which include advertisements for hair- and skin-care products and makeup. If it's a body cream, the model will have beautiful, flawless skin, without any bruises or scratches or tattoos. If it's a hair ad, she'll have healthy, beautiful hair. For fashion ads, on the other hand, designers usually select a celeb or model who is either the It Girl of the moment or one who embodies what's happening in fashion, depending on what look the designer is trying to sell that season. Other times, especially in smaller markets, the advertiser will choose a model whose look appeals to local consumers.

Real-people models are also often chosen to appear in advertisements. For more information, see Chapter 20.

Getting Booked for an Advertisement

Like all other modeling jobs, advertising jobs start with a go and see set up by your agent. Before you go, your agent will tell you what it's for and the terms of the contract—for instance, that they'll want you to be exclusive to them for 3 months, meaning you won't be able to appear in an ad for one of the client's competitors during that period.

The go and see is similar to any other one (see Chapter 14 for more information); you want to arrive on time and be as friendly and personable as possible. Depending on who the advertiser is, you should dress as simply as possible, in jeans and a T-shirt or sweater. If it's an ad for a fashion designer, you could wear something more fashion-forward (although it's by no means necessary). If it's for an advertisement that involves a body-conscious product, the client might ask you to wear a bathing suit underneath your street clothes so they can get a good look at your figure. They'll also probably take a Polaroid of you in the bathing suit.

If the client decides they want to book you for the ad, they will call your agent and state the terms of the contract—the amount you'll be paid, the time period in which the ad will run, and the format of the ad.

Clients may request that you wear a two-piece bathing suit such as this one underneath your clothes when you go on castings for some advertisement jobs so they can see your body.

(Photographer: Kwame Brathwaite; model: Laura McLafferty)

Reality Check

When you're asked to wear a bathing suit on a go and see, don't wear a suit that will get more attention than you. Your best bet is a solid-color, two-piece suit. Avoid thongs and patterns, which are too distracting. Wearing a bra and panty instead of a suit is too intimate and, therefore, not appropriate. A one-piece, on the other hand, hides too much.

The major reason you would turn down the job is if the money isn't good enough, especially if it's early in your career. Often once you appear in an ad for one product, even if it's just for a short period, more likely than not you'll never be hired to represent a competitive product. For instance, if you do a shampoo ad in the first or second year of your career, for the next 8 or so years you're working as a model, there's a strong possibility that you'll never represent another shampoo product again. You and your agent need to decide if the money being offered is ample compensation.

Another reason you might decide against doing an advertisement is if it's for a product that's not considered high-end or reputable, such as cigarettes or a feminine hygiene product. Once you do an ad for a product like that, it says to the industry that you couldn't get anything better, and it's unlikely you'll be considered for more prestigious jobs (ads for cosmetics or clothing, for instance) in the future.

Modeling for an advertising job can be very creative work, although other times it can be very tedious; it all depends on the individual job. You may be shooting only one or two clothing changes (as opposed to doing 12 different "looks" when you're doing a catalog shoot), but you could find yourself in the uncomfortable position of hanging off the Eiffel Tower for the whole day so the photographer can get the shot he wants. I once did a job for a body-wash advertisement in which I had to pose for 3 hours in a "waterfall" constructed in the studio.

Reality Check

In general, try not to do ads for products that will end up limiting your career. This means steering clear of feminine hygiene, cigarette, and alcohol ads, which are all considered down-market advertisements.

Generally, though, advertisers pamper the model and treat her well. They often provide a car service to and from the location, and they have nice catered lunches. The whole day is about you. They want to make you feel your best so that good feeling will be reflected in the ad and (hopefully) in sales.

Endorsements: A Model's Stamp of Approval

To land an endorsement is to hit the lottery. With an endorsement, a company signs you on to represent its products and the company for a relatively long period of time for a sizable amount of money. For example, L'Oréal might hire you to endorse its hair-care, makeup, and skin-care products for 3 years at a rate of $1 million a year. But you might be required to work only a relatively few number of days—20, perhaps—to earn that money. Granted, only a few models—less than 1 percent—ever land endorsement deals, but it can happen!

When a company signs a model to do an endorsement, it's not just thinking about how pretty she is. It's thinking about how she will affect the bottom line. Will sales increase? Will customer numbers increase? Will the stock price go up? It's not just about being fun and fabulous on the cover of *Seventeen*; it's a whole other level.

Although celebrities are being used more and more often, occasionally a model will get lucky. Landing an endorsement deal means that not only are you considered to have an extremely valuable, desirable image, but you are also an integral part of a major corporation. An endorsement deal means that your image is pleasing to people and that you have what it takes to be the face and voice of a major corporation (which is why these models are often called spokesmodels). Showing your image is how the company communicates its message to the public. You have the power to affect the value of the company's stock on the stock markets, and that, in turn, can affect millions of people.

Some models and celebrities who've landed endorsement deals include the following:

- Christie Brinkley (Cover Girl—for 3 decades!)
- Halle Berry (Revlon)
- Gisele Bündchen (Victoria's Secret)
- Carolyn Murphy (Estée Lauder)
- Beyoncé (L'Oréal)
- Liya Kebede (Estée Lauder)
- Adriana Lima (Maybelline and Victoria's Secret)
- Catherine Zeta-Jones (T-Mobile and Elizabeth Arden)

One of the reasons models and celebs make so much money when they endorse products is because usually the biggest names land endorsement deals, and they can command sky-high dollars. Also, an endorsement is considered an exclusive deal, meaning the model or celeb cannot represent competitive products. Someone with a Revlon deal can't represent Estée Lauder, for instance, because they're both cosmetic companies.

If a model or celebrity has more than one endorsement deal, each product she represents must be in a different category, as well as equally reputable. For instance, if a model is representing Maybelline, you won't see her doing feminine-hygiene endorsements, which are considered less respectable. She can, however, endorse a brand of high-end cell phones or a well-known clothing company because none of these businesses competes with the other and all are considered high-end products with the same level of appeal.

An endorsement contract can prohibit a model from representing a less reputable product because when a model endorses a product, she represents both the product and the image of the company. She's the spokesperson. And a blue-chip company doesn't want its spokesmodel appearing on a late-night TV ad hawking miracle knives or pocket fishing gear because it reflects badly on the company.

Endorsement deals also have clauses that govern personal conduct because your behavior is a reflection on the company. If you're the spokesperson for a major cosmetic company, and you lose your temper with your assistant and throw a bottle of perfume at her, and the story winds up in the tabloids, that makes you look bad. It also makes the company you represent look bad.

Also, during the term of the endorsement deal, your contract might specify that you can wear only the clothes of the designer you're endorsing (if it's a fashion company) or the makeup of the company that signed you (if it's a cosmetic company). These are minor restrictions, but you should be aware of them.

Model Scoop

I was the spokesperson for Clairol Balsam Color for 3 years, appearing in all their ads during that time. After I had worked with them for a while, they found that I could do more than just pose, that I could hold my own in business situations. Because I could discuss the product intelligently, I was asked to represent Balsam Color in interviews with the press. They also asked me to make appearances on their behalf at the *Essence* awards (an award show sponsored by *Essence* magazine honoring people in the entertainment industry), in-house business meetings, and charity events. For me, what was even more important than the money I made was the wonderful opportunity it offered me to represent a major corporation and become accustomed to being a spokesperson.

If you want to land a major endorsement deal, you need to keep your reputation clean from the moment you start working as a model. You don't want to be known as the girl who parties too hard, who's impossible to work with, or who's always having public spats with her boyfriend because that sort of behavior is a red light to major corporations handing out endorsement deals, no matter how beautiful you are.

Although the advantages far outweigh the disadvantages, there's a downside to doing endorsements. When a model lands an endorsement deal, she's the hottest model in town because she's endorsing a major company and making a lot of money. Many other models (and people in general) will be saying to themselves, "I wish I had her job."

Roshumba's Rules

If you have an endorsement deal, try to keep your image fresh by keeping up your editorial work and adding more things to your life, such as preparing for a career after modeling or going back to school.

But when the endorsement deal expires, she could be thought of as old news. For the rest of her career, she could be known as the *old* DKNY model or the *old* Estée Lauder model. By that point, many models have been in the business a long time and are ready to retire. But if not, it can be hard getting clients to think about her in any other terms than as the former spokesmodel for some other company.

On Camera: Modeling for TV Commercials

TV commercials offer you a way to reach a much broader audience and become more recognizable than with magazine work or even print advertisements. People have to go out and buy a magazine to see you, but TV requires no effort from consumers—they don't even have to turn the page—and you're being exposed to a much broader audience.

With TV commercials, you're being seen in a whole different medium. You're coming across live and in full color into people's living rooms, which gives consumers a chance to see your personality in a way that's not captured in a still ad. This could help you land other clients, too, when they see how well you can project in a TV ad.

In addition, TV commercials pay very well because you might also earn *residuals* every time the commercial runs during a set period of time, as well a fee for your modeling services. (Your agent negotiates the rate.) If the client decides to rerun the commercial after the initial cycle, if they use it outside the United States, or if they use it in another medium (for example, on the Internet), they have to pay you additional sums.

Catwalk Talk

A **residual** is a payment an actor or model receives every time the commercial she appears in is broadcast. For a national commercial that gets heavy play, this could be a significant amount of money.

When it comes to TV commercials, you can't really predict who's going to be selected to represent what. TV is a medium that's very different from print ads. Clients try to pick people who are extremely consumer-friendly, whom customers will like, and to whom customers can relate. Some models are more appealing on TV than in print ads.

It's also essential that the viewer believes the model really uses the product. If a size-0 model is selected to star in a Jell-O pudding commercial, no one will believe she eats pudding. Or if a 15-year-old model is cast as the mom of three, it won't create a believable image. When it comes to TV commercials, it's all about believability. This is why when you go to a *casting* for a TV commercial, the client will ask you a lot more questions than you'll be asked on other go and sees, such as "Do you like pudding? Did your mom make Jell-O?" The camera will pick up on any credibility gaps.

Because there are so many different types of products, all sorts of models, as well as actors and real people, can find themselves cast in TV commercials. Not only are they booked to sell clothes, cosmetics, and accessories, but they're also used to sell other consumer products, from cars to soap. You can get the quirky young woman selling Diet Coke, the wholesome teenager selling Noxema, or the androgynous model selling Lee Jeans.

Your regular agent probably won't be handling your television commercial bookings. Although some agencies have in-house TV commercial departments that handle TV commercial bookings for all the models in the agency, most have an agreement with an outside company that handles TV work for all the agency's models. You will probably find yourself being sent out on TV commercial auditions from the time you sign with the agency. Usually when a casting director calls the agency looking for *talent*, she may say something like, "I'm looking for a redhead with long hair with a country-girl sort of look." If the agency just signed a brand-new 13-year-old redhead, she will be sent to the casting, along with any older, more experienced redheaded models.

> **Catwalk Talk**
>
> **Casting** is the television industry's term for auditions for television commercials. Usually, you'll meet first with the casting director, who narrows down the number of possible candidates for the client, who will probably want to meet you before booking you.

> **Catwalk Talk**
>
> The models, actors, or other performers working at a still photo shoot, on a TV commercial or movie set, or at a live performance are called the **talent**.

The ABCs of TV Commercial Castings

Castings for TV commercials are quite different from other go and sees. First of all, you usually don't need to take your book. You will need to bring your composite, though. At the first meeting, you'll usually meet with the casting director and the assistant. They'll ask you to stand in front of a video camera so they can tape you, to see how you look on a live camera. You might be asked to walk around. They might film your body from the left, from the right, and straight on, and then do close-ups of your face from every direction.

If the commercial includes dialogue, you might be asked to read it. They might also ask you to do something completely strange, such as pretend you're eating the most delicious piece of chocolate cake or imagine you're on a desert island. You'll need to try to act that out, even if it makes you feel pretty stupid. What's even more disconcerting is that generally, you often get no feedback whatsoever from the client.

TV commercial auditions can be very embarrassing and uncomfortable. My only advice for getting through them is to try to remember we've all been there and try not to freak out too much. Instead, try to be yourself and enjoy the moment. Hopefully, you'll learn something new, such as which angles best suit your body and facial expressions on a live camera.

Shooting a TV commercial can take anywhere from 1 day to 2 weeks, depending on the concept, product, location, and what's needed from the model. TV commercials can be filmed in a studio or on location, such as a big house, a beach, or a restaurant. The setup of a TV-commercial shoot is a lot more complicated than the setup of a still-photography shoot because the cameras move.

Also usually a lot more people are involved in a TV shoot. In addition to the commercial's director, who usually worked with the advertising agency to come up with the concept, the camera operator and one or two of his assistants are there. Numerous union workers set up the lights and cameras and do whatever else is necessary to create the set and keep it running smoothly. The hairstylist, makeup artist, clothing stylist, and all their assistants are present. The clients themselves will be there, along with the art director and other personnel from the ad agency. Craft service employees will be there to provide the food for everyone.

TV commercial shoots are much more structured and time-conscious than print photo shoots. Everyone is on the clock, and if the shoot goes into overtime, the budget can quickly skyrocket.

TV commercials challenge you to express and sell yourself in a totally different way. On your first few shoots, your best bet is to talk to the director, the camera person, and the art director to get a better understanding of what they're looking for, what image they're trying to project, and what they want from you. Keep asking questions throughout the shoot to be sure you're giving them what they need.

Roshumba's Rules

If you're working on a TV commercial, find out when you're needed on the set and be sure you're dressed and ready in time. Schedule your personal phone calls and snacks around the shoot. The cost of shooting a TV commercial is so high, you don't want to do anything to cause a delay.

The Downside of Commercials

TV commercials require exclusivity from the model, meaning that if you're doing a TV commercial for one product and somebody wants to book you to represent a similar product, you won't be able to do it, even if they want to pay you more.

Also the actual work of filming a TV commercial can be very draining. It often requires much more energy than other types of modeling work, and you might be required to do a lot of things you're not used to. Because the technical aspects of filming are so complicated, many more logistical problems tend to arise, which can make shoots more of a headache.

Even with these few cons, whenever you have a chance to appear in an advertisement or TV commercial, or are asked to endorse a product, congratulations! This is a sign the industry highly values your beauty and marketability.

The Least You Need to Know

- ◆ Modeling in print advertisements can pay well and offer a way for a model to develop her mass-market appeal.

- ◆ Landing an endorsement deal is as lucrative—and as rare—as winning the lottery.

- ◆ TV commercials are a good way to learn how to work in front of a live camera and can be quite profitable.

Chapter 20

Specialty and Real-People Models

In This Chapter

- ◆ Big is beautiful: plus-size models
- ◆ Beauty over 35: elegant models
- ◆ Opportunities for men and children
- ◆ Work for parts and real-people models

In addition to the Gisele Bündchens, Heidi Klums, and Elle Macphersons of the world, many other beautiful models come in all sorts of sizes, shapes, sexes, and ages. There are beautiful size-14 plus-size models, exquisite over-35 models, gorgeous male models, and adorable child models.

Models who don't meet the stringent requirements for fashion models outlined in Chapter 3 fall into the category of "real-people" models. Although there are fewer opportunities for these types of models than for fashion models, they still exist. One major source of work for real-people models is parts modeling, in which just one part (hands, legs, or feet) appears in the photographs. The second major source is character modeling, in which models portray real people (young moms, concerned pharmacists, grandfathers, and so on).

In this chapter, I discuss the types of work each of these models does, the qualifications to get involved, and how you can get started in the exciting world of specialty and real-people modeling.

Big and Beautiful Plus-Size Models

The market for plus-size models (generally defined as models who wear a size 12 and up) has boomed in the last decade, mainly because the fashion industry has finally realized that the average American woman wears a size 14 and cannot relate to super-skinny regular models. Plus-size models are booked to model the same type of clothes regular fashion models model, including lingerie, bathing suits, sportswear, and evening dresses. They appear in magazines, catalogs, runway shows, and advertisements.

Plus-size models are larger than regular models, but they're healthy, tall (between 5'8" and 5'10"), toned, and well proportioned. They may be large-boned, with broad shoulders, full hips, full breasts, and maybe a bit of a tummy. They may wear a woman's size 12 to 20 (but most wear 14 to 16).

Plus-size model Natalie Laughlin strikes a sexy pose.

(Photo: Fadil Berisha)

Plus-size models come in all types, including Classic Beauty, Athletic Girl Next Door, Oddball, and Exotic.

Plus-size models do a lot of catalog work, and they have a growing presence in television commercials and commercial print (advertisements).

In New York, Wilhelmina, Click, and Ford all have plus-size divisions. In local and secondary markets, most agencies aren't large enough to have a separate division for plus-size models, so they're handled by an agency's regular bookers.

"New York is where most plus-size models work," explains plus-size model Natalie Laughlin. "But before they come to New York, most work in smaller markets, such as Miami, Atlanta, Chicago, Seattle, Toronto, and L.A., to build their books. But you have to be patient—it doesn't happen overnight.

"For any model, especially a plus-size model, testing is really important," advises Laughlin. "Test constantly for your book. Unfortunately, you usually have to spend some of your own money because photographers don't want to test with you, because they don't want to show plus-size models in their book (although that's changing). But by testing, you can find that freedom within yourself to move. A lot of plus-size models, when they start out, are inhibited by their bodies, and they feel uncomfortable moving. When you are in front of the camera (whether it be for a job or for a test), create an idea in your mind of the attitude you want to project—this may come out of a made-up story or emotional relationships.

"Staying in shape is also important," she says. "Being a plus-size model doesn't mean you're not in shape. It's really important to exercise. You have to eat right, drink lots of water, and get enough sleep."

Because there's no uniform size for plus-size models, plus-size models sometimes wear padding (breast pads, hip pads), explains Laughlin. "So if the clothes don't fit on your body correctly, you use the pads to fill you out."

In general, there aren't open calls and model searches for plus-size models looking for agents, but there are exceptions: *America's Next Top Model* has featured plus-size contestants, and *Mo'Nique's Fat Chance* was a modeling contest for plus-size women. To find an agent, an aspiring plus-size model's best bet is to e-mail photos of herself to agencies that handle plus-size models. (See Chapter 6 for information on taking snapshots, and Chapter 7 for information on sending them to agencies.)

The Elegant Department

Elegant models—fashion models over 35—have become very popular over the last few years. As baby boomers have aged, advertisers and fashion designers have moved toward using models who appeal to this huge group of consumers and have found that 50-year-olds just don't identify with 14-year-old models. Therefore, a whole new category of models 35 and over has emerged.

Elegant models have a range of clients, including runway, advertising, and editorial. Most of their work, however, is modeling for catalogs. Catalogs use older models because they need to appeal to a variety of people, and they're not so trend-driven. Elegant models may also appear in specialty ads for designers who are trying to draw people of all ages. In addition, they may do product endorsements, especially for cosmetic products such as wrinkle creams geared toward older consumers.

> **Catwalk Talk**
>
> An **elegant model** (also known as a *classic model*) is a model or celebrity who's over the age of 35. Elegant models can be famous actresses or former "regular" models who have returned to the business. Some of the most popular include Christie Brinkley, Susan Sarandon, Elizabeth Hurley, and Julianne Moore.

Elegant model Dianne DeWitt is living proof that models are beautiful at any age.

(Photo: Martin Brading)

Elegant models can include any type, from Classic Beauty to Amazon, Exotic, and Athletic Girl Next Door.

Like their younger counterparts, elegant models are tall and slim, with well-proportioned bodies. They must have striking features and beautiful skin, teeth, hair, and nails. It's very important for elegant models to stay slim, youthful, and attractive and to keep their skin in its best condition. They shouldn't look unnaturally young, but they should look youthful, the best their age can look. They may need to take more vitamins, use special moisturizers and skin treatments, work out more, watch their diets more carefully, and avoid smoking.

In general, there are no open calls and model searches for elegant models looking for agents. Most elegant models have experience in the business and use their contacts to establish themselves as elegant models.

If you've never modeled but think you have what it takes to be an elegant model, e-mail pictures of yourself to agencies that handle elegant models. In New York, certain large agencies (Wilhelmina, Ford) have elegant model divisions. The Bryan Bantry agency in New York handles many elegant models, the majority of whom are former cover girls. In smaller markets, elegant models may be handled by an agency's regular bookers, not by a special division. Call some of the agencies near you to find out if they handle elegant models; if so, e-email or mail snapshots of yourself to them to see if they'd be interested in handling you. (See Chapter 6 for information on taking the right kind of snapshots, and Chapter 7 for information on sending them to agencies.)

Male Models

The male model market has exploded due to the rise of models such as Ashton Kutcher, Ryan Snyder, Karl Lindman, and Jason Lewis.

Male models walk the runway in the major menswear fashion shows twice a year in Milan, Paris, New York, and London. They appear in shows for major men's designers, including Giorgio Armani, Gucci, Prada, Joseph Abboud, Paul Smith, Ralph Lauren, and Calvin Klein. They also appear in men's magazines, such as *GQ*, *Esquire*, and *Details* in the United States; *Uomo Vogue* in Italy; *Vogue Homme* in Paris; and *Arena* in London.

Male model Ryan Kopko is too sexy for his shirt.

(Photo: Kwame Brathwaite)

Male models must be tall, generally at least 6' and up to 6'2", and fit a size 40 regular to size 42 long jacket. Like female models, they need to look good in clothes, have good skin, and have an appealing, vibrant personality. Also like female models, male models come in many of the same categories: Athlete, Oddball, Classically Good-Looking.

> **Roshumba's Rules**
>
> Male models generally start their careers slightly later than female models—at 18 to 20—but can work much longer, conceivably until their mid-30s. Some male models in their 40s are still working regularly.

Like top female models, male models travel constantly, doing the fashion shows and photo shoots all over the globe. Like female models, when they're not traveling and working, they have to keep themselves looking their best, eating healthfully and taking care of their body.

In New York, the most important agencies handling men include IMG, Wilhelmina, Ford, Major, NY Models, DNA, Click, and Request. Even in smaller markets, agencies generally have a men's division. Like female models, male models do test shoots and assemble a book when they've acquired an agent. It usually takes longer for men to launch their careers because there's less work for men than for women.

Many modeling searches and conventions have opened their doors to men. But an equally good option for an aspiring male model is to e-mail or mail snapshots of himself to agencies that handle male models in the city where he wants to work. (See Chapter 6 for information on taking snapshots, and Chapter 7 for information on sending them to agencies.)

Child Models

Every mother of a cute kid has wondered if her child has what it takes to be a child model. Patti Abbott-Claffy, a child modeling and talent agent in Philadelphia who helped launched Brooke Shields' modeling career, shares her insider secrets on breaking into the business.

These photos of child models Christiana Anbri and Stephen Schmidt give the viewer a sense of their friendly, outgoing personalities.

(Photos: Art Lynch)

Child models do magazine work (for both children's magazines and adult magazines that focus on families), advertisements, endorsements, TV commercials, and industrial work (training videos for corporations, corporate manuals, and brochures, particularly in the booming health-care and pharmaceutical industries).

Because it's such a specialized field, child models are handled by agencies who deal exclusively with children.

Before a child reaches the age of about 5, there's not a tremendous amount of work, except for the occasional job for a baby. This is mostly because working with very young children is so difficult. Once a child wears size 5 clothing, the amount of work increases tremendously, assuming the child is mature and cooperative. "They're able to get cooperation at age five," explains Abbott-Claffy. "That has a lot to do with it."

Looking younger than her age has many advantages for a child model. "What you get with that is a really intelligent child who's more disciplined, a child who can really withstand more pressure and longer hours, yet she looks five," says Abbott-Claffy.

For catalog and fashion modeling, being a perfect size (a child who fits perfectly into a child's size 5 or 6) is an advantage. For commercials, industrial work, and editorial, children are hired by age, not by size. Between the ages of 12 and 14, it's harder for children to work, because they're at an awkward age—they're no longer a child, but they haven't reached maturity.

Also, it can be difficult for a child to work after she loses her baby teeth but before her adult teeth are in. Generally, there are two options, according to Abbott-Claffy: wait it out, or get flippers. Flippers are a removable dental appliance that fits over teeth to make it look like the child still has all her baby teeth intact.

Years ago, only classic, all-American *P&G children* could get bookings. "Now we get calls on just about all types," says Abbott-Claffy. "Exotic is in; racial mixes are definitely in. The child you choose generally jumps out at you when you're meeting them in the first two minutes, personality wise, looks wise, the way they use their eyes when they speak to you," she explains. "That, coupled with discipline. You have those who are precocious and adorable, but you can't get them to pay attention. Their attention span doesn't allow them to focus and follow directions yet. It's the combination of a sparkling personality and terrific listening skills, plus the ability to follow directions [that makes for a successful child model]."

Catwalk Talk

The **P&G (Procter & Gamble) child** is a child with perfect all-American features, like the kind of kid featured in classic P&G commercials for products such as Life cereal, Crest toothpaste, or Charmin toilet paper.

Although a few children will make enough as child models to finance their college educations, this is not the norm. In general, the money made will be "the icing on the cake," as Abbott-Claffy puts it, not a major source of income. According to Abbott-Claffy, "The top kids do [make enough to pay for college], if all the factors are there. But it can become a full-time job for mothers for really successful, in-demand children. There are children whose college is paid for, but it's not common. Those who hang in for the long run seem to be more profitable."

The hourly rate for print shoots runs from $50 and up. An average is $75 an hour. Starting out, a child model may accept a lower pay rate to get the experience.

Getting the Parents Involved

Because the parent must accompany the child to all go and sees and auditions, it's key that parents understand what they're getting into. "I not only interview the child, but if I have an interest in the child, I sit down and talk to the parent to find out whose main desire this is," says Abbott-Claffy. "It should be fun for the child. If it's not fun, I don't want to participate. You don't want a child who doesn't love it because you have to love it to put in the time, or the child will get stressed and eventually crumble from the pressure. Also, I don't want to see a child responsible for making the parents happy."

Being the parent of a child model is a huge investment of time. "Being available, particularly for print and commercials," says Abbott-Claffy, "is one of the most important things. Sometimes you get a call in the morning for a booking that afternoon. If you don't have the time to really put into it, the child won't be able to work. If you do have the time, you're ahead of the competition. It seems those moms who can drop everything seem to book more. You must have the type of family life that allows that. Many of the families that work a lot have the grandparents involved."

It's also important that parents not pressure children, that they find success in the small victories, and that they not emphasize bookings over everything. "I believe you should treat each audition, each interview, as being successful," says Abbott-Claffy. "The idea that your child can go in there and represent themselves, they've done what 98 percent of the population hasn't done. Most seven- and eight-year-olds could not walk into an interview and introduce themselves. The self-esteem you can gain, if you treat each time as a success, whether or not you book the job, is great."

Reality Check

If your child isn't feeling well, call and cancel the appointment. "Yesterday I met with a little girl who wasn't feeling well," says Abbott-Claffy. "She was very cute, but she was acting shy. Her mother said she'd been really sick and that she wasn't normally like this. We really liked her look, but we can't risk our reputation by having that happen [on a job]."

Finding Your Child Model an Agent

Con artists waiting to take advantage of naive parents who want to get their children into modeling abound. To give you a heads-up about bad business practices, here are standard operating procedures for finding an agent and getting your child started as a child model.

To find an agent, send informal snapshots to the agencies you're interested in working with. Don't spend a lot of money on professional portraits. "I prefer they don't have professional pictures done before they [see me]," says Abbott-Claffy. "A lot of times, the parents think they've got what I'm looking for and it's not at all what I'm looking for. A good department store photo showing the personality that costs $20 is all we need. A snapshot that Mom took of the child by herself, especially in outdoor light, is also perfect. We don't like to get those Christmas pictures with friends and family, the kind of snapshot that is really busy. It should be just the child, and not with a hat pulled down or anything so you can't see what they look like."

The only money you should pay an agency is a commission on fees your child earns for working. Although some agencies will charge an interview fee, an evaluation fee, or a consultation fee, it should never be more than $25 to cover administration costs, according to Abbott-Claffy. Charging registration fees or any kind of fee just for representing your child is not legitimate.

Taking Test Photos

When the agent has agreed to represent the child, professional test pictures need to be taken that will be used for the child's portfolio, head shot, and comp card. "I give them recommendations of photographers, and they go to whomever they want to," says Abbott-Claffy. It should never be outrageously expensive because children change so quickly that photos need to be retaken often. You shouldn't pay more than a couple hundred dollars. If someone is coercing you into using only one photographer, especially one who is charging outrageous fees for taking professional photos, beware!

> **Roshumba's Rules**
>
> There's a great difference between a portrait photographer and a photographer who shoots for modeling and commercials. In a photo taken by the portrait photographer, the personality doesn't necessarily come through.

Eventually, the test photos will be replaced by tear sheets in the child's portfolio, just like for fashion models. Starting out, however, the child can work with just a comp card and a head shot.

Parts Models

A parts model is a model who specializes in modeling certain body parts such as the legs, feet, hands, or back—basically any part of the body, but rarely the face. Parts models can be hired to do a variety of work—editorial work, advertising, TV commercials, catalogs, even films. Parts models generally don't meet the requirements to be fashion models—maybe they're not tall enough or don't have the right look—but they have at least one standout part, such as beautiful hands, gorgeous legs, or perfect feet.

Aside from having the physical qualifications of a great part, an aspiring parts model needs to have plenty of patience and the ability to keep her part still while photographers adjust lights, backdrops, and props to get ready to shoot.

Parts models generally get started a little older than regular models; between the ages of 18 and 20 is common. As long as your part stays beautiful, you could model for up to 20 years or more. The work can be very intense and tedious, yet it can be a long, lucrative career for someone with fantastic legs, standout feet, or lovely hands.

Parts for Parts

A fair amount of parts modeling work is available. Just think about all the ads and commercials you see for sandals, nail polish, jewelry, hair ornaments, hosiery, and more.

Hand models model jewelry and nail products, or anything where a magazine, advertiser, or catalog would want to focus attention on the hand. Their hands may also occasionally double as the hands of regular models. A hand model's hands should have a perfect shape—long and elegant fingers, well-manicured nails and cuticles, no sun damage, and no scars.

Leg models model hosiery, footwear, shaving products, and body creams. They need to have long, lean, toned legs with no scars, bruises, tattoos, or scratches.

Foot models model shoes, socks, footcare products, and toenail polish. They need to wear size 5½ to 7 medium-width shoes. They need to have medium to high arches, without any bunions, toenail fungus, crooked toes, badly proportioned toes, or calluses.

Reality Check

If you're considering parts modeling, keep in mind that you need to take amazing care of your part. Although this might sound simple, it can have a major effect on your lifestyle. For example, many hand models wear gloves constantly, even on a hot summer days, to protect their hands from sun and wind damage.

Body parts modeling jobs, as well as all other types of modeling jobs, are available in any market, small or large, where advertising is created. Some established parts models in the fashion capitals can have full-time careers, depending on the type of work they're doing and their success in booking clientele on a regular basis. When they have built a name for themselves as a parts model, they can find themselves in steady demand, and they may even work over and over for the same clients. In secondary and local markets, however, the work is more sporadic, and it may be difficult to have a full-time career as a parts model. Still, it can be a good source of extra income.

Parts modeling pays more in the larger markets, where the big national ads are booked. And when a model is established as a great foot model, for instance, she can command higher rates.

Finding a Parts Agent

In the fashion capitals, agencies such as Wilhelmina and Parts Models have parts modeling divisions. Like regular models, parts models have portfolios and composites and online examples of their work. When clients call looking for a hand or foot to use in an ad or magazine story, the model's portfolio is sent to that client.

Because parts modeling is a small, rather specialized field, no model searches or open calls for aspiring parts models are held. Instead, to get started, call an agency that represents parts models and find out what their preferred procedure is for seeing new models—whether you should e-mail photos, drop by the agency, or make an appointment.

Roshumba's Rules

It's fine if the snapshots of your part are taken by a friend or family member who's handy with a camera. Spending loads of money having professional pictures taken is a waste of money when you're first starting out.

If the agency wants to see some snapshots, and you're a foot model, have several pictures taken of your feet perfectly groomed with no color on your toes. Also take some shots of your feet with your toes polished in a colored nail polish and foundation applied to your feet to smooth out the color and texture. Also, do a shot of your feet in high heels (without stockings). Take several pictures of each "look" from a variety of angles.

A leg model should take several pictures of her (makeup-free) legs in different poses—some where she's barefoot, some wearing high heels, some wearing sneakers. Take some photos straight on, some in profile, some with the feet in the model-T pose (the classic beauty pageant pose, with feet together, one pointing straight ahead, and the other pointing outward).

A hand model should take photos from several angles of her well-groomed (moisturized, nails filed neatly) hands with unpolished nails. Then she should polish her nails in a natural-color polish and take pictures of them from several angles. Try to find natural-looking poses, and feel free to use a prop, such as a flower or champagne glass.

Select and print the best ones or e-mail them to the agent. (It's fine to have them developed at the drugstore.)

Real-People and Character Models

Character modeling, also known as real-people modeling, is available in almost every market and is often more accessible than fashion modeling. Character models portray real people in all areas of advertising and TV commercials, as well as in industrial training films, in music videos, and as retail models. Think about any career or field of interest, and a publication or TV program probably targets that audience. And where there's a magazine or a TV show, there are advertisements. A real-person model can be a florist, a health-care worker, a teacher, a jubilant grandmother, or a young mom with laundry woes.

One of the great things about character modeling is that experience, height, weight, and classic features are rarely factors in determining whether a model is hired for a job. Most important is that he or she has the right look for the role. Kate Moss may have all the modeling experience in the world, but if the job is a print ad for a hospital that features a typical-looking female doctor, it would be difficult for Kate to fit that bill.

Roshumba's Rules

Just because character models are more like real people than their supermodel counterparts doesn't mean they don't have to have that special sparkle that sets all models and actors apart.

Character models have to be skilled at expressing different emotions through their facial expressions. They benefit from having strong acting skills, especially for booking TV commercials. If you're interested in pursuing character modeling work, consider taking acting classes or on-camera classes (classes that teach on-camera techniques, speaking, working your best angles, and character development and projection) to develop those essential acting skills.

Although character models generally don't make as much as fashion models, this still can be a lucrative area. A lot depends on what kind of jobs you're doing. As with fashion models, print advertising bookings pay better than editorial bookings. Television commercials also generally pay well.

Do Real-People Models Need Agents?

In my opinion, all models need an agent or someone representing them. Agents are the first to find out when a job is being cast. A model working alone doesn't have the resources to find out about every potential booking, nor would it be appropriate for her to call around to ad agencies and potential clients. Also, agents screen clients so a model isn't sent into a dangerous situation. Finally, agents handle billing, collections, and other aspects of the money side of things.

Real-people models are handled by *commercial agents* (sometimes also called *talent agents*) as opposed to fashion-model agents. Some work in modeling agencies, while others work in agencies that specialize in real people. (In smaller agencies, especially in smaller markets, one agent may handle both.)

When a job is being cast, the client calls the agent with a description of what type of model the client is looking for and sends appropriate models on a go and see. Character models generally have comp cards with three or four pictures representing different looks (see Chapter 12 for more information on comp cards) or a regular *theatrical head shot* taken by a professional photographer with a resumé printed on the back. Your agent will make the arrangements for this. As with regular modeling, don't pay for expensive head shots or comp cards before you have an agent—it's a waste of money.

Catwalk Talk

A **commercial agent** handles models who don't fall into the traditional fashion-model category. They book models for commercial work (print ads, TV commercials) as opposed to editorial or artistic work. A **theatrical head shot** is an 8×10-inch photo of an actor or model's head and face given out to casting agents on auditions to help them remember the models they've interviewed.

If you're interested in becoming a character model, call some of the reputable commercial, talent, and modeling agencies in your area and find out which ones have a commercial division. They may request that you e-mail them a photo, or they may make an appointment for you to visit them.

The Real-People World of Television Commercials

No other area of modeling offers more opportunities for real people than television modeling. The need exists for every age, type, and ethnicity. Household products need homemakers to help sell them, copier machines need businesspeople, bologna needs cute little kids, and the guy who gets sand kicked on him at the beach needs to look kinda nerdy! Even men who look like Santa Claus (or women who look like Mrs. Claus) can find work doing holiday commercials.

Television work is available just about everywhere, in cities large and small. Locally produced commercials, like those you see for car dealerships and other local retail and service establishments, all provide work for local models. (Usually these commercials don't have the budget to fly models and actors in from around the country.) As is the case with advertising print work, though, the bookings for large national commercials take place in the big cities.

Bookings for television commercials are generally handled by specialized agents who handle only TV; many large agencies have TV departments. (In some smaller markets, an agency might not have formal departments but still handles all types of bookings.) Your regular modeling agent may be able to refer you to someone. If you don't have one, ask any acquaintances who do TV work who represents them. Otherwise, call the reputable agents in your area to find out who handles this kind of work. If and when you are invited for an interview, be prepared to be auditioned on-camera.

Industrial Training Films

Industrial training films and corporate videos are used to train people for a specific career or for working at one company. When a new worker is hired at the big bank downtown, for instance, he might be shown a video outlining various work-related procedures. These films feature actors/models who physically resemble the real people you would find working in these and many other fields.

Actors/models are also used for product demonstration videos that often run in house-wares stores like Bed Bath and Beyond and Linens 'n Things.

These sorts of films are produced in any area of the country where manufacturing or commercial hubs need training videos, which makes it a great area for aspiring models outside the fashion capitals and in very large cities.

The pay for training videos is a fraction of what a TV commercial offers. It could be as little as $50 plus a free lunch. But this is a good foot in the door and a treat opportunity for a model or actor to get video footage of herself so she can begin putting together a *sample reel* of her work (and that is valuable!).

> **Catwalk Talk**
>
> A **sample reel** is a video-tape of all of an actor or model's on-camera work, including television commercials and industrial training films. Think of it as a portfolio spotlighting an actor's/model's best clips.

To get involved with industrial training films, you need to have a commercial agent who can send you out on auditions.

Extra Work

The customers in the background in the Wendy's commercial? The guy walking his dog in the back of a UPS ad? They're extras. Like real-people and character actors, extras look like real people—kids, students, young marrieds—not necessarily like fashion models. Extras appear in the background for music videos, print ads, commercials, TV shows, and movies.

Working as an extra is a great way to get into the business. The best way to find out about opportunities is through show-business industry publications such as *Backstage* or *Variety*, or your local newspaper. To find out more about opportunities, you can also contact the Screen Actor's Guild (SAG; www.sag.org) or the American Federation of Television and Radio Artists (AFTRA; www.aftra.org).

Whether you have a great part or embody the look of a specific character type, you might be able to find work as a real-people model.

The Least You Need to Know

- Plus-size models (fashion models who are generally size 12 to 16) are an increasingly busy category of models.

- Elegant models (fashion models over the age of 35) have also become busier than ever.

- Male models have gone from obscurity to celebrity, thanks to the popularity of male supermodels.

- The field of child modeling can be a lucrative, fun-filled opportunity if parents avoid the many pitfalls.

- People who don't fit the height, weight, age, and other requirements for fashion models can find work as parts models and character models.

- Real-people models are used in print advertisements, television commercials, industrial training films, and music videos.

Part 6

Personal and Career Management

Throughout her career, a model needs to look her best every single day. In Part 6, I discuss how to take care of yourself from head to toe, including hair, skin, teeth, and nails. I also talk about ways to maintain your model figure with a healthful eating plan.

I talk about personal management, too, and how to deal with fame and the downsides of modeling (drugs, alcohol, partying, bad boyfriends, eating disorders). Forewarned is forearmed: if you know what to look out for, you'll be a lot less likely to fall prey to one (or more) of these traps.

When a model has gotten her career off the ground, she'll want it to keep building momentum so she can get as much out of the business as possible. I give you advice (as well as tips from other experts) about how to manage and maintain your career so you work as often as possible, make as much money as you can, and have a career that lasts for a good long time. I also discuss how to manage your money, why you need a qualified accountant, how to set up a savings plan, and how to spot scams. Finally, I talk about planning for your future; the career span of a model is often relatively brief, and it's vital that she start planning for the future sooner rather than later.

21

The Outer You

In This Chapter

- ◆ Making healthful food choices
- ◆ A model exercise program
- ◆ Makeup tips for your most beautiful look
- ◆ Keeping hair, skin, nails, and teeth picture-perfect

A model depends on her looks; therefore, it's vital that she knows how to take care of herself so her physical appearance is always at its best. Not only are eating healthfully and exercising mandatory, but so are getting frequent haircuts, hair coloring, manicures, pedicures, facials, waxing, and dental cleanings.

In this chapter, I describe everything a model needs to know and do to keep herself looking picture-perfect. I also let you in on some of my secret tips that have helped me to look my best over the years.

Model Meals

If I had a nickel for every time I've been asked if models eat, I would probably be very rich. Not only do models eat, but many of them eat extremely fattening foods—hamburgers, french fries, and ice cream.

Although many models may indulge in eating fatty foods, it's usually done in moderation. For the most part, models have healthful diets, not only because they have to but, because it's the nature of the business. The fashion industry in general is very health-conscious. Magazine editors, photographers, hairstylists, makeup artists, and fashion designers tend to be an international group, and they usually bring with them different and often more healthful eating habits.

America is known for its frequent snacking, huge portions, and greasy fast food. In other countries, such as France and Italy, the focus is on sitting down and enjoying a meal, which also allows people to pay attention to what they're eating. Dining is looked at as a special time, a time to relax, let go, and socialize. Processed and fast foods are rarely a big part of the diet.

For breakfast, usually just coffee and a croissant or a breakfast bread is eaten—not fat- and calorie-laden bacon, eggs, hashbrowns, and toast. Lunch is usually a balanced meal, consisting of meat or fish, vegetables or salad, bread, and a light dessert. Usually nothing else is eaten until dinner, which is a repeat of lunch as far as a type of food: meat, fish, or poultry; vegetables or salad; bread; and a light dessert. (In Italy, the diet differs in that pasta is a big part of each main meal.) This might sound like a lot of food, but the portions are very small.

The quality of food is also very important. Superfresh fruits, vegetables, and fish; whole grains; fresh bread; and lean cuts of high-quality meat are the staples of the diet. For the most part, the fashion industry has these eating habits as well—the catered meals on photo shoots are also usually very fresh and healthful.

> **Reality Check**
>
> While it's true that people believe models are super-humanly thin, I think many of them don't realize that models, especially during the prime years of their careers, are usually very young—between 16 and 25. At this age, it's quite normal to be thin, so actually, models aren't so abnormally thin if you take their ages into consideration.

> **Model Scoop**
>
> Many models are vegetarians, and I, too, went through a period of about 5 years when I was a vegetarian. At first, I was a vegan, meaning I ate nothing that came from an animal, which included milk, cheese, eggs, meat, and fish. Instead, I consumed mostly whole grains, beans, vegetables, and fruit. This change was too drastic and did not agree with my body. I felt tired, my skin lost its glow, and I lost a lot of body fat; it did not look good. So I added eggs and fish back into my diet, which I found was the perfect balance for me. It also made it much easier to find things to eat when I traveled. Today, my diet consists mainly of grilled fish, seafood, and salads, but I do have a weakness for potato chips and cookies, and I occasionally indulge in other treats like pizza and ice cream.

What Does Roshumba Eat?

For the person who is in good shape and has the ideal weight for her age and height, I suggest she eat balanced meals and not snack too much in between or eat too many fatty foods or breads.

Following is a sample of what I might eat in a day. This meal plan works very well for me and helps me maintain my model figure. You should make adjustments for your caloric needs, your age (you need fewer calories as you get older), your activity level (athletic people require more calories to maintain their weight), and your own personal tastes.

Roshumba's Rules

If I go over my ideal weight of 120 to 125 pounds, I cut out breads, dairy, fried foods, and desserts. As long as I don't overindulge in these foods, I'm able to maintain my weight.

Breakfast:

◆ 1 or 2 eggs, boiled or poached (scrambled or fried are okay occasionally) *or* 1 cup yogurt *or* ½ cup cottage cheese

◆ 1 or 2 slices whole-grain toast *or* 1 small muffin or bagel *or* 1 cup oatmeal

◆ Fresh fruit or juice and tea or coffee

Lunch:

◆ 3 to 4 ounces grilled fish, seafood, (lean) meat, or poultry

◆ Salad and/or vegetables

◆ Grains or beans (½ cup rice, pasta—whole wheat is preferable, beans, or couscous or 1 slice bread)

◆ Fresh fruit

◆ 1 cup yogurt (optional)

Dinner:

◆ 3 to 4 ounces grilled fish, seafood, (lean) meat, or poultry (If you had fish for lunch, have poultry or meat for dinner, and vice versa.)

◆ Salad and/or vegetables

◆ Grains or beans (½ cup rice, pasta, or couscous or 1 slice bread)

Portion size plays a big role in the number of calories consumed, so pay attention to how much you're eating, not just what you're eating.

Model Moves

Exercise not only makes you look good, but it makes you feel good, too. Although models are often naturally thin, most of them do exercise. It's important to establish some sort of exercise routine that will keep your body toned and in shape, alleviate stress, and burn calories. Develop your own regimen of moderate exercise that includes cardiovascular work (walking, running, swimming, or biking, which gets your heart pumping), strength training (weight lifting or calisthenics that increase your strength and tone your muscles), and stretching (which keeps your muscles flexible). Try to exercise at least four times a week.

Most models work out regularly to keep their bodies toned and strong.

(Photographer: Kwame Brathwaite; model: Laura McLafferty)

Model Scoop

I love to exercise, although I'm not really into going to the gym. I prefer working out in the privacy of my own home. I have a whole collection of DVDs I love working out to ones that incorporate stretching, toning, and aerobics. When I wake up in the morning, the first thing I do is turn on a DVD and work out for ½ hour, 5 days a week. Usually I choose aerobic workouts designed to burn calories and fat, and tone and tighten my muscles. Sometimes I alternate these with yoga, depending on my mood or what I feel my body needs.

The Stress on Tresses

Those luscious locks may be your ticket to big money, which is why it's important to keep them looking their best. Hair advertisements can be a very lucrative source of money for models with beautiful, healthy hair.

Be sure you keep your hair clean, well conditioned, and well groomed. Get ¼ to ½ inch trimmed off your ends every 2 weeks to 4 weeks to get rid of split or damaged ends and keep your cut in tiptop shape. If you color or highlight your hair, get the color redone at least once every month, or as soon as your roots start showing. Even though it's expensive to maintain, it will cost you a lot more if clients don't book you because of your unsightly roots.

If you're working every day, hairstylists are probably applying buckets of hair products to your hair on a daily basis. That's why you want to be sure you keep your hair as clean as possible. Because many hair products contain alcohol, which can dry out hair, I try to wash my hair as quickly as possible after a shoot—usually as soon as I get home.

 Reality Check

Be extremely cautious about who you let color your hair. You don't want to end up with a bad color job, which could stop your career in its tracks. Ask your agent or other industry professionals for recommendations. Try to stick to the same colorist every time, to limit the possibility of a hair disaster.

Whenever you're working with hairstylists at a job, talk to them before they start working to let them know what condition your hair is in. If you've just been through 3 grueling weeks of fashion shows where your hair has been blown and styled 5 times a day, and it can't take the strain anymore, let the stylist know and ask (politely) if he or she could be extra gentle.

Roshumba's Rules

Most models' hair does experience some damage, especially if they're working a lot. If your hair starts to show the signs of damage, treat yourself to a deep-conditioning hair treatment once a week (you can find deep-conditioning products in the hair-care section of the drugstore). You might also want to make an appointment at a salon that does special hair-conditioning and repair treatments.

The morning before a shoot, don't do much to your hair because whatever you do, the hairstylist is probably going to undo. Just be sure your hair is clean, conditioned, and tangle free.

The Skinny on Skin

Skin is so important to the success of a model's career. Most models have naturally good skin. Even though makeup can cover a lot of flaws, such as acne, when clients are selecting a model, they want someone who's as perfect as possible when first starting out. In the modeling industry, makeup is used as a beauty enhancer, not a camouflage. That's why skin texture, glow, color, the size of your pores, and the way the light reflects off your skin are so important.

Roshumba's Rules

Drinking lots of water—at least 8 glasses a day—is one of the best things you can do for your skin. It flushes out your body and keeps your skin well hydrated and moisturized.

If you suffer from acne flare-ups or other skin conditions, you should consult a dermatologist, who can recommend a number of treatments. The truth is, a model without good skin might have a tough time getting bookings.

I keep my skin in tip-top shape by drinking lots of water, wearing sunblock, and steaming my face once a week to clean my pores. I also moisturize my entire body from head to toe daily.

Insider Makeup Tips

Model or not, it's to your advantage to learn about makeup. The first thing you should do is study what you look like in your natural state, without any makeup; how you look with some makeup on; and what you look like fully made up. This helps you learn which makeup looks enhance your face and which detract from your natural beauty.

Basic makeup includes foundation, concealer (as needed), powder, blush, eye shadow, lipstick or gloss, mascara, and groomed brows. Medium makeup includes basic makeup plus eye liner, eye shadow in the crease, and lip liner. Glamour makeup (which is worn mostly at photo shoots or special occasions) includes basic and medium makeup plus contouring under the cheekbones, false eyelashes, and more dramatic colors on the eyes and lips. (For a look at all three types of makeup, check out the photos in the book's color insert.)

Here are some quick and easy tips on applying makeup, in the order you should apply it:

1. Start by placing small dots of foundation on your forehead, cheeks, nose, and chin. Use a cosmetic sponge to blend.

Applying foundation with a sponge gives a more sheer, even application.

2. Use concealer only where it's needed. Dot it on and then pat it with your ring finger to blend.

3. Dip a fluffy powder brush into loose powder, tap off any excess, and then dust over your face.

4. Using an eye shadow brush, sweep powder eye shadow from your lash line to your brow and then blend.

5. Wipe any excess mascara from the wand with a tissue. Then, holding the wand horizontally, sweep through your lashes. Reapply to the top of your lashes only.

6. Using your brow brush, brush your eyebrows up and slightly out.

Applying a dark eye shadow in the crease of the eye enhances the eyes and gives them more depth and drama.

7. Dip your blush brush in the blush and tap off any excess. Place the brush on the apple of your cheek, and stroke back toward your ear. Most of the color should be on your cheek. If you make a mistake, use your powder brush to "buff" it out.

Apply blush to the apple of your cheek, sweeping the brush out toward your ear.

8. Slick on lip gloss with your finger. For lipstick, dip your lip brush in the lipstick. Outline your lips with the brush, starting from the center and working out toward the edges. Fill in the bottom lip and then press (don't rub) your lips together. The excess from the bottom will color your top lip and eliminate the need for blotting.

9. Use a small brush to sweep a darker, coordinating tone in the crease of your eye.

10. Dip an eyeliner brush in a dark eye shadow (black, navy, or gray), and dot a line along the upper and (if you want) lower lash lines. For an even more dramatic look, use an eye pencil to line around your inner lash line.

11. For less mistake-prone contouring, sweep translucent powder under your cheekbones to highlight bone structure.

Apply lip liner first and then fill in with lipstick.

Lining the eyes helps define their shape and gives them a dramatic look.

12. False eyelashes usually come in clusters of three lashes and in three different lengths—short, medium, and long. Apply the longest ones on the outside corner of your lashes, the mid-length ones in the middle of your eye, and the shortest ones close to your nose.

> **Reality Check** _____
>
> Because some people are allergic to the adhesive used on false eyelashes, many manufacturers recommend that you do an allergy test before you apply the lashes. Follow the directions on the package.

To apply false lashes, pick up the individual cluster with a tweezers and then dip the base of the lash in the adhesive that comes in the eyelash kit. Gently set the base of the false lash exactly where you want it and then hold it there for a minute with the tweezers. Repeat until your lashes have the desired fullness. Be sure to glue the false eyelash to your eyelashes, not your skin. Apply mascara to blend the false eyelashes with your natural ones.

Picture-Perfect Nails

When you go to a photo studio, your nails should be clean and buffed, or clean, buffed, and polished with a natural polish. Your cuticles should be smooth and in healthy condition. In general, clients don't want to see long red talons on a model's hands, and they don't appreciate when girls come in with chewed-up nails and bleeding cuticles. Go for short nails with a square or rounded shape.

I get a manicure every week. Sometimes I have my natural nails manicured; other times I get nail extensions (acrylic nails). If I do get nail extensions, I don't leave them on for more than a month and then I take them off so my nails can breathe. Also, I don't get those long "cat claw" type of extensions. Mine are a short, manageable length that look natural and healthy. At home, I have a nail file, a nail buffer, clear nail polish, some colored nail polishes, and cuticle oil. If I'm not able to get to the manicurist, I do my own nails.

Reality Check

Take care of your hands. Wear sunscreen to protect them from the sun so they don't get dry, discolored, or splotchy. I also protect mine from the cold by wearing gloves. When it comes to washing dishes and doing housework, I always wear rubber gloves to protect them from chemicals, detergents, and hot water, which can dry out hands tremendously and leave them rough looking.

Apply hand moisturizers as often as possible. Not only will this keep your hands looking their best, but it will smooth your cuticles and moisturize your nails. Also massage a cuticle oil into your cuticles once a week to keep them healthy.

Roshumba's Rules

If I have a shoot coming up and I want my feet to look their best, I slather Vaseline on my feet, wrap them in plastic, and then put on socks before I go to bed.

Keeping your feet in prime condition is also important because very often your feet will be showing on-camera—for instance, if you're wearing sandals or if you're barefoot. Models are notorious for having the worst feet because they're always having to squeeze them into shoes that aren't the right size. Also, working in high heels all day can damage the feet, as does all that running around on go and sees and other appointments.

To be sure my feet look their best, I get a pedicure every 2 weeks to slough off the calluses and dead skin and keep the cuticles healthy. I generally get a natural or clear polish on my toenails, unless the client has requested a specific color.

The Least You Need to Know

◆ Models do eat, but they eat reasonable portions of healthful food.

◆ Most models exercise regularly; it's a good habit to develop.

◆ Models should know how to apply their own makeup to look their best.

◆ It's vital that models take good care of their hair, skin, nails, and teeth.

Chapter 22

The Inner You

In This Chapter

◆ Drugs, alcohol, and eating disorders

◆ Bad relationships

◆ Rejection and stress

◆ Work slowdowns

Staying physically fit and emotionally and mentally healthy is vitally important for models, but this can be extremely tough, given the fashion industry's emphasis on physical beauty and the continual rejection models have to deal with. It can all take an enormous toll on models' self-esteem.

I've survived many years in this business, and I've seen it all—the rejection, the stress, the exhaustion, the drug and alcohol problems, the bad relationships, the work slowdowns. Although many models fall victim to these problems, many others manage to reap the benefits of a modeling career without self-destructing.

In this chapter, I give you the benefit of my experience in the modeling business so you'll be prepared for any obstacle that comes your way.

The Downsides of Modeling

We've all heard the stories of how great the perks of modeling can be: the money, clothes, parties, and travel. But there are two sides to every story, and the other side of modeling can be pretty frightening. Here's the real scoop on the dark side of modeling and how you can avoid falling prey to drugs, alcohol, overspending, eating disorders, and bad relationships.

Drugs: Just Say No

The modeling world is a world full of excesses. Yes, drugs are around, and, yes, models do take them. For a very long time, industry professionals denied this. But in the past decade or so, the fashion industry has acknowledged drugs' existence and the fact that they are frequently used and abused by many people in the industry.

But even though drugs are so readily available, most models don't use them; it's not a given that you'll start using drugs or become an addict once you're a model. Models who get into drugs tend to be young, just starting out in the business, rather insecure, and looking for a way to either ease their fears, control their weight, or fit in with the cool crowd.

> **Reality Check**
>
> Some people might feel it's okay to take drugs occasionally or recreationally, or say it's possible to take them without getting addicted, but why even take the chance? It has been proven over and over again by musicians, actors, comedians, models, and everyday people that indulging in drugs is a quick trip down a dead-end street.

Drugs are also not too hard to come by when you're a model. They're available in photo studios, backstage at runway shows, in nightclubs, and on street corners. On top of that, it is possible to have them delivered to almost any location.

I'm not going to preach to you and tell you what to do and what not to do. I just want to warn you that drugs destroy. They can take away everything you have worked so hard to earn. Not only will they rob you of all your material possessions (an addict will sell everything or steal anything to get her fix), but they will also take away your health, beauty, youth, and dreams.

Alcohol Abuse

Drinking alcohol is very easy to get caught up in and addicted to, especially because it's everywhere in the fashion industry and it's accepted as one of life's necessities. Models are regularly offered champagne before fashion shows—even if the show is at

9 A.M.—because of the party atmosphere surrounding fashion shows and because it's supposed to take the edge off and calm the models' nerves.

A glass of champagne is fine. But imagine if a model does three to five shows a day in all the major markets—Milan, Paris, and New York—for 6 weeks straight and drinks champagne at each show. In addition, she may have wine with both lunch and dinner and then drink a couple cocktails at a party each night. That adds up to a great deal of alcohol consumption.

Models might not even notice how much they're drinking, and people in the fashion industry think it's normal to drink socially. But the truth is, all these "social drinks" could lead to a serious drinking problem. Many models and other fashion industry professionals do have problems with alcohol. So be aware of the possibility that drinking too much can happen very easily in the fashion industry, and even though it might seem acceptable, in the end, it could destroy or damage your career—not to mention your health.

Shopping Till You Drop

Working as a model exposes you to the finest things in life, including designer clothes, accessories, and luxurious jewelry. When I first started modeling, I knew nothing about Chanel, Prada, and Gucci. But after working with many of the designers of these garments and accessories, and meeting other models, fashion editors, agents, and photographers who owned these products, I found myself wanting to have them, too. For a while, I went crazy, buying everything in sight—clothes, shoes, bags, and jewelry—until one day, my accountant said to me, "Roshumba, it's okay to have nice things, but take it easy; you don't need to own the world."

Remember, a modeling career is short-lived, and when your money is gone, it's gone. Spend in moderation.

> **Roshumba's Rules**
>
> As hard as it may be, especially when you're around beautiful, expensive things all day, try not to over-shop. It's okay to have some of the finer things in life, but you don't need 10 of everything.

Dieting and Eating Disorders

Although in many people's minds, dieting and eating disorders are associated with modeling, the majority of models are naturally thin and don't suffer from eating disorders. But for those models who don't have a healthy relationship with food and/or are not naturally thin, staying model-slim may be an enormous challenge. Unless you plan to have a career as a plus-size model (which offers more limited work), you need to maintain your weight so you're able to wear a sample-size dress.

> **Reality Check** _____
>
> Don't freak out if you suddenly find you've gained a few pounds. It's true that your agent and clients might notice, and you might be asked to lose weight. But try to deal with it calmly and sensibly so you don't endanger your physical or mental health. Step up your exercise program, consult a registered dietitian, or join a reputable weight-loss program such as Weight Watchers.

But diet pills, crash diets, fad diets, purging (vomiting), fasting, and other gimmicks are not the answer to staying slim. Maybe you will lose weight initially, but once people stop these practices, they tend to regain the weight—and then some—very quickly. Plus, they take a toll on your heath and well-being.

> **Catwalk Talk** _____
>
> **Anorexia** is an eating dis-order. Sufferers eat little or nothing because they think (erroneously) that they're fat even though they're often severely underweight. **Bulimics** consume huge amounts of food at one time and then purge it by vomit-ing, abusing laxatives, or exercis-ing excessively.

Excessive, overzealous dieting can also sometimes trigger eating disorders in certain people. People with eating disorders, which include *anorexia* and *bulimia*, are obsessed with food, weight, and appear-ance to such an extent that their health and daily lives—including their modeling careers—are nega-tively affected.

Anorexics literally starve themselves, eating and drink-ing little even though they suffer terrible hunger pains. Although they might be bone-thin and very much underweight, they think they're overweight. They have a terror of gaining even the smallest amount of weight. At the same time, they go to extremes to keep their eating habits secret. Even within a short period of time, anorexia can damage vital organs such as the heart and brain. In addition, menstrual periods may cease, nails and hair may become brittle, the skin may dry out and turn yellow, and the body may become covered with soft hair. Ultimately, it could kill you.

Bulimics consume huge amounts of food at one time and then rid their bodies of the excess calories by vomiting, abusing laxatives, or exercising obsessively. Because this "bingeing and purging" is done in secret, and because many bulimics feel terrible shame about their actions, bulimia can be hidden from others for years. Still, it takes a terrible toll on the body. The acid in vomit wears down the outer layer of the teeth, causing them to become discolored. Scars can form on the hands from being cut by teeth due to pushing down the throat to induce vomiting.

Eating disorders often develop as a means of dealing with emotional pain, low self-esteem, stress, traumatic events, and stringent diets. Early treatment is the most effective, so if you think you might have a problem, get help now! Ask your agent or family doctor for a referral to a psychologist, social worker, or psychiatrist who treats patients with eating disorders.

Boyfriends Who Aren't Your Friends

When people of the opposite sex see models in advertisements, especially where they're selling things with sexual overtones, they get the idea that models are sex objects, that they're easy or loose.

But in their private lives, most models are not sexually promiscuous. Many are married, in committed relationships, or so busy with their careers that they just don't have time. Still, others throw caution to the wind and have sex with everyone they can. Some are trying to sleep their way to the top, some are lonely and far away from home, some haven't yet realized they don't have to sleep with everyone who asks them, and some are just naturally sexual.

Reality Check

Don't use sex as a way to fill a void in your life. If you're feeling lonely, make some friends outside the business, volunteer your time, or call your family. If you think you may have an emotional problem, get professional psychological help as soon as possible. Know that you can have a very successful, happy, and fulfilling career without sleeping with anyone you're not totally in love with or committed to.

If you find yourself being pressured sexually by any man, be he a photographer, an agent, or a fan, and you are not comfortable or interested, let him know that you are a professional, are in a relationship, or are just not available for anything that's not work related.

Modelizers are men who date only models. Although some are obnoxious and aggressive, others are sensitive, available guys who hang around at every model-related event. Watch out! This is the guy who is probably the most dangerous modelizer of them all. His shyness and sensitivity might appeal to many models who are away from home for the first time, feel a little lonely, and are rather insecure. He may also be appealing because he'll go out and escort models at a moment's notice, walk their dogs, pick up their dry cleaning, and do whatever errands are necessary. Don't be fooled by his niceness; this type can be a leech.

Now don't get me wrong—not all sensitive, shy, accommodating guys are modelizers. Many are just wonderful men who possess these qualities. Be sure you're not getting in with a bad type. Is his ambition just to be around and date models and live a fun, glamorous lifestyle at the model's expense? Check whether he works and can support himself, whether he has his own career goals and accomplishments, and whether he has his own apartment. Can he take you out to dinner, is his career a priority in his life, and, most important, do you feel safe, secure, and mentally, emotionally, and financially supported when you are with him? If not, he might be using you, in which case, you don't want him to be a part of your life.

No matter how cute he is, how charming he is in public, how much money he makes, or how much you fear being alone, a bad relationship is not worth it.

Overcoming Rejection

Although it may seem like a dream job, probably in no other business in the world will one human being receive so much rejection as in the modeling industry. So if you decide you want to become a model, get ready! Plan to have doors slammed in your face and hear very blunt criticisms of your body and features ("Her butt's too fat," "Her boobs are too small," "No Asian girls," "Her jaw's too square").

If you really want to have a modeling career, swallow your pride, grab your portfolio, and hit the pavement. The truth is, there is something for every type of model because every client is looking for something different.

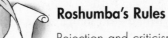

Roshumba's Rules

Rejection and criticism never feel good. When I first started out, I took each negative comment as a slap in the face. After a while, though, my skin toughened when I realized it wasn't personal.

Hopefully, you'll quickly get past the shock of learning how cold and cruel the modeling world can be. Keep in mind that you're not being critiqued on the inner you, but on your "product"—your face, body, hair, skin, and so on. Although it's not a great feeling, it helps if you know that wasn't meant as a personal insult. Believe me, I've heard people slander models' race, physical attributes, height, weight, eyes, nose, ears … you name it. Generally, clients are polite and don't say anything negative, but sometimes the comments are incredibly mean.

The smallest thing—maybe something you've never even noticed about yourself—can be cause for a client not to book you. Perhaps they're looking for a girl with really skinny calves to sell a shoe that wraps up the leg, and your calves are just medium. Or maybe the client is shooting a collection of dark-colored clothing and feel the clothes won't stand out against your dark skin. You can't help any of these things, and there's nothing you can do to change them, so don't let them upset you. Just move on to the next go and see, where the client may be looking for someone with just your shape of calves or just your color of skin. Always remember that whenever a client evaluates you, it's always in terms of what they need to sell the product, as well as their own personal tastes.

Fortunately, your agent is there to act as a buffer against harsh criticisms and mean-spirited rejections. A good agent will usually sugarcoat a client's words. If a client has some constructive criticism, however, and mentions something that you can improve on—your teeth need to be straightened, you need to gain a few pounds, you need to let your hair color go back to its natural state—your agent may pass along the message.

Reality Check

What you definitely *don't* want to do is curse at clients, scream at them, criticize them back, or show them any disrespect, even if they rudely rebuff you or say something insulting. If someone rejects you, say "Thank you for your time," take your book, and walk away.

Don't deal with rejection in a negative way, by overeating, having one-night stands, or drinking or taking drugs to numb the pain. After you've binged on ice cream, slept with someone indiscriminately, or gotten drunk, the rejection will still be there in the morning. Not only that, but it will be compounded by the extra weight you gained, a hangover, a drug addiction, and maybe finding yourself pregnant or with a sexually transmitted disease.

> **Roshumba's Rules**
>
> When you're feeling rejected, talk to your agent. A good agent can be your own personal cheerleader. She'll tell you, "Okay, you didn't get this one, but I know you'll get the next one; keep your chin up."

Instead, talk to some uplifting friends who always make you laugh or feel good about yourself. Or call your parents, who will tell you they love you no matter what those people said. Maybe you could read a book of positive affirmations.

Getting Through Work Slowdowns

At various stages of your career, it's only natural that you experience work slowdowns. When you're first starting out in the modeling business, it might seem like not much is happening with your career. Even though you've done numerous test shoots and been on a million go and sees, the bookings are only dribbling in.

Don't panic! This happens to just about everyone. The best way to deal with this is to stay optimistic. Realize that you're the new kid in town and that it may take a while to make yourself known. Also remind yourself that if an agency signed you, someone believed you have the potential to become a model.

> **Roshumba's Rules**
>
> Until your career gets started, focus on making yourself a better model by doing as many test shoots as possible and by getting to know your agent and the other staff at the agency better.

Once a week or so, drop by and talk with the agents, both your own and the others in the agency. While you're there, introduce yourself to the managers who run the agency. Keep it light and friendly. This shows you're optimistic and that you're gung-ho, which will renew their faith in you and remind them who you are. Be sure, however, that you're not being a pest, that you're not hanging around the agency moping and pouting. A career that isn't taking off is frustrating to your agent, too. Your whining may turn them off completely.

In the meantime, try to make some new friends; invite other models, makeup artists, or test photographers you meet at go and sees or on jobs to have coffee, go to lunch, see a movie, whatever. Develop some interests outside modeling. If you haven't yet graduated from high school, this is a good time to focus on getting your diploma. (You can even sign up for online courses to complete your GED or get college credit.) If you're new in town, take this opportunity to learn the city; ride the subway, take long walks, and learn your way around. Also explore some of the local cultural institutions—museums, landmarks, galleries, theaters. When your career takes off, you'll probably have very little time to enjoy these things.

Finally, if you're sitting around poor and broke, consider getting a job. Many models get jobs waitressing or hostessing in restaurants, bars, and clubs (in fact, some hot spots hire only models), temping, or working in retail stores. (See Chapter 9 for more information on the best types of jobs for models.)

Model Scoop

When I was trying to get my modeling career off the ground in Chicago, I had a full-time job in the medical field. Even though I was having trouble booking modeling gigs, the medical job was a great self-esteem booster. Not only was I helping people, but I also knew I had something to fall back on if modeling didn't work out. Another thing I always loved doing was coloring in coloring books. Whenever I was down and distracted, I would get out my crayons and color Mickey Mouse and Snow White! Something about seeing all those colors calmed me and made me feel happy because I was focusing on something other than the fact that I wasn't modeling.

Later in your career, you might find that several regular clients are no longer booking you. Don't be bitter or angry about these shifts; recognize that change is an inevitable and even natural part of being a model, and move on to the next chapter. Talk to your agent and really focus on seeing other clients. Now's the time to go on a new round of go and sees and establish a new set of clientele.

All in all, modeling can be a very cold-hearted, harsh business. The rewards are great, but so is the toll it can take on your emotional self. That's why it's so important to know what you're getting into, so you can develop coping mechanisms to insulate yourself from the harshness of the modeling world.

The Least You Need to Know

◆ Drug and alcohol abuse, overspending, eating disorders, and bad relationships can all derail a modeling career.

◆ Your new modeling career may change the attitudes of old friends and family members toward you.

◆ Constant rejection is an intrinsic part of the modeling game. Learning not to take it personally is the best way to deal with it.

◆ Successful models learn to deal with stress and work slowdowns in positive ways.

Chapter 23

Managing Your Career and Your Money

In This Chapter

- ◆ Establishing clientele and finding your niche
- ◆ Balancing the different types of modeling work
- ◆ The importance of role models
- ◆ Planning for the future: life after modeling
- ◆ The pros and cons of accountants, lawyers, and managers
- ◆ Healthy beauty: medical insurance for models

You've come a long way, baby! By this point, you've found an agent, persevered through many go and sees, and survived your first few photo shoots.

This is where so many models get in trouble. They get caught up in living above their means, thinking their careers will last forever and that they'll be bringing a check home all their lives. But after 10 years or so of hard work as a model, you don't want to find yourself working as a checker at a grocery store because you lost all your money or you didn't save anything, and all you have to show for all your hard work is a 5-year-old Prada bag.

It takes careful planning, strategizing, and managing to get as much as you can out of a modeling career, to ensure that you make the most money and work for the best clients you can, work consistently, and have the kind of career that evolves, grows, and lasts for more than a few years. What about insurance? And how will you wisely manage the money you've made? Believe me, those dollars will be there one day and gone the next if you don't know how to handle money and don't keep an eye on how you spend and invest it.

Nice and Steady: The Beauty of Establishing Clientele

Just as a car salesperson establishes clientele—meaning she develops and builds relationships with customers who come back to her again whenever they need a new car—successful models also establish clientele. Developing and building relationships with certain clients and certain *teams* can be very beneficial to your career. The ideal situation is to have several clients and teams with whom you work all the time. First of all, working for regular clients means steady work and a reliable source of income. Also, once you've established clientele, they'll call just you and book just you; you don't need to spend time running around on go and sees.

> **Catwalk Talk**
>
> In modeling, a **team** refers to the behind-the-scenes people who work together to help the model look her best. This includes the photographer, hairstylist, makeup artists, clothing stylist, and all their assistants.

Working for one client also enables you to become familiar with a certain style and format of shooting, to become friends with the members of the team and with a certain group of models. The more you work with one team, the better your work can become. As hard as you try, you can't reach your potential or do your best work at a one-time-only job. But working with the same team, the more you learn, the more you inspire them—and they inspire you—and all your work becomes better.

> **Reality Check**
>
> The disadvantages of having a work relationship evolve into a friendship is that if something happens in the personal relationship—maybe you don't see eye to eye on something—that personal rift could end up affecting your work. If things are really bad, the client may no longer book you because the situation is so uncomfortable.

Although you obviously want to establish clientele for professional reasons, it's also great to have a chance to establish personal relationships and friendships in what can be a very lonely business. This is more important than it may sound because once you're a part of the fashion world, you might find it difficult to build relationships with "ordinary" people outside the business. They often don't understand your world and your lifestyle, which is why it's so great if you have the opportunity to develop relationships with people in the fashion world who can relate to your problems and everyday existence.

Model Scoop

For a long time, *Elle* magazine was my home. I was an "*Elle* girl" for 3 or 4 years and did photo shoots for them every month. I became really close friends with *Elle's* creative director, Regis Pagniez. Whenever *Elle* or Regis would host or attend private parties, charity events, and famous dinners, I was always invited. Although Regis has since retired, he is still a very dear friend I know I can count on to this day.

As great as it is to establish clientele whom you work with frequently, be sure you don't neglect to pursue new clients as well. If you don't continually replenish your list of clientele, you could find yourself stuck with just one client. So even though you might have strong relationships with a few clients, you should always keep trying to form and nurture relationships with new ones.

Balancing Editorial, Advertising, Runway, and Catalog Work

It's great to have a niche, but it's also important to try to work in as many different aspects of modeling as you can. Models often make the mistake of doing only one type of work: all they ever wanted was to appear on a runway in Paris. That's great, but they need to focus on having a fabulous career, not just one fabulous moment.

Modeling in different arenas gives you wider exposure, and also, every aspect of modeling feeds off the others. Somebody might see you in a fashion show, love your look, and book you for an advertisement. Somebody else might see you in an ad and want to use you in their catalog. Working in a variety of areas also gives your career more longevity than is possible with a single-minded focus.

Reality Check

Although it might be tempting, don't get lazy and focus on only one type of work. Even though it might be easier in the short term, a single-minded focus won't be to your benefit. Always be sure you're being sent on go and sees for a variety of jobs, including fashion shows, TV commercials, catalogs, and advertisements, especially early in your career.

Ideally, you'll be doing some editorial work (to keep your image fresh and your face in front of the fashion industry), TV commercial and advertising work (to make money and to broaden your audience in the mass market), runway work (to solidify your place as a fashion model), and catalog work (to pay the bills and establish long-term clientele).

Another reason to work in as many aspects of modeling as possible is that the fashion industry is notoriously fickle. If a client stops booking you because they found a new model, you'll want to have another client or another aspect of modeling to fall back on. Not only will you expand the possibilities of your career, but you'll also learn new skills, meet new people, and at the same time grow as a talent.

Although not everyone will be able to work in all aspects of modeling (or even in more than one), it's very important that you at least give it a try.

That's why a good relationship with your agent is key, so you make the right decisions and take advantage of all the opportunities that present themselves. Once they're gone, they're usually gone for good.

Planning for a Future Beyond Modeling

Models have a limited career span, which is why it's so important to start making plans for your post-modeling future in the third to fifth year of your career.

Ask yourself what you want to be doing in 5 years:

- ◆ Do you want to have made enough money so you can just quit the business, get married, and have a family?

- ◆ Do you want to use modeling to segue into another career as a magazine editor, a fashion writer, a fashion designer, an actress, or a broadcast personality?

- ◆ Do you love modeling and want to keep doing it as long as you possibly can?

Whatever choice you make, you need to map out a game plan so you can accomplish your goals. During this process, talk with your agent about your plans to be sure she knows what you're up to so she can help you. Your decision about your future will affect how she'll promote you and structure your career so she makes sure you get what you want out of the business.

Reality Check _____

The process of planning for your future can be very difficult. While you're trying to take classes or pursue various other interests, you'll still be modeling full-time, and it's not a good idea to turn down too many jobs. When I started to prepare for my future, instead of signing up for classes that would force me to cancel jobs, I worked with a coach and took classes on weekends, which made scheduling easier.

The Final Curtain: Leaving the Business

It's much better to walk away from the modeling business than to have the business walk away from you. Hopefully, by the time your career is coming to an end, you'll have figured out what you want to do with your future and will have already started doing it. The end can come anywhere between the eighth and fifteenth years of your career, but in general, most models have 10-year career spans.

The conclusion of your modeling career can come in several ways. Your agent might tell you to consider retiring, that the natural cycle of your career has come to an end. Or maybe for the past year, your bookings are down to one a week, and even that's not always guaranteed.

Roshumba's Rules _____

Your work might slow down between the eighth and fifteenth year, and this might be the first time you'll have the time to pursue a college degree, if that's your ambition. When you start attending school full-time, it might be almost impossible for you to travel for modeling jobs.

I think that it's better to retire yourself than to be asked to leave. If you want to continue modeling, transfer to your agency's elegant division, or find an agency that handles elegant models. Even if you're not working every day, if something comes up, you'll still have representation.

Model Scoop _____

You might be inspired by the success of many ex-models. Many models, including myself, have gone into acting, as have: Rebecca Romijn, Eva Longoria, Cameron Diaz, Andie MacDowell, and Rene Russo. Many others have gone into fashion design: Elle Macpherson has a very successful lingerie collection, Elizabeth Hurley has her own swimwear line, and Christy Turlington has designed a line of yoga clothes. Kathy Ireland has parlayed her fame into numerous ventures, including clothing, furniture, and housewares.

This is also a good time to seriously pursue acting, if that's your ambition. You'll want to dedicate the necessary time and energy into learning your craft, going on auditions, and trying to find an agent.

If you want to start your own business, this can be the time to do it. (Depending on the business, you might be able to start it earlier—sometime after your fifth year in the business.) Most self-owned businesses, especially service businesses such as restaurants, health clubs, and nightclubs, are so time-consuming that you probably can't manage running them while pursuing a modeling career.

A Model Plan for a Financially Sound Future

When a model starts out, especially if she hasn't had to think about money management before, she might not have a real grasp of money—what it takes to earn it and how to handle it. Maybe her parents just gave her money whenever she needed it.

Roshumba's Rules

Follow the one-third plan: pay your bills with one-third of the money you earn, have fun with one-third, and put one-third in a savings account. Even if you don't follow this plan exactly (at the beginning of your career, you might not be able to afford to save one-third of your salary), be sure you save at least a portion of the money you make.

Starting out, many models find themselves making more money in a week than they could make in a year at their local Burger King. When their careers take off, they might not realize that although they're making a lot of money really fast, it can disappear as quickly as it comes in, and once it's gone, it's not coming back!

Three to five years later, they're no longer earning top dollar, and they're no longer quite as in demand. Suddenly, they realize they have a very luxurious lifestyle and no way to keep it up. They may have an expensive shopping habit, a luxe apartment, vacation homes, and cool sports cars, but they didn't plan how they would maintain these things after they stopped making the big bucks.

The moral: plan ahead from the very first paycheck.

Planning for the Future, Right from the Start

The day you get your very first paycheck, you should open checking and savings accounts. (Ask your agent for the name of a local bank that has a good reputation.) Later, you'll want to open an investment account as well. A checking account enables you to write checks to pay your bills and other expenses. With a savings account, you can deposit money that you're going to keep, not spend.

It's vital that models learn to manage their own personal finances.

Model Investments

Models often make a lot of money in the first few years of their careers, then a medium amount of money, and finally very little as their careers come to an end. This is just a fact of life for models, and it will be far less devastating if you continue to adjust your lifestyle according to your income level.

When you find your career slowing down, really start socking away every cent into savings, because soon you might not be earning anything. Start by limiting your expenses as much as possible. You don't need to go out to dinner every night; instead, find another hobby besides shopping and save money by learning to cook.

When it comes to your investments, be serious and conservative. Get involved with an investment professional who's been in business a long time and has a good track record and an upstanding reputation. Work with an established financial company that can give you sound advice as far as stocks and other investments go.

Roshumba's Rules

When it comes to your money, speak up, be involved, and tell your investment counselors yes, no, and maybe later. Read *Money* magazine, *The Wall Street Journal,* and *Fortune* on a regular basis to find out more about the financial world.

Be sure you get (and read!) monthly statements that let you know what's happening with your money. Insist on documentation for all your stock purchases, retirement accounts, and other investments.

Scam Alert!

Many con artists lurk around the modeling industry in the hopes of finding their next victim. They've lured in many models with their get-rich-quick schemes. Some con artists set up investment companies where they buy risky stocks using models' money. Others want to open their own businesses, such as health clubs, nightclubs, restaurants, and resorts.

To a young model who is inexperienced in dealing with large amounts of money, these plans might sound like good investments. Some of them might be, but I think it's a much better idea to buy stock in an established company. Giving money to such shady people can mean a quick trip on the road to financial ruin. Steer clear of the happy-go-lucky guy or gal who asks you for money.

Remember, if it sounds too good to be true, it probably is. If someone tells you that if you invest in his restaurant you'll double your money in 6 months, grab your wallet and run. Only a minuscule number of investments yield those returns. Be very suspicious if someone promises you'll double your money.

Even when you get married, you should follow the same rules until you've passed several major anniversaries. Too many models find that those great guys they married quickly turn into total money grubbers, especially when the relationship sours.

Even if the guy makes more money than you, you should always have a prenuptial agreement when you get married. As bad as divorce is on a personal level, it's a lot worse when you have to give him half of everything you own, pay his debts and taxes, and pay him alimony when you split up. And believe me, it does happen!

Model Scoop _____

I know several prominent models who have been burned financially in divorce court. When one highly paid model split up with her husband, he got to keep the million-dollar house she had paid for, plus *she* had to pay *him* alimony. Another model got married and had children right away. When she and her husband got divorced, she had to pay him off to stop him from harassing her. Another model was dating a guy who talked her into buying an apartment. She put up all the money and paid all the bills, but he had co-signed the loan, so when they split up, he was entitled to half, even though they'd been dating for only a short period.

Charge It! The Credits and Debits of Credit Cards

Because models are on the road so much, they definitely need to have a major credit card. Although the client pays for your hotel room, you are responsible for extra things such as telephone calls, pay-per-view movies, and snacks and beverages from the minibar. You'll need a credit card to secure the telephone and other necessities.

At the same time, credit cards can be very dangerous. When you hand that credit card to the salesclerk, it can give you the false impression that you're just signing a paper and then walking away with something for free. It's a great convenience, but you have to be careful not to abuse it. When the bill comes, the credit card company wants its money. So before you charge anything, be sure you already have the money to pay the bill at the end of month.

The One Certainty in Modeling: Taxes

When most people receive a paycheck, their employers withhold a significant amount of money for income and Social Security taxes, which the employer then pays to the government on the worker's behalf. When a model receives a check from her agency, however, no income or Social Security taxes have been deducted from the check. This is because the model isn't an employee of the agency; she is an independent contractor, meaning she is self-employed, someone who works for herself, not for a company.

Because no taxes are withheld from her paychecks, a model has to pay her own federal and state taxes on a quarterly basis. She has to set aside a certain percentage of each paycheck so she'll have enough money to pay her taxes four times a year. (To be on the safe side, figure a third of your income will go to taxes.) Because the tax laws are so complicated and change all the time, most models have accountants who figure out how much they owe every quarter. Your accountant will let you know how much you need to pay each quarter, but you'll write the check to the IRS.

Reality Check _____

Some models give their accountants power of attorney (which means they have the power to sign the models' name on checks) to ensure that all their taxes and bills are paid on time. But I think giving anyone that type of power over *your* money is crazy because it's a power that can be abused very easily, and you'll be the one who's thousands of dollars poorer.

Don't ever blow off paying your quarterly taxes. Don't get behind in your payments because the IRS will come after you in a big way—and that's one of worst things that can happen to you financially. The IRS will assess you penalties and interest on the amount you owe, and your bill can quickly skyrocket. In extreme cases, a lien (or freeze) could be put on all your accounts so you won't be able to spend a cent without the IRS's approval.

If you can't pay your taxes on time, talk to your accountant, who can try to set up a payment schedule with the IRS.

Calculating Why You Need an Accountant

Have I convinced you by now that you should probably get an accountant? If not, and if you still think you can handle all your own taxes, investments, and so on, read on.

No matter how financially savvy they may be, most models benefit from having an accountant. Tax laws are always changing, and you need someone who's really knowledgeable when it comes to doing taxes for models. For one thing, models have write-offs other people don't have, including makeup, certain clothing items, manicures, pedicures, car services, and taxis. They can deduct these expenses from their income so they don't have to pay taxes on them. But it's best to have an accountant's advice on this.

In addition to taking care of taxes, accountants can help you keep track of how much you're earning, saving, and investing. They can give you advice on savings and investments and tell you whether this is a smart time to invest in Wall Street or whether it's better to keep your money in a less-risky money-market account. Accountants can refer you to financial planners and stock brokers who can help you invest your money. They also try to get you to evaluate your expenditures so you're not spending mindlessly or foolishly and instead e saving and investing as much as you need to for the future.

Your accountants can also counsel you on setting up a retirement account (SEP or IRA). The rules for these often change, and an accountant who keeps up on the latest revisions in the law can help you maximize your investments in these.

The best way to find an accountant is to ask your agency for a referral. Or maybe your family has one they've used for years. When you're looking for an accountant, be sure you can develop a long-term relationship with the person you hire. You'll want to be able to talk to your accountant about money matters, taxes, investments, retirement planning, and ways to avoid or delay paying taxes, so you want someone you can relate to.

A caution on accountants: It's very important that your accountant be legitimate, professional, and trustworthy. I've heard about many scams involving celebrities who wanted to focus only on the artistic aspects of their career, leaving accountants, friends, spouses, or managers to handle their money. Too many of them find out years later that their accountants have lost all their money through incompetence and bad investments. When huge sums of money are flying around—and if you're earning it and they aren't—people often feel entitled to more than they're being paid.

Also writing your own checks and paying your own taxes makes you more responsible and involved with your personal finances, which ultimately is to your advantage. You're the one who earned it and put it in that checking account, so you should be the only one who can take it out. Only you know how hard you had to work to get it.

Financial Rx: Medical Insurance

It's probably the last thing you'd think of buying when you get that first paycheck, but it's one of the most important: insurance. Medical insurance isn't as much fun to buy as a Calvin Klein jacket, but it is one of the smartest investments you can make.

Although it's a remote possibility, if a medical emergency were to happen, it could quickly wipe out all your savings and put you in debt for years because of the high cost of medical care in this country. Unlike most people who get medical insurance through their jobs, models don't because they're considered self-employed.

Ask your agent, other models, or other industry professionals if they know of any good medical plans. Also, when you do a TV commercial, you might be eligible for the medical insurance plan of the TV actors' union, the Screen Actors Guild (SAG). (You are required to earn a certain minimum amount to qualify.)

Roshumba's Rules

Although it's costly, you might also want to consider getting disability insurance, which provides you with an income in case you get hurt and can't work for a significant amount of time.

The Big Guns: Lawyers and Managers

Although your agent can handle most standard contracts, when it comes to any very detailed or complicated contract, you'll probably need to hire a lawyer. Lawyers are necessary whenever you're negotiating an endorsement deal or a TV or movie contract. In general, these contracts contain highly technical language only lawyers can really understand.

Lawyers can also negotiate difficult situations or disagreements between you and the client, which spares your having to deal with a negative situation. A good lawyer can also suggest ways of making the most of contract opportunities.

It's best to have a lawyer who has experience in negotiating contracts for artists, especially if she's a specialist in the field of books, TV, modeling, or performing. Your agent or other industry professional can probably recommend a good lawyer who has experience working with other models.

If and when your career starts branching out to the point that you're doing not just modeling, but also TV, films, and endorsement deals, as well as developing your own product lines, you might want to consider getting a manager. Many models end up having managers because they can be lifesavers for very successful or very busy models, especially those who want to break into show business.

When you have many different things going on—modeling for TV commercials, runway shows, and magazines; going on acting jobs, producing a calendar; starting a regular broadcasting career—you might end up having four or five different agents. It can be a little hectic having to coordinate all this yourself. A manager can coordinate your whole schedule so you have only one person to deal with.

Roshumba's Rules

Ask a potential manager who else she manages. If she represents people you're aspiring to be like, such as successful actresses, that's a good sign.

Finding a manager can be a bit tricky. Most likely, your agent won't be very helpful because he might be concerned about someone invading his territory. Your best bet is to ask other models or professionals in the field you want to get into, whether it's TV, broadcasting, or movies. Also, your film or TV agent, accountant, or lawyer might be able to refer you to someone.

Good managers always make you feel like you're their first priority. They take your phone calls or get right back to you. They're always on top of your schedule. They encourage you to better yourself, to take acting classes or see certain movies, and they keep you informed of what's happening in the field you want to get into. You get the impression that they're constantly seeking new opportunities for you, that one of their first priorities is making sure you're accomplishing what you want.

Six months to a year after you start working with a manager, evaluate the relationship. How successful has she been in helping you accomplish career goals? If she's not getting the job done, she might not be so good for you.

The Least You Need to Know

◆ Establishing clientele ensures a steady source of work.

◆ Selecting good role models can have a positive impact on your career.

◆ Publicists can be key for models with high-profile careers.

◆ It's important to start planning for a future beyond modeling years before it happens.

◆ Smart models start saving and investing from their very first paycheck.

◆ Paying taxes on time and using credit cards responsibly are essential for a model's financial security.

◆ Most models need an accountant, and some might benefit from hiring lawyers and/or managers.

Appendix A

Catwalk Talk Glossary

agent   A person in a modeling agency who recruits new models, markets them to clients (including magazines, advertisers, and fashion designers), and guides their careers.

Amazon   Named after a tribe of ferocious, powerful warrior women in Greek mythology, Amazon models are tall, muscular, and imposing looking.

American Federation of Television and Radio Artists (AFTRA)   The union that represents television actors and radio personalities.

anorexia   An eating disorder. Sufferers eat little or nothing because they think (erroneously) that they're fat.

Better Business Bureau (BBB)   A private, nonprofit organization with offices around the country that provides reports on local businesses.

body shot   A picture of a model in a bathing suit that shows her body from head to toe.

booker   *Booker, agent,* and *model manager* are interchangeable terms that all refer to the person in an agency who develops you as a model, books you for jobs, and oversees your career.

booking   Any job a model is hired to do. When a model is hired for a job, whether it be to pose for a magazine or advertisement or to appear in a runway show, she is said to be "booked" for the job.

bulimia   An eating disorder. Sufferers consume huge amounts of food and then purge it by vomiting, abusing laxatives, or exercising excessively.

call time   The time a model is expected to arrive at the job. It's the time the work of the day begins, when the model and other team members go on the clock—that is, start getting paid.

callback   When an agency or client asks you to come back for a second interview because they're considering representing or hiring you, their request is referred to as a callback.

castings   Another word for go and sees. In the United States, the term *castings* usually refers to go and sees for TV commercials. In Europe, the term *castings* is used more often for all types of go and sees.

catwalk   *See* runway.

celebrity model   An actress, singer, or other well-known person who models in an ad, a magazine story or cover, or a fashion show.

Chameleon   Named after a lizard that's able to change its color so it can blend into the landscape, Chameleon models change their appearance frequently to stand out from their environments.

client   On a magazine shoot, the client is the fashion editor. On a catalog shoot, it's the representative or art director from the catalog company. On an advertising shoot, it's the corporate client.

collections   Refers to the collective showing of designers' new fashions in one particular city. The New York collections take place when all the top New York designers show their latest designs for the season.

commercial agent   A person who handles models who don't fall into the traditional "fashion model" category. Commercial agents book models for commercial work (print ads, TV commercials), as opposed to editorial or artistic work.

commercial models   Models who work primarily in local and secondary markets and appear mainly in catalogs and advertisements.

composite (or comp) card   A card that features several different shots of a model and is given out to clients so they can get an idea of the model's look.

confirmed   If the client definitely wants to book you, you are said to be confirmed.

conflict of interest   When a model appears in two advertisements for similar products, thus undermining her ability to sell either one.

contact sheet   A large sheet of photographic paper that has mini prints of numerous pictures the photographer shot. Most photographers download the pictures they take and work with them directly on the computer, but often they'll have a contact sheet printed as well.

contouring   In makeup terms, contouring means applying a foundation in a darker or lighter color to shade and shape a model's face, to enhance facial features or create the illusion of high cheekbones or a slender nose.

cover try   A photo shoot that's done in the hopes that it will be good enough to appear on a magazine cover. The photo itself must be striking, and the model must look her best.

day rate   The amount of money a model earns for a full day of work. A model's experience, her popularity, and her client's caliber all have an effect on her day rate.

eating disorder   An emotional and physical problem that expresses itself through the abuse of food and the body. Eating disorders include anorexia, bulimia, and compulsive overeating.

editorial   Refers to any work that will appear in a magazine's editorial (as opposed to advertising) pages. It includes stories about the latest fashion and beauty trends, as well as lifestyle (sex, relationships, job, and money) pieces.

editorial models   Also known as high-fashion models, editorial models work in the fashion capitals, where they appear in magazine stories, designer fashion shows, and high-end advertisements.

elegant (or classic) model   A model or celebrity who's over the age of 35. They can be famous actresses or former "regular" models who have returned to the business.

fashion boards   Also known as teen boards, these are groups sponsored by malls that provide models for modeling events at the mall.

fashion capitals   Milan, Paris, and New York City are the three fashion capitals of the world because so many fashion and cosmetic companies, fashion magazines, advertising agencies, and models are based there.

fashion credits   In return for being allowed to borrow clothes from designers for fashions shoots, a magazine identifies the designer of a garment next to the picture of it.

fashion editor   Also known as the fashion stylist or the sittings editor, this person selects the clothes to be photographed for a magazine story and makes sure the magazine's vision is being captured.

fashion spread   A story spotlighting a particular fashion trend that takes up two whole pages of a magazine. It appears toward the back of the magazine, where there are no advertisements.

fashionista   A person, often someone who works in fashion or retail, who follows every trend. She is always wearing the latest styles, carrying the most fashionable purse, and sporting the hottest sunglasses.

featured model   The first and/or the last model to appear in a runway show. At the end of the show, she walks down the runway on the arm of the designer. She may be a celebrity, the designer's favorite model, or a famous supermodel.

Federal Trade Commission (FTC)   A government agency headquartered in Washington, D.C., that enforces consumer protection laws.

fittings models   Models who work in a designer's studio trying on the unfinished clothes; the designer then makes any adjustments to the garment so it fits perfectly.

foundation   Sometimes called base, this is the first makeup product an artist applies to your face. It smoothes out any minor discolorations and flaws, and creates a perfect canvas for the rest of your makeup.

go and see   An interview for a modeling job. It's called a go and see because a model *goes* to the client's office so they can *see* what she looks like in person.

haute couture   Ultraexpensive clothes custom-made to fit the few women wealthy enough to afford them. They are made of the most expensive, luxurious fabrics, with exquisite details and hand-sewn seams.

head shot   A head shot is an 8×10- or 9½×11-inch photo of an actor's or model's head and face. They are given to potential clients to help them remember the models they've interviewed. They're used mainly for TV work.

hobby modeling   Also called modeling for experience, it is done primarily for the experience and fun of modeling. Hobby modeling is usually unpaid.

image   A physical embodiment of an idea or concept. A company will hire a model that best represents its image.

in-store modeling   Also called informal modeling. Models dressed in clothes from the store walk around and let the customers see the clothes up close as they shop.

live-action camera   A video or film camera that captures movement.

local markets   Any city that's not a fashion capital (New York, Paris, and Milan) or a secondary market (Chicago, Los Angeles, and Miami).

look books   Photo albums that are put together by clothing companies so consumers can look at all of that season's styles in one place. Look books can be in-store photo albums or printed brochures given to fashion editor and retail buyers and/or mailed out to customers.

masthead   The masthead of a magazine lists everyone responsible for putting together the publication, including the editor in chief, the fashion editors, and the model editor.

measurements   One of the statistics supplied to prospective agents and clients, usually written as a series of three numbers—for example, 34-24-34. The first number is the bust size, the second is the waist measurement, and the third is the hip size.

meet and greet   A short interview judges and agents conduct with participants at a model convention. You'll be asked basic questions, such as where you live, what grade you're in, and why you want to be a model.

model editor   The magazine staffer who books all the models featured in a magazine, including those used in fashion stories, beauty pieces, and all the other features in the magazine (pieces about jobs, relationships, advice, and money, for example).

model manager   *See* agent.

model search   A contest a modeling agency or magazine holds to find potential new models. Model searches are held in cities all around the country, often at local malls.

modeling agent   *See* agent.

modeling conventions   Events where agencies can recruit aspiring models. Unlike model searches, they charge sizeable entrance fees and usually last several days.

mother agency   The agency that discovered you, marketed you, and developed your career. If you've changed agencies in the course of your career, your mother agency is your base agency, located in the city you call home.

overexposed   A model is said to be overexposed when she has been working too much in one market—she's appeared in every fashion show, magazine, and ad. Clients get bored with looking at her face and stop hiring her.

P&G child   Shorthand for the Procter & Gamble child, this common industry term refers to a child with perfect, all-American features.

panic attack   An extreme reaction to a situation that wouldn't be cause for abnormal distress for most people. It's characterized by an extreme sense of anxiety, fear, and stress.

plus-size clothing   Women's clothing in sizes 12 or 14 and larger. It's modeled by plus-size models, who are larger than regular models.

portfolio   An album of specially selected pictures you take with you to job interviews.

profile shot   A shot of the side of your face or body.

publicist   Also called a public relations specialist, this person handles all your contacts with the press, including magazine and newspaper interviews, photo shoots, and appearances on radio and TV shows.

ready-to-wear   Unlike haute couture garments, which are custom-made, ready-to-wear clothes are mass-produced. Nearly all the clothes you see at the local mall fall into the ready-to-wear category.

real-people models   Represent a type, such as a mom, a cute kid, a kindly granddad, a balding regular Joe, or a businesswoman. These models appear mainly in ads and TV commercials.

residual   A payment an actor or model receives every time the TV commercial she appears in is broadcast. For a national commercial that gets heavy play, this could be a significant amount of money.

resort wear   A line of clothing that appears between fall and spring collections. Usually casual, it was traditionally worn at resorts in warm-weather climates by people escaping cold winters.

runway   Also known as the catwalk, a long, narrow stage that juts out into the audience. At a fashion show, the models walk down the runway, which allows the audience to see the clothes up close.

Screen Actors Guild (SAG)   The union that represents actors in films.

sample reel   A videotape sampling of an actor's or model's on-camera work, including TV commercials and industrial training films.

secondary markets   Refers to second-tier fashion cities in the United States, including Chicago, Los Angeles, and Miami.

set   The area in a photo shoot where the pictures are actually taken. The cameras, the lighting, and any necessary backdrops or props are set up on the set.

straight-on shot   A photo in which your head and/or body are facing the camera.

supermodel   A model who is so successful she becomes a household name, well known to an audience outside the fashion industry. Heidi Klum and Gisele Bündchen are supermodels.

talent   The models, actors, or other performers working at a still photo shoot, on a TV commercial or movie set, or at a live performance.

team   The behind-the-scenes people who work together to help the model look her best. This includes the photographer, the hairstylist, the makeup artist, the clothing stylist, and all their assistants.

tear sheets   Pages torn from a magazine, newspaper, or other periodical. A model tears out any pages on which she's pictured and puts them in her portfolio.

test shoots for your book   Special photo shoots done mostly by beginning models to gain modeling experience and to get photos to put in their portfolio.

testing photographers   Photographers who do test shoots with aspiring models. They are often the assistants of major working photographers and are usually aspiring to become working photographers in their own right.

theatrical head shot   *See* head shot.

three-quarters angle   In a photo, you're facing slightly off to one side, halfway between the straight-on and profile shots.

vouchers   Special model time sheets. A model's agency gives these forms to her. At the end of a shoot, the client signs the voucher, verifying the model worked and should be paid.

Waif   A superskinny, undernourished-looking, not classically pretty model. Waifs were the talk of the fashion world in the early 1990s.

wardrobe   The clothes you'll be wearing on a photo shoot, as well as the area where you'll get dressed. It's where the fashion stylist works and where the model changes from her street clothes into the garment being shot.

wrapped   Another word for "finished." "We're wrapped," is the official word from the photographer or client that the shoot is over, that the work of the day has been completed, and that the model and the team can pack up and go home.

Model Knowledge: Essential Books and Websites

These books and websites are great sources of additional information on fashion, beauty, modeling, and models.

Model Reads

Aucoin, Kevyn. *The Art of Makeup*. New York: HarperCollins, 1996.

Beale, Lucy, and Angela Jensen. *The Complete Idiot's Guide to Better Skin*. Indianapolis: Alpha Books, 2004.

Begoun, Paula. *The Beauty Bible: The Ultimate Guide to Smart Beauty*, Seattle: Beginning Press, 2002.

Brown, Bobbi, and Annemarie Iverson. *Bobbi Brown Beauty: The Ultimate Beauty Resource*. New York: HarperCollins, 1997.

———. *Bobbi Brown Teenage Beauty: Everything You Need to Look Pretty, Natural, Sexy and Awesome*. New York: HarperCollins, 2001.

Emme, and Daniel Paisner. *True Beauty: Positive Attitudes and Practical Tips from the World's Leading Plus-Size Model*. New York: Perigee, 1998.

Fried, Stephen M. *Thing of Beauty: The Tragedy of Supermodel Gia*. New York: Pocket Books, 1994.

Gross, Michael. *Model: The Ugly Business of Beautiful Women.* New York: Warner Books, 1994.

Martin, Richard, and Harold Koda. *Christian Dior.* New York: Metropolitan Museum of Art, 1996.

Milbank, Caroline Rennolds. *Couture.* New York: Stewart, Tabori and Cheng, 1997.

———. *New York Fashion: The Evolution of American Style.* New York: Harry N. Abrams, 1996.

Pochna, Marie-France, and Joanna Savill (trans.). *Christian Dior: The Man Who Made the World* Look *New.* New York: Arcade Publishing, 1997.

Summers, Barbara. *Black and Beautiful: How Women of Color Changed the Fashion Industry.* Amistad, 2001.

———. New York: *Skin Deep: Inside the World of Black Fashion Models.* Amistad, 1999.

Teboul, David. *Yves Saint Laurent 5, avenue Marceau, 75116 Paris, France.* New York: Harry N. Abrams, 2002.

Vreeland, Diana. *D.V.*, Cambridge, MA: Da Capo, 2003.

Walker, Andre, and Teresa Wiltz. *Andre Talks Hair.* New York: Simon & Schuster, 1998.

Wallach, Janet. *Chanel: Her Style and Her Life.* New York: Nan A. Talese, 1998.

Widdows, Lee, and Caroline Cox. *Hair & Fashion.* London: Victoria & Albert Museum, 2005.

Model Websites

www.bbb.org
Better Business Bureau website—information about modeling scams

www.bossmodels.com
Boss modeling agency

www.bravoTV.com
Official site of *Project Runway*

www.clickmodel.com
Click modeling agency

www.elitemodel.com
Elite modeling agency

www.elle.com
Elle magazine site

www.fordmodels.com
Ford modeling agency

www.ftc.gov
Federal Trade Commission website—
information about modeling scams

www.giselebundchen.com.br
Gisele Bündchen's official site
(in Portuguese)

www.heidi-klum.de
Heidi Klum's official site

www.idmodels.com
ID Model Management

www.imgmodels.com
IMG modeling agency

www.imta.com
International Modeling and Talent
Association model convention

www.majormodelmanagement.com
Major Model Management

www.marilynagency.com
Marilyn modeling agency

www.mc2mm.com
MC2 modeling agency

www.modelingadvice.com
Lots of interesting information and
posts about modeling scams

www.models.com
Modeling industry news, plus information about top models and agencies

www.mtv.com
Official MTV site; information about
8th & Ocean and links to fashion
specials

www.newyorkmodels.com
New York Model Management

www.nextmodels.com
Next modeling agency

www.qmodels.com
Q modeling agency

www.seventeen.com
Seventeen magazine site

www.Style.com
Official website of *Vogue* and *W*

www.trumpmodels.com
Trump modeling agency

www.tyrabanks.com
Tyra Banks's official website

www.cwtv.com/shows/americas-next-top-model
Official site of *America's Next Top Model*

www.victoriassecret.com
Victoria's Secret website

Directory of Modeling Agencies

The following is a list of modeling agencies in the international fashion capitals and in the secondary markets in the United States. To the best of my knowledge, these are all legitimate agencies, but inclusion here does not necessarily mean I endorse any particular one.

New York

Abrams Artists Agency
275 Seventh Avenue, 26th Floor
New York, NY 10001
646-486-4600
abramsartists.com

Boss Models
1 Ganesvoort Street
New York, NY 10014
212-242-2444
bossmodels.com

Click Models
129 W. 27th Street, Penthouse
New York, NY 10001
212-206-1616
clickmodel.com

Cunningham, Escott & Dipene
257 Park Avenue South, Suite 900
New York, NY 10010
212-477-1666
cedtalent.com

Elite Model Management
404 Park Avenue South, 9th Floor
New York, NY 10016
212-529-9700
elitemodel.com

Ford Models/Children
111 Fifth Avenue
New York, NY 10003
212-219-6500
fordmodels.com

Ford Models
111 Fifth Avenue
New York, NY 10003
212-219-6500
fordmodels.com

Gilla Roos Representatives
16 W. 22nd Street, 7th Floor
New York, NY 10010
212-727-7820
gillaroos.com

ID Model Management
110 Greene Street, Suite 702
New York, NY 10012
212-206-1818
idmodels.com

IMG Models
304 Park Avenue South, 12th Floor
New York, NY 10010
212-253-8884
imgmodels.com

Major Model Management
381 Park Avenue South, Suite 1501
New York, NY 10016
212-685-1200
majormodelmanagement.com

Marilyn, Inc.
300 Park Avenue South
New York, NY 10010
212-260-6500
marilynagency.com

MC2 Model Management
6 W. 14th Street, 3rd Floor
New York, NY 10011
646-638-3330
mc2mm.com

New York Model Management
596 Broadway, #701
New York, NY 10012
212-539-1700
newyorkmodels.com

Next Management
15 Watts Street, 6th Floor
New York, NY 10013
212-925-5100
nextmodelsusa.com

Q Model Management
180 Varick Street, 13th Floor
New York, NY 10014
212-807-6777
qmodels.com

Trump Model Management
91 Fifth Avenue, 3rd Floor
New York, NY 10003
212-924-0990
trumpmodels.com

Wilhelmina
300 Park Avenue South
New York, NY 10010
212-473-0700
wilhelmina.com

Chicago

ARia Model & Talent Management
1017 W. Washington, Suite 2C
Chicago, IL 60607
312-850-9671
ariatalent.com

Arlene Wilson Management
430 W. Erie, #210
Chicago, IL 60610
312-573-0046
arlenewilson.com

Elite Chicago
58 W. Huron
Chicago, IL 60610
312-943-3226
elitemodel.com

Ford Chicago
1017 W. Washington, Suite 2C
Chicago, IL 60607
312-243-9400
fordmodels.com

Stewart Talent
58 W. Huron
Chicago, IL 60610
312-943-3131
stewarttalent.com

Miami

Elite Miami
1200 Collins Avenue, Suite 207
Miami Beach, FL 33139
305-674-9500
elitemodel.com

Ford Models
1775 Collins Avenue, Suite 216
Miami Beach, FL 33139
305-534-7200
fordmodels.com

Irene Marie Management Group
728 Ocean Drive
Miami Beach, FL 33139
305-672-2929
irenemarie.com

MC2 Model Management
846 Lincoln Road, Penthouse
Miami Beach, FL 33139
305-672-8300
mc2mm.com

Michele Pommier Models
927 Lincoln Road, Suite 200
Miami Beach, FL 33139
305-674-1733
michelepommier.com

Next Management
1688 Meridian Avenue, Suite 800
Miami Beach, FL 33139
305-531-5100
nextmodelsusa.com

Wilhelmina
930 Washington, 4th Floor
Miami Beach, FL 33139
305-672-9344
wilhelmina.com

Los Angeles

Cunningham, Escott & Dipene
310-475-2111
cedtalent.com

Elite Model Management
345 N. Maple Drive, Suite 397
Beverly Hills, CA 90210
310-274-9395
elitemodel.com

Ford Models
8826 Burton Way
Beverly Hills, CA 90211
310-276-8100
fordmodels.com

Next Management
8447 Wilshire Boulevard, Penthouse
Beverly Hills, CA 90211
323-782-0010
nextmodelsusa.com

Nous Model Management
117 N. Robertson Boulevard
Los Angeles, CA 90048
310-385-6900
nousmodels.com

Q Model Management
8618 W. 3rd Street
Los Angeles, CA 90048
310-205-2888
qmodels.com

Wilhelmina West
7257 Beverly Boulevard
Los Angeles, CA 90036
323-655-0909
wilhelmina.com

Paris

City Models
21, rue Jean Mermoz
Paris
France
75008
33-1-53-93-33-33
city-models.com

Elite
21, avenue Montaigne
Paris
France
75008
elitemodel.com

Ford Models Europe
3 rue de Choiseul
Paris
France
75002
33-1-53-05-25-25

IMG Models
8, rue Danielle Casanova
Paris
France
75002
33-1-55-35-12-00
imgmodels.com

Marilyn Agency
4 avenue de la Paix
Paris
France
75002
33-1-53-29-53-29
marilynagency.com

Next Management
188, rue de Rivoli
Paris
France
75001
1-53-45-13-00
nextmodels.com

Success
11-13, rue des Arquebusiers
Paris
France
75003
33-1-42-78-89-89
successmodels.com

Viva Models
15, rue Duphot
Paris
France 75001
33-1-44-55-12-60
vivamodels.fr

Milan

Note: Phone numbers in Italy can be either 6 or 8 numbers.

Christian Jacques Women/CJ Men
Via Voghera, 11/A
Milano
Italy
20144
39-02-5810-7440
cjmodel.com

Elite Model Management Milano
Via San Vittore 40
Milano Italy
20123
elitemodels.com

The Fashion Model Management
Via Monte Rosa 80
Milano
Italy
20149
39-02-480-861
fashionworld.it

IMG Models Milan
Piazzale Biancamano n8
21021 Milano Italy
39-02-6203-3037
imgmodels.com

Joy Model Management
Via S. Vittore, 40
Milano
Italy
20123
39-02-4800-2776
joymodels.com

Directory of Key Foreign Tourist Offices

I've included these key tourist offices as a source of reference if you're ever looking for hotels, information on transportation, or answers for any number of questions.

England

British Tourist Authority
551 Fifth Avenue, 7th Floor
New York, NY 10176
212-986-2200 or 1-800-462-2748
www.visitbritain.com

In Britain:

Britain and London Visitor Centre
1 Regent Street
London SW1Y 4XT
020 8846 9000

France

French Government Tourist Office
444 Madison Avenue, 16th Floor
New York, NY 10022
514-288-1904
www.franceguide.com

In Paris:

Espace du Tourisme
Place de la Pyramide Inversée
Le Carrousel du Louvre
(Postal address: 99 rue de Rivoli)
75001 Paris
33 1 44 50 19 98

Italy

Italian Government Travel Office
630 Fifth Avenue, Suite 1565
New York, NY 10111
212-245-5618
www.italiantourism.com

In Milan:

Azienda di Promozione Turistica
1 Via Marconi at Piazza Duomo
Milano
39 02 725241

Japan

Japan National Tourist Organization
1 Rockefeller Plaza, Suite 1250
New York, NY 10020
212-757-5640
www.jnto.go.jp

In Toyko:

Tourist Information Center
Tokyo Kotsu Kaikan Building 2-10-1
Yurakucho
Chiyoda-ku Tokyo 100-0006
81-3-3201-3331

New York

NYC & Company
810 Seventh Avenue, 3rd Floor
New York, NY 10019
212-484-1200
www.nycvisit.com

Index

C

M

S

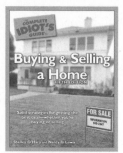

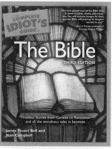
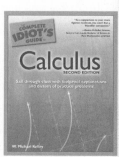

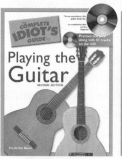